NEW WORLD COURTSHIPS

RE-MAPPING THE TRANSNATIONAL
A Dartmouth Series in American Studies

SERIES EDITOR
Donald E. Pease
Avalon Foundation Chair of Humanities
Founding Director of the Futures of American Studies Institute
Dartmouth College

The emergence of Transnational American Studies in the wake of the Cold War marks the most significant reconfiguration of American Studies since its inception. The shock waves generated by a newly globalized world order demanded an understanding of America's embeddedness within global and local processes rather than scholarly reaffirmations of its splendid isolation. The series Re-Mapping the Transnational seeks to foster the cross-national dialogues needed to sustain the vitality of this emergent field. To advance a truly comparativist understanding of this scholarly endeavor, Dartmouth College Press welcomes monographs from scholars both inside and outside the United States.

For a complete list of books available in this series, see www.upne.com.

Melissa M. Adams-Campbell, *New World Courtships: Transatlantic Alternatives to Companionate Marriage*

David LaRocca and Ricardo Miguel-Alfonso, editors, *A Power to Translate the World: New Essays on Emerson and International Culture*

Rob Kroes, *Prison Area, Independence Valley: American Paradoxes in Political Life and Popular Culture*

Etsuko Taketani, *The Black Pacific Narrative: Geographic Imaginings of Race and Empire between the World Wars*

William V. Spanos, *Shock and Awe: American Exceptionalism and the Imperatives of the Spectacle in Mark Twain's* A Connecticut Yankee in King Arthur's Court

Laura Bieger, Ramón Saldívar, and Johannes Voelz, editors, *The Imaginary and Its Worlds: American Studies after the Transnational Turn*

Paul A. Bové, *A More Conservative Place: Intellectual Culture in the Bush Era*

John Muthyala, *Dwelling in American: Dissent, Empire, and Globalization*

Winfried Fluck, Donald E. Pease, and John Carlos Rowe, editors, *Re-Framing the Transnational Turn in American Studies*

MELISSA M. ADAMS-CAMPBELL

NEW WORLD COURTSHIPS

Transatlantic
Alternatives to
Companionate
Marriage

DARTMOUTH COLLEGE PRESS
HANOVER, NEW HAMPSHIRE

Dartmouth College Press
An imprint of University Press of New England
www.upne.com
© 2015 Trustees of Dartmouth College
All rights reserved
Manufactured in the United States of America
Typeset in Sabon by Integrated Publishing Solutions

For permission to reproduce any of the material in this book, contact
Permissions, University Press of New England, One Court Street, Suite
250, Lebanon NH 03766; or visit www.upne.com

Library of Congress Cataloging-in-Publication Data

Adams-Campbell, Melissa M.
   New world courtships: transatlantic alternatives to companionate
marriage / Melissa M. Adams-Campbell.
      pages cm—(Re-mapping the transnational: a Dartmouth series in
American studies)
   Includes bibliographical references and index.
   Summary: "The first scholarly study to recover a geographically
diverse array of eighteenth- and nineteenth-century countertexts that
actively compare culturally diverse marriage practices from Canada to
the Caribbean"—Provided by publisher.
   ISBN 978-1-61168-831-3 (cloth: alk. paper)— ISBN 978-1-61168-832-0
(pbk.: alk. paper)— ISBN 978-1-61168-833-7 (ebook)
1. Marriage in literature.   2. Courtship in literature.   3. Sex in literature.   4. Man-woman relationships in literature.   5. Literature—18th
century—History and criticism.   6. Literature—19th century—History and
criticism.   7. Man-woman relationships—Cross-cultural studies.   8. Companionate marriage—Cross-cultural studies.   I. Title.   II. Title: Transatlantic alternatives to companionate marriage.
   PN56.M28A33 2015
   809'.933543—dc23

                                                              2015008498

5 4 3 2 1

CONTENTS

Acknowledgments   ix

Introduction: Mapping Marriage   1

1   Why Marriage Mattered Then   21

2   Comparing Rights, Comparing Stories   42

3   Making Room for Coquettes and Fallen Women   70

4   A Postcolonial Heroine "Writes Back"   97

5   Bungling Bundling   113

Epilogue: Why Marriage Matters Now   140
Notes   147
Bibliography   177
Index   197

ACKNOWLEDGMENTS

Over the years, many people have assisted in the thinking, writing, and making of this book. It is a sincere pleasure to finally thank them in these pages. For helping me to conceive and reconceive the dissertation project that evolved into this book I would like to thank Jonathan Elmer and Deidre Lynch as well as committee members Mary Favret and Kirsten Sword. Your thoughtful feedback and continual mentoring have made all the difference in my success. Many others at Indiana University (IU) provided guidance and support for this project, including the faculty in the English and gender studies programs, members of the Center for Eighteenth-Century Studies, English graduate secretary Beverly Hankins, and IU's ever-helpful librarians. I am so fortunate to have made lasting friendships with IU friends Jim Berkey, Jon Blandford, and Ana Owusu-Tyo who helped me to think, write, and laugh more than they will ever know. A special shout-out here as well to Celia Barnes, Michael Brown, JoEllen Delucia, Melissa Jones, Chad Luck, Jessica Lewis Luck, Tobias Menely, Sarah Murphy, Kristen Renzi, Brandi Stanton, Roger Stanton, Courtney Wennerstrom, and Paul Westover.

At Knox College, I would like to thank current and former members of the English department, especially Monica Berlin, Robert Hellenga, Ed Niehus, Audrey Petty, Natania Rosenfeld, Lori Schroeder, Rob Smith, and Barbara Tannert-Smith, as well as the McNair program staff and the incredible Knox librarians for rigorous intellectual discussion, excellent opportunities for research and teaching, and constant kindness and support during my undergraduate education and beyond. Carley Robison deserves special mention for nurturing my love of old books. Thanks for setting me on the path, friends.

I am fortunate to have many generous colleagues who have offered welcome assistance in reading chapter drafts, relaying professional advice, and proffering much-needed friendship. At Ball State University, I thank current and former faculty members Amit Rahul Baiysha, Adam

Beach, Jill Christman, Patrick Collier, Cathy Day, Frank Felsenstein, Jacqueline Grutsch McKinney, Robert Habich, Pamela Hartman, Joyce Huff, Deborah Mix, Rai Peterson, Elizabeth Riddle, Will Stockton, and many other kind colleagues and staff who supported me intellectually and emotionally through difficult years as a new professor and a new mom. I well remember your many kindnesses.

At my current institution, Northern Illinois University (NIU), thanks especially to Phil Eubanks and Amy Levin for generously mentoring and supporting pretenure faculty. For making sure I get money and supplies and generally understand how things are done, my eternal thanks to Jan Vander Meer and all the staff at NIU. Thanks to Deborah DeRosa, David Gorman, Kathleen Renk, and Diana Swanson for reading drafts of this material and offering advice and friendship. Elizabeth Schewe has read and reread multiple drafts of this manuscript and offered invaluable feedback and friendship. Thanks also to NIU colleagues Gulsat Aygen, Scott Balcerzak, Joe Bonomo, Nicole Clifton, Lara Crowley, Tim Crowley, Michael Day, Sue Deskis, Jeffrey Einboden, Ryan Hibbet, Tom McCann, Doris McDonald, Amy Newman, Bradley Peters, Jessica Reyman, Timothy Ryan, Mark Van Wienen, and many others who have welcomed me to the department. I am also grateful to J. D. Bowers, associate vice provost for University Honors, who offered sound advice on the shape of this manuscript and adeptly commented on drafts of this work, and to both J. D. and Anne Birberick, vice provost of academic affairs at NIU, for extending my transnational research and teaching opportunities by selecting me to lead NIU's study-abroad program for honors students in Montreal.

I want to thank generous Chicago-area colleagues who have mentored and encouraged me along the way: Jim Chandler, Hillary Chute, Heather Keenleyside, Anna Kornbluh, Eric Slauter, Robin Valenza, Abram Van Engen, and Tim Yu. I am especially grateful for good conversations, convivial dinners, and play dates with Heather Keenleyside, Michael Green, and Wilder Keenleyside Green.

I have been fortunate to have benefited from the financial and intellectual support of many institutions. I am grateful to have received the Kenneth Johnston Dissertation Fellowship for Romantic Studies at Indiana University as well as a research and artistry grant from Northern Illinois University's Office of Sponsored Projects, which enabled me to include the interviews with Mohawk community members in chapter 2. I first realized that I should go to Akwesasne while I was a participant in the 2010 National Endowment for the Humanities summer institute program "From Metacom to Tecumseh: Early Native American Resistances Movements" at the Newberry Library led by Scott Stevens, then director of the Newberry's Darcy McNickle Center for American Indian and Indigenous Studies. Many thanks to Scott and the wonderful staff at the Newberry, to the faculty who presented, and to my fellow participants. Thanks also to Rebecca Bales who initially encouraged me to get in contact with Mohawk leaders regarding my research interests. I presented early drafts of chapter 2 at the Newberry's American Indian Studies Seminar Series (AISSS) and at Dartmouth College's Futures of American Studies Summer Institute. Special thanks to LaVonne Ruoff at AISSS and Ivy Schweitzer at Dartmouth for your gracious mentoring and support of this work.

Spending time at Akwesasne gave me a new understanding of how and why research ought to be done. I would like to say nia:wen to the tribal staff who approved my research request, to Wolf Clan Faithkeeper Richard Mitchell, Bear Clan Mother Louise McDonald, and especially to Akwesasne Museum program coordinator Sue Ellen Herne for her assistance on the ground at Akwesasne. Thanks to all of you for sharing your knowledge with me; I am humbled to listen and share your words with others. For assistance in the Mohawk spelling of Handsome Lake's "Good Message," special thanks to Rohonwa'kiéh:rha at Akwesasne. You make your mom and your community proud! Thanks also to Mohawk storyteller Kay Olan for sharing stories with me and my NIU students and for many hours of good conversation.

I would like to offer special thanks to the Northern Illinois University library staff, especially Lynne Thomas at the Rare Books Room and the library's digitization services staff for reproducing the images included in the book's introduction. I would also like to thank several students for research assistance: Jonathan Pierrel at Ball State for translation assistance in chapter 3, Rachel Skinner at Northern Illinois University for transcribing the interviews in chapter 2, and Jen Fife for research assistance in chapter 5. For proofreading the earliest draft of this manuscript I owe many, many thanks to longtime friend and initial copy editor Rosemarie Connolly. Her suggestions and corrections enabled me to send the book out in a timely manner.

Special thanks to Richard Pult, Susan Abel, and everyone at UPNE who helped in the making and marketing of this book, and to the copyeditor, Anne Rogers, and indexer, Michael Tabor. I have been so pleased with the experience. I am most grateful to the Re-Mapping the Transnational series editor, Donald E. Pease, for helping this book to find a home.

A tremendous debt of gratitude goes to Ivy Schweitzer and Duncan Faherty for your thoughtful evaluations of this book; it is substantially stronger for your constructive feedback and sharp revision suggestions. Any failings are all my own. I thank the Johns Hopkins University Press for permission to reprint portions of chapter 3, which originally appeared as "Romantic Revolutions: Love and Violence in Leonora Sansay's *Secret History, or The Horrors of St. Domingo*" in *Studies in American Fiction* 39, no. 2 (2012): 125–46.

Finally, thanks to my family for always cheering me on. My mother, Brenda Adams, never doubted that I could do this work. Her perseverance through life's difficulties showed me the true meaning of strength. My father and stepmother, Chuck and Jacque Adams; my brother, Jeron Adams; and nephew, Damen Adams, have been supportive in every way. Thanks, too, to Betty Adams, Theresa Adams, Margaret Cooke, Cindy King, and Cheryl Moreno-Buxton for modeling what it means to be strong women. To Charles Adams, Tim Adams, Sam Buxton, Ray Cooke, and Scott King—thanks for your love. To the Fishers and Campbells, thank you for including me in your families; I am grateful every day for your kindness and warmth. My husband, Tim, has been there from the beginning, reading drafts and consistently giving the best feedback on my work. Thank you for sharing this life with me. My son, Charlie, is my constant joy. I am so grateful for you, dear boy. And although she will not arrive before this book goes into print, I welcome here our newest addition to the family.

NEW WORLD COURTSHIPS

INTRODUCTION: MAPPING MARRIAGE

IN AN INTERVIEW ABOUT *The Marriage Plot* (2011), the US novelist Jeffrey Eugenides admires the tightly constructed marriage plots of Jane Austen, Henry James, Gustave Flaubert, and Leo Tolstoy. In the classic marriage plot, events are organized around a single heroine's seemingly ordinary task of finding and securing an appropriate husband. These plots present companionate marriage—that is, marriage based on personal choice and mutual affection—as the heroine's ultimate reward for the many trials she endures throughout courtship. Rather than dismissing courtship and marriage as quotidian, these plots convey the gravity of a young woman's decision. The choice of a husband not only determines the heroine's personal, social, economic, and geographical future, but also publicly marks her attainment of maturity. Her choice, actually limited to a yes or no, is essentially irreversible. Beyond this, though, the choice of an appropriate husband symbolically expresses the heroine's moral character and worth; in choosing a worthy mate, she proves herself worthy of regard.

"The" Marriage Plot?

Eugenides's description of the marriage plot will be familiar to readers and scholars of nineteenth-century fiction. Austen, James, and the other writers he mentions have been so influential to the study of the novel that this very particular European marriage plot has come to be "the" marriage plot, canonical beyond measure. Indeed, foundational histories of the novel establish the marriage plot as central to the rise of the novel.[1] Eugenides explains his 2011 novel as a lamentation on "not being able to write a novel with a proper marriage plot because so many social conditions had changed. It was no longer possible to do that." Although he believes that it is no longer possible for American writers to use the marriage plot because "we no longer live in a world where marriage is the end all be all of life and divorce might actually lead you to suicide," Eugenides makes the case that the marriage plot continues to influence our romantic expectations: "Today . . . it exists in our heads. . . . It still forms our intentions and expectations, especially romantically."[2] Whether these plots are celebratory or critical of the heroine's quest to find a husband, in Eugenides's account, the power of the marriage plot lies precisely in how it establishes a shared and long-lasting romantic imaginary with seemingly universal cultural meaning.

New World Courtships argues that novelistic representations of courtship, marriage, and romantic life from the mid-eighteenth through the early nineteenth centuries are considerably more diverse than this standard account suggests. Alongside the canonical marriage plots familiar to readers of Austen and James are many strange and mostly forgotten transatlantic marriage plots with decidedly non-European scenes of courtship and marriage ceremonies. These *comparative marriage plots*—plots that include significant story lines focused on comparing cultural differences in courtship and marriage practices—offer an alternate vision of what marriage meant in the eighteenth and early nineteenth centuries and how it served as a point of encounter between different, diverse cultures. Evident in Anglophone Atlantic world novels such as *The Female American* (1767), *The History of Emily Montague* (1769), *Secret History; or, The Horrors of St. Domingo* (1808), *The Woman of Colour* (1808), and *The Life and Adventures of Obadiah Benjamin Franklin Bloomfield M.D.* (1818), comparative marriage plots demonstrate how novelists around the time of Austen struggled to represent the diversity of Atlantic world courtship practices reported in colonial documents, missionary accounts, and popular volumes of travel literature.[3] I argue that in these novels, comparative marriage plots undermine monocultural assumptions about what constitutes or should constitute normative sociopolitical institutions, especially marriage.

I use the phrase *New World* cautiously, but purposefully. The phrase has been rightly criticized as rhetorically emptying the North American continent of its extensive and culturally distinct populations of indigenous peoples. The Americas were and are populated by diverse groups of people with long-standing and rapidly evolving marriage traditions. Many of the courtship and marriage practices outlined in this book were not "new" to the Americas, although some did arise from the unique relationships and sexual dynamics that developed among various colonizing European groups, Native peoples, and enslaved black populations across several generations of settlement. Instead, I use the phrase *New World* to indicate the surprising critical insight—the creative possibilities for reimagining courtship and marriage—achieved by the culturally diverse comparative framework deployed by these texts. Whether they support the status quo or imagine new possibilities for arranging sexual relations and family units, the comparative marriage plots traced in this book allow for a moment of reflection and uncertainty. In this way, this study is an exercise in reading against the grain, as it searches for moments when the meanings of marriage across several European metropoles and their colonies are, however briefly, destabilized. *New World Courtships* lingers on such moments of uncertainty and destabilization, which are also the horizon of "new" possibilities.

At the outset, then, it will be useful to review what some historians have called the rise of the conjugal or nuclear family, and with it, the widespread eighteenth-century discursive tradition of the companionate-marriage ideal. As a number of historians and social theorists have argued, in the eighteenth century the desire for a freely chosen marriage based on mutual romantic love transformed generations of previous Western thought on the purpose and function of marriage. Whereas in earlier periods romantic love and sexual passion were not exclusive to or required for marriage and reproduction, Niklas Luhmann argues that the demand for romantic love in marriage led to a remarkable intensifying of heterosexual intimacy.[4] By the end of the eighteenth century, individual choice replaced parentally arranged marriage as a new social ideal among the upwardly mobile gentry. While actual social practices did not necessarily align with this ideal, there was a growing sense that affection ought to be the proper basis for marriage.

This shift toward affectionate, romantic marriage necessitated a new and elaborate culture of courtship including chaperoned and unchaperoned visits, carriage rides, outings, and the presentation of gifts. These courtship rituals can be seen in the nascent novel, increasing the likelihood that readers would incorporate these practices in their own courtships. As young people increasingly chose their own marriage partners, so too did they see the time before marriage as a necessary period for assessing the suitable qualities of and compatibility with a future mate.

The adoption of romantic love as a social ideal occurred at different rates in various populations. Edmund Leites describes a new emphasis on emotional companionship in seventeenth-century Puritan discourse on marriage, a shift from previous classical rhetoric on the virtues of same-sex friendships.[5] Even as sexual attraction and compatibility were recognized as beneficial to Puritan marriages, they were not (yet) considered an adequate basis for establishing marriage. In *The Family, Sex and Marriage in England,* Lawrence Stone argues that an intensive restructuring of the English family occurred across the long eighteenth century.[6] Stone tracks what he calls the transition from the restricted patriarchal family with its authoritarian family relationships and large households, which might include grandparents, extended family, and servants, to the closed nuclear family with its more intimate relationships and greatly reduced household. The nuclear family, as Stone describes it, was more private and withdrawn from the community, less dependent on kin, and more affectionate. Stone's thesis largely draws on evidence from an emerging bourgeois literary print culture, and so it cannot accurately describe social conditions on the ground or show the nuances of class differences in family structures. Although Stone's work has been criticized for, among other things, describing companionate marriage as normative before it in fact becomes a mainstream practice, I find the term *companionate marriage* useful to describe a social *ideal* within a discursive tradition of novels and conduct books targeted at Anglophone women readers.[7]

In describing the shifting attitudes toward marriage as "yoke mates to soul mates," Stephanie Coontz outlines two significant social changes that enable the rise of companionate marriage: the shift to wage labor that made young people less dependent on land or parentally controlled inheritances and new Enlightenment ideas such as the right of the individual to pursue happiness.[8] This Enlightenment emphasis on the individual and contractual nature of marriage has been traced back to the political reformulation of the Glorious Revolution, when the relation between the monarch and his subjects was renegotiated as a voluntary agreement.[9]

The slow transition during the course of the eighteenth century from previous domestic economies, where men and women labored in the home to produce trade goods and household necessities, to wage labor outside the home led not only to a historically new phenomenon, the male breadwinner marriage, but also to an increase in the belief that men and women ought properly to operate in separate spheres.[10] By the nineteenth century, this line of thinking divided humanity into two gender-based categories with supposedly inherently distinct traits. The male sphere was active, rational, and engaged in public life, while the female sphere was compassionate, domestic, and private. The complementary coming together of the two spheres in heterosexual marriage was thought to produce a well-rounded and whole family. Jürgen Habermas theorizes this two-spheres phenomenon by arguing that the development of an intimate private sphere of the family in the eighteenth century made possible the development of a rational public sphere. Thus, the privacy of the family—specifically the bourgeois nuclear family emerging from a freely chosen and mutually affectionate companionate marriage—is, for Habermas, the seedbed of personal and political freedom.[11]

What is crucial in this study is how novels in this period proclaim Anglophone women's new ability to contract affection-based marriages as a signifier of freedom, specifically translating personal marital choice into nationalist claims for British superiority. Surprisingly, these period claims have been recirculated by well-meaning historians and literary scholars. For instance, Stone claims that companionate marriage benefited women and led to more equal marital relations, while Ian Watt describes the rise of the novel as "connected with the much greater freedom of women in modern society, a freedom which, especially as regards marriage, was achieved earlier and more completely in England than elsewhere."[12] Because the marriage plot has traditionally been understood to express the ideological norms and values of a particular nation, Judith Roof argues that canonical Euro-American marriage plots establish "an irresistible merger of family and state."[13] However, the comparative marriage plots studied in this book specifically compare other cultural systems and priorities for making marriages in the Americas alongside the emerging British companionate-marriage ideal, often with the effect of unsettling the normative "merger of family and state" found in canonical marriage plots. For instance, in chapter 2 I trace how Frances Brooke compares Wendat (Huron) and Haudenosaunee (Iroquois) women's political rights and systems of arranged marriage with the much-touted freedom British women had to choose spouses in *The History of Emily Montague,* while in chapter 3 I turn to Leonora Sansay's interest in contractual nonmarital sexual relations in the Caribbean in *Secret History,* especially the relationship between white planters and black and biracial *ménagères* (housekeepers), which regularly included both domestic and sexual services. These writers' comparative marriage plots make it possible to recognize that sex and marriage have not always and everywhere been private or irreversible relations.

The comparative lens employed by novels such as *The History of*

Emily Montague and *Secret History,* among others, suggests that one of the reasons these texts have been so long ignored is precisely that they do not easily align with the focus on the nation that is arguably still central to literary studies. However, recent turns toward Atlantic and transnational studies allow literary scholars to reassess the privileged position of the nation and the literary critical emphasis on national literatures.[14] My comparative practice is rooted in what Susan Stanford Friedman calls "locational" feminism, a strategy that demands both an immersion in particular cultural contexts and attention to the ways that local practices are bound up in national and transnational geopolitics and their discourses.[15] In *New World Courtships,* comparison is more than a methodology. The long history that lies behind my methodology itself becomes an object of study as I consider the ways that Enlightenment novelists themselves engage in a comparative methodology to establish and critique evolving ideals of marriage. Theorizing about the function of comparing marriage practices in Anglo-imperial Atlantic novels offers a more complex picture of the ideological work of romance in the processes of colonial governance *and* in the history of the novel. This book describes how and why Atlantic world differences in courtship traditions and novels about those various traditions have mattered since the eighteenth century.

A Novel History of Companionate Marriage

As Shulamith Firestone observes in her radical feminist treatise, "Love, perhaps even more than childbearing, is the pivot of women's oppression today. . . . The panic felt at any threat to love is a good clue to its political significance."[16] Although Firestone has been rightly criticized for an essentialist view of sex difference that is at odds with her Marxist dialectical framework, her critique of the negative effects of romantic love as it exists in patriarchy remains compelling. She argues, "It is not the process of love itself that is at fault, but its *political,* i.e., unequal *power* context" that makes it destructive; however, as it currently exists in this unequal power relation, "romanticism is a cultural tool of male power to keep women from knowing their conditions."[17] More recently, Anna Jónasdóttir observes that "love work" is unevenly distributed between partners in heterosexual marriages, and that "men tend to exploit women's capacities for love and transform these into individual and collective modes of power over which women lose control."[18] This book follows in this tradition of feminist debates about women's agency and investments in romance and romance narratives.[19] It, too, is concerned with how novels promote certain romantic relations as normative and whether those relations are good for women.

While feminist literary critics have long recognized the ways that the novel's insistence on the marriage plot has shaped women's lives, they have largely traced these effects through a historically and culturally specific British and Anglo-American companionate-marriage paradigm.[20] Studies by Joseph Allen Boone, Nancy Armstrong, and others demonstrate how the courtship plot's inevitable conclusion in marriage conservatively maintains the status quo and restricts women's possibilities. For instance, Boone argues that "the movement toward stasis in the canonical love-plot, be the resolution comic or tragic, functioned to preclude, by repressing from the audience's overt consciousness, any serious dismantling of the social order."[21] Of course, the reigning social order both inside and outside the fictional space of the love story is defined by hierarchical gender patterns and assumptions, which Armstrong controversially argues take precedence in the nineteenth century over previously dominant social issues such as class difference.[22] These and other important critiques of the romance tradition trace the conservative ideological content in hegemonic romance culture, but they tell only part of the story. In contrast to the conservative nature of many marriage plots, Anne DuCille insists that nineteenth-century African American women writers use the marriage plot as a means of achieving respectability so that the heroine can go on to accomplish meaningful racial uplift projects in her community.[23] Although the novels in DuCille's study are not comparative in the ways that I outline, these texts demonstrate how nineteenth-century African American women's marriage plots did not prevent women from participating in the public sphere. By telling a different story, DuCille highlights the ways that the field of feminist literary studies itself shaped "the" marriage plot.

This study seeks to widen the scope of feminist analyses of fictional marriage narratives by attending to novels with a comparative focus on Atlantic marriage practices. One of the central claims this book makes is that Anglophone novels with comparative marriage plots frequently unsettle Enlightenment hierarchies of human progress in ways that cultural comparisons in other genres do not. That is, comparisons of various marriage traditions and gender practices in the Americas operate differently in fiction. This book traces those differences as they unfold in settings as various as Great Britain, colonial Virginia, lower Canada, Haiti, Jamaica, and newly independent Pennsylvania. This range of geopolitical contexts not only enriches our understanding of gender and marriage relations in each locale, but also enables a broader scope with which to recognize the diversity of marriage plots in the history of the novel and the diversity of gender systems in an earlier Atlantic world.

Feminist literary critics have rigorously outlined the narrative mechanics of marriage plots and their ideological content in their attempts to explain why marriage plots prove so satisfying to readers. In *Writing beyond the Ending,* Rachel Blau DuPlessis argues that the discovery of mutual love that drives the plot of so many early novels leads to one of two inevitable endings for a woman in love: marriage or death.[24] Of these two conclusions, marriage offers the positive social recognition that women are taught to desire; marriage means social stability and the attainment of adulthood. Moreover, these canonical plots conclude at the altar. Readers have little interest in the couple's quotidian married life. Here, marriage *is* a woman's story. Rachel Brownstein describes the heroine's propulsion toward marriage as securing "an achieved, finished identity." The appeal of this plot, Brownstein notes, is "the tantalizing, misleading illusion of the self perfected through a resolution of the female destiny—by the idea of becoming a heroine. . . . Young women like to read about heroines in fiction so as to rehearse possible lives and to imagine a woman's life as important—because they want to be attractive and powerful and significant, someone whose life is worth writing about, whose world revolves around her and makes being the way she is make sense."[25] Like Eugenides in the opening example, both DuPlessis and Brownstein note the powerful ideological hold that canonical marriage plots have on women readers and later generations of writers.

For DuPlessis, the rigid conformity to the two conclusions of female protagonists' stories in nineteenth-century fiction becomes a challenge that later twentieth-century writers such as Virginia Woolf, H.D., and others will purposefully revise and write "beyond." One of the surprising discoveries of working with previously overlooked comparative marriage plots such as the story of a biracial Jamaican women in *The Woman of Colour* (1808) is how a century before DuPlessis marks the trend in white Anglophone women writers, the anonymous author of *The Woman of Colour* turns to the solution of writing beyond the ending to critique the limitations of the British marriage plot. In chapter 5 I argue that the author moves beyond marriage to purposefully revise the possibilities for biracial colonized women such as Olivia Fairfield. In these and other examples, I trace how in contrast to the eighteenth-century discourse of women's marital freedom, comparative marriage plots allow for a critical awareness of the narrow options women are granted within the canon-

ical marriage plot and within the sociopolitical life of the Anglophone
Atlantic world. Although the comparative plots explored in this book
are not easy multicultural celebrations of difference, the comparative lens
they deploy makes visible how the marriage norms of the British Atlantic
world and the narratives about those norms are only one of a range of
options for making marriage.

One facet of feminist debates about the conservative or progressive
nature of romance narratives has centered on the ways that traditional
marriage plots trap women in the private sphere. More recent studies by
Helen Thompson and Elizabeth Maddock Dillon use courtship novels
as a site for questioning the supposed division between private romantic relationships and public political agency.[26] For instance, Thompson
asks if feminist scholars may be limiting what counts as recognizable
female agency by focusing exclusively on acts of resistance. She argues
that many British heroines' acts of compliance with patriarchal demands
actually render patriarchy visible, showing readers the absurdities of female passivity. In the early American context, Dillon demonstrates how
marriage is a tool for ratifying citizen-subjects and instantiating the
division of gendered private and public spheres, rather than reflecting
preexisting separate spheres. Both Thompson and Dillon offer significant
and sophisticated readings of the ideological function of marriage in the
emergence of liberal political institutions in Britain and the United States;
however, both these accounts exist within the monocultural logic of British
and Anglo-American marriage traditions. The Americas, and texts written
about the Americas, contain many different marriage traditions—including
traditions that fundamentally threaten the primacy of the patriarchal companionate-marriage ideal.

This book turns to an Atlantic world model of marriage comparison in
order to extend the geographic borders as well as the cultural and racial
delimiters of "the" marriage plot. The comparative elements in these marriage plots decenter the primacy of monogamous heterosexual couples
and their romantic attachments in favor of other relationships, duties,
and life choices. These plots make room for questions about whether
companionate marriages are actually more progressive than other styles
of marriage and whether marriage should be the ultimate aspiration,
especially for women. The texts featured in *New World Courtships* do
not abandon their romantic ideals or colonizing hierarchical schemas
for evaluating others; yet, in the moment of comparison, what seems
natural and inevitable about marriage becomes recognizable as simply
one among many structuring systems for organizing sex, marriage, and

families, and their relationships to the state and/or empire. This moment of comparison leads, too, to the critical insight that patriarchal marriage systems could change. This book attends to the ways that Anglophone novelists in the mid-eighteenth to early nineteenth centuries repeatedly describe a shift in conceptualizing romance after encountering marital diversity in the circum-Atlantic world.

Representing Marital Diversity in the Anglophone Novel

In the established canon of transatlantic novels, there are already obvious resources for exploring representations of Atlantic world marital diversity. In *Oroonoko* (1688), for instance, Aphra Behn is keenly aware of the challenges slavery poses to marriage. However, her novel is not comparative in the same manner as the novels I study, which integrate on-the-ground comparisons of actual local marriage practices into their plots in order to consider and question companionate-based British marriage relations. The tragedy of *Oroonoko* is that slavery disrupts the royal Oroonoko's patriarchal marriage rights, not that such rights exist. Ultimately, Behn is not particularly invested in the ways that the system of slavery alters marriage relations and gender expectations in the Americas.[27]

Daniel Defoe's *Moll Flanders* (1722) is another familiar text where colonial marriage figures prominently. However, Defoe is not interested in the diversity of colonial American marriage practices, nor in comparing those traditions. He does not attempt to represent the complexities of competing indigenous, European-imported, or Creole legal, religious, and social practices in the Americas. Rather than documenting the productive messiness of Atlantic world marriages, *Moll Flanders* renders colonial marriage relations profoundly unnatural with its memorable Virginia-based incest plot. In doing so, it ushers in a whole strain of novels from Edgeworth's *Belinda* to Brontë's *Jane Eyre* that characterize romantic entanglements in the Americas as a threat to proper British marital alliances.[28]

In contrast to *Moll Flanders* and *Oroonoko,* the comparative plots taken up by *New World Courtships* portray marital diversity in the Atlantic world as sources of possibility. They openly reflect on the merits of organizing marriage and family relations differently. While not necessarily critical of normative companionate-marriage expectations, these texts recognize and validate the existence of other cultural systems for making marriage.

Lydia Maria Child's 1824 historical novel *Hobomok* is perhaps the best-known example of what I am calling a *comparative marriage plot,* although it has not generally been recognized as such.[29] The first publication in Child's long writing career, *Hobomok* draws on colonial-era primary source materials to represent richly detailed and culturally distinct seventeenth-century Puritan and Native fictional worlds. The novel follows Mary Conant, the daughter of a stern Puritan immigrant, as she evaluates her romantic options. After Mary's inflexible father rejects her favorite suitor, Charles Brown, because of his Anglicanism, Brown leaves the colony and reportedly dies at sea. Devastated by the news and, perhaps, rebelling against her father's oppressive patriarchal authority, Mary marries Hobomok, a Wampanoag friend and ally of the Puritans. Mary lives with Hobomok and raises her biracial child in the Wampanoag village until Charles Brown returns. Upon seeing Brown, Hobomok immediately sacrifices his family, grants Mary a divorce, and leaves the village, never questioning that this is what she would want in her heart. After Hobomok's sudden departure, Mary freely marries Brown and assimilates her biracial child into colonial culture.

Hobomok's treatment of interracial marriage and miscegenation has received considerable scholarly attention. Many scholars acknowledge Child's progressive political sensibilities and champion her feminist revisions to the frontier romance genre, often characterizing the novel as a protofeminist response to James Fenimore Cooper's *Leatherstocking Tales.* But they are brought up short by the way that *Hobomok*'s conclusion participates in racist nineteenth-century "vanishing Indian" rhetoric.[30] They are right to note this and to be troubled by it. Child does make Hobomok sacrifice his love and abandon his family so that his white wife can marry her "true" (white) love and assimilate her child into white colonial culture. She does, ultimately, validate the white companionate couple and American manifest destiny. What, then, does her comparison of Mary's suitors accomplish?

By juxtaposing Mary's plausible romantic options, Child uses a comparative marriage plot to question and critique patriarchal marital regulations in the novel's seventeenth-century colonial setting as well as in Child's own nineteenth-century period. During the course of the novel, she presents Native marriage practices as a logical and valid system with its own cultural integrity, infusing her depictions of Wampanoag peoples with as much primary-source-derived historical detail as she gives to her Puritan characters. What's more, she suggests that Native marriage traditions may, in fact, be more progressive and accommodating than

Anglo-American marriage practices in either the seventeenth or the nineteenth century. This is not to say that Child's depictions are either historically accurate or politically correct—this is still a nineteenth-century
historical novel with a notable "vanishing" agenda. Nevertheless, Child
textures the lives of her Native characters with the kind of ethnographically rich, quotidian detail that Mark Rifkin identifies in contemporary
Native writing as a strategy of simultaneously remembering tradition and
resisting US governance.[31] In short, Child's comparative marriage plot is
not free from racism, but her comparative feminist approach is worth
recuperating more fully.

　　Child devotes considerable energy to representing seventeenth-century
Puritan and Native New England communities with realistic details
drawn from period sources. She peoples her novel with the names of
both Puritan and Native historical persons such as Bradford, Higginson,
Morton, Massasoit, Squanto, and Hobomok. However, her novel is not
a celebration of the triumph of Puritan New England. Child includes
several episodes in which disagreeable Puritan elders bitterly debate the
finer points of theology, more anxious to correct religious "toleration"
than to build community.[32] Their open hostility toward one another
spreads outward as Child depicts the Puritans' distrust of their Wampanoag allies and repeatedly shows Puritan elders making derogatory comments about competing sects of dissenters, Puritan women, and Native
peoples alike. Child's detailed and historically documented representations of Puritan bigotry become a critical lens on Puritan patriarchy as
well when their rigidity in matters of faith carries over into tyrannical
control of their children's romantic lives. For instance, Mary Conant's
father flatly rejects his daughter's wealthy and attractive Anglican suitor,
practically driving her into the arms of Hobomok. Child builds readers'
sympathy for Mary's difficult situation by creating an overall negative
impression of seventeenth-century Puritan society as intolerant, frac-
tious, and restrictive. Child similarly textures her depictions of Wampanoag peoples with the same level of historical detail she gives to Puritan
characters and settings. For instance, she describes disagreements between Wampanoag leaders Corbitant and Hobomok regarding the desir-
ability of a continuing alliance with the Puritans. As with the theological
debates in the Puritan community, these disputes fade to the background
as Mary's interracial romance with Hobomok takes precedence. Child
notably makes her most strident critiques of Anglo-American patriarchy
through comparisons of Puritan and Wampanoag attitudes about gender
and marriage.

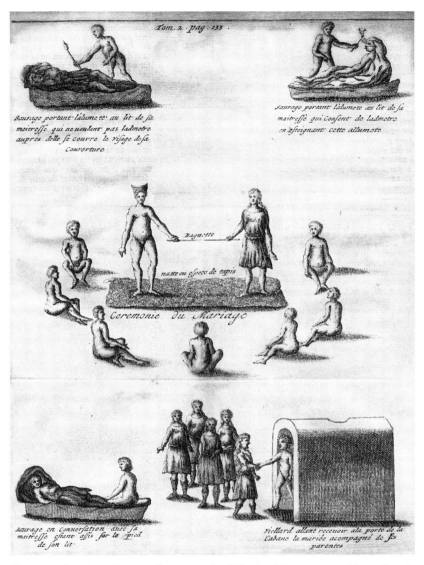

Figure 1. A series of images demonstrating Wendat (Huron) courtship and wedding customs from Baron Lahontan's *Mémoires de l'Amérique Septentrionale ou la Suite des Voyages de Mr. Le Baron de Lahontan* (1703). Courtesy of Rare Books and Special Collections, Northern Illinois University.

Child offers glimpses of a more tolerant and balanced Native gender system among Northeast Woodlands groups by portraying, for instance, the specifics of an "Indian" wedding ceremony with details from Baron Lahontan's memorable account of Wendat (Huron) courtship and wedding rituals in his *Mémoires de l'Amérique Septentrionale* (1703).[33] Setting aside questions of Lahontan's credibility and the misguided use of Wendat traditions in lieu of appropriate ethnographic data on Wampanoag marriage practices, Child's attempt to locate ethnographically rich primary-source details on Native marriage traditions demonstrates her investment in portraying Wampanoag characters with cultural and historical integrity. We should read Child's turn to historical sources such as Lahontan's not as a repetition of obvious stereotypes, but rather as a serious attempt at cultural relativism before such a concept had a name.

Lahontan's account of Wendat courtship and marriage ceremonies has obvious appeal for Child. Lahontan describes and illustrates Wendat courtship in vivid detail. If a young man wants to pursue a lover, he takes a torch to her bedside and shines the light on her. If she agrees to spend time with him, she uncovers her face. If she prefers to reject this suitor, she covers herself with her blanket. This takes place in her parents' home with their ostensible supervision. In the illustration accompanying Lahontan's text (figure 1), the two sit beside each other chatting in bed (a tradition akin to colonial New England bundling, which I explore in chapter 5). A Wendat woman may accept or shun the attentions of multiple suitors, engage in close physical contact (including premarital sex), and enter a one-year trial marriage with no loss of social status.[34]

In *Hobomok*, Child imaginatively extends the autonomy of Wendat courtship and marriage to Mary Conant. For instance, even as she attempts to defuse her readers' resistance to Mary's interracial marriage to Hobomok by suggesting her heroine's mentally and emotionally fragile state, Child gives Mary considerable agency in setting the terms of her marriage. Mary proposes to Hobomok; she requests that they relocate to Hobomok's "wigwam"; she consents to an "Indian" marriage ceremony and exchanges vows of love with her husband. She is remarkably in control of the situation, in fact. Details of the wedding ceremony follow Lahontan's basic outline. Mary's wedding ceremony is witnessed by four of Hobomok's relations, who "joined in a dance, singing in a low tone." The couple circles their home, hand in hand, reentering the dwelling and taking hold of the opposite ends of a witch-hazel wand (see figure

Figure 2. Detail of a Wendat wedding ceremony with mat and rod, as shown in Baron Lahontan's *Mémoires de l'Amérique Septentrionale ou la Suite des Voyages de Mr. Le Baron de Lahontan* (1703). Courtesy of Rare Books and Special Collections, Northern Illinois University.

2). The elderly "Indian" officiant reminds the couple of their respective duties: Hobomok must "hunt plenty of deer for his wife, love her, and try to make her happy," while Mary "should love her husband, and cook his venison well, that he might come home . . . with a light heart." The couple publicly declares their love. Hobomok then takes the wand and breaks it into pieces, distributing them among the witnesses as a record of the event/relationship. The company sings and dances around the couple three times, tobacco is smoked, and the guests leave: "The ceremony of that morning was past recall; and Mary Conant was indeed the wife of Hobomok."[35] Although it is difficult to assess whether such details are accurate, Child remains remarkably neutral in her protoethnographic presentation of Mary's "Indian" wedding ceremony.[36] Unlike many accounts that deride Native cultural traditions, Child reserves judgment on the particularities of the event. In terms of plot, Child does not endorse Mary's spousal choice; neither, though, does she ridicule the proceedings. Rather, Child imbues her version of a Native marriage ceremony with pomp and ritualistic detail, legitimizing indigenous forms of marriage and the authority of Native peoples to regulate their own marriages.

The detail with which Child infuses Mary's "Indian" marriage scene suggests not only a desire for historical accuracy, but also an activist's

attempt to reimagine history from nonpatriarchal perspectives.[37] For instance, she clearly chooses Lahontan's picture of indigenous gender relations over William Wood's *New England's Prospects* (1634), a more
regionally appropriate but highly critical account of Native women. In
his chapter on Pequod and Narragansett women, for instance, Wood
describes the misery of Native women as they compare their situation
with the romantic affection English women supposedly receive: "Since
the English arrivall comparison hath made them [Native women] miserable, for seeing the kind usage of the English to their wives, they doe
as much condemne their husbands for unkindnesse, and commend the
English for their love."[38] Wood's account is a typical example of what
David Smits identifies as the "squaw drudge" stereotype: the notion that
Native women were forced to perform the most intense labors, such
as drawing water, tending fields, and gathering fruits and nuts, while
"lazy" American Indian men took on tasks such as hunting, fishing,
and diplomatic negotiations primarily associated with the aristocracy
in Europe.[39] Smits outlines a second crucial aspect of this stereotype:
the supposed lack of conjugal affection in American Indian marriages,
evident in Wood's claim that Native women are "miserable" after comparing their lot with the "love" English women receive. As I discuss at
length in chapter 2, this stereotype fundamentally misrepresents the significant spiritual, social, and political roles that Northeast Woodlands
Native women possess in relation to their work. The simple fact that
Child rejects both Wood and the widely circulated "squaw drudge" stereotype, emphasizing instead Hobomok's romantic devotion and his
public vows of love, suggests her commitment not only to comparing,
but also to reevaluating existing attitudes toward Native spiritual, cultural, and romantic values. By taking readers inside Hobomok's wetu and
recognizing the formal wedding rituals as rituals, Child acknowledges
the authority of this community to regulate their own marriages as they
see fit.

More radically, Child's comparison leaves open the possibility that
Native marriages (as represented by Lahontan) may offer women more
freedoms than Anglo-American marriage practices do. Where Mary's father forbids her marriage to Charles Brown, Lahontan's fictional Wendat
character Adario describes, in dialogue form, his daughter's insistence
and acknowledged right to marry as she chooses. Speaking to Lahontan,
Adario explains that even though he disapproves of his daughter's choice,
she will have her way: "She has a mind to't; and that is enough in our
Country. . . . I am oblig'd to comply with my Daughter's demands." Adar-

io's unnamed daughter rejoins, "What do you think Father! Am I your Slave? Shall not I enjoy my Liberty? Must I for your fancy, Marry a Man I do not care for? How can I endure a Husband that buys my Corps[e] of my Father, and what value shall I Have for such a Father as makes Brokerage of his Daughter to a Brute?"[40] In contrast to Wendat courtship and marriage arrangements—in which premarital sex was normal, women had the final say in a marriage partner, and divorce had relatively few social consequences—the norms regulating Anglo-American romantic relations in the seventeenth and nineteenth centuries are incredibly restrictive. Women who engaged in premarital sex are regularly shamed and ostracized, fortune was still a prominent consideration despite the increasing rhetoric of companionship, and divorce was difficult to obtain. Even when married, Anglo-American wives were considered *feme coverts,* "covered" by their husbands in the sight of the law.[41] Although Child does not directly draw this comparison, her comparative plot juxtaposes Puritan and Wendat romantic traditions in such a way as to allow readers to judge for themselves.

In this light, Child's attention to indigenous divorce proceedings exceeds the current critical consensus that it is a plot device used to "vanish" Hobomok and symbolically remove and/or assimilate the nation's considerable American Indian population. The ease and availability of divorce in many Native communities provide a model for ensuring conjugal happiness and peaceful family relations that Child holds up for her nineteenth-century readers to consider. Indeed, in many Jesuit missionary reports, the lack of divorce in Catholic marriages was a serious barrier for many Wendats to Christianity.[42] In this context, Native divorce policies ensure women's and men's individual happiness, and it is precisely the language Hobomok uses to describe his own divorce proceedings. In a remarkable affidavit that combines New England print culture and indigenous record-keeping systems—the sticks held by witnesses of the wedding ceremony—Hobomok requests that the colonial governor validate his "Indian" divorce proceedings, initiated when Mary's former suitor, Charles Brown, returns. The document notes that Hobomok has requested that the wedding sticks be burned, the ritual necessary for divorce: "this I doe, that Mary may be happie."[43] Hobomok's sacrifice is not only a racist fantasy of ending the "Indian problem"—though it certainly *is* that—it is also an instance when comparison opens a New World of marital possibilities. Under the rules governing Native marriage contracts, as Child depicts them, Mary and Hobomok are freer to consent to marriage and end their marriage than are seventeenth-century Puritans or nineteenth-century US citizens. *New World Courtships* recovers precisely such comparative views of marriage as well as the historical conditions and cross-cultural contexts that make this comparative line of sight available.

Chapter 1 explores the significance of comparative analyses of courtship traditions in three Enlightenment genres: popular "marriage-rites" compilations such as *Hymen: An Accurate Description of the Ceremonies Used in Marriage, by Every Nation in the Known World* (1760) by "Uxorious"; Scottish Enlightenment stadial theory, especially *The Origin of the Distinction of Ranks* (1771) by John Millar; and an early transatlantic novel, *The Female American* (1767) by Unca Eliza Winkfield (pseudonym). Restoring the Enlightenment emphasis on comparing marital diversity illuminates the disruptive potential of New World settings and cultural practices in a variety of genres; such power is especially evident, though, in the narrative practices and hybrid points of view frequently employed in transatlantic Anglophone fiction. In its comparisons of the "commonly domestick" nature of most women's stories with the pleasures of Native women's mobility and romantic autonomy, *The Female American* challenges the nationalist and imperialist comparative agendas of "Uxorious" and Millar.

Chapter 2 moves from genre studies to consider comparisons in a more specifically grounded geopolitical context: the complex interactions of British, French, Wendat, and Mohawk women in mid-eighteenth-century Canada. Interweaving contemporary Mohawk oral traditions with Frances Brooke's Canadian novel *The History of Emily Montague* (1769), this chapter explores the binary Brooke establishes between Mohawk women's right to "chuse a chief" versus British women's right to "chuse a husband." While Brooke insists that romantic rights are more important than a voice in the public arena, Mohawk oral tradition shows how Mohawk women's stories decenter romance narratives, enabling women in the past and present to move beyond the marriage plot and imagine more options for community engagement and personal satisfaction.

Chapter 3 continues to trace women's romantic relationships, now transitioning to the Caribbean. Interrogating stereotypical reports of Caribbean sensuality and lasciviousness, Leonora Sansay's *Secret History; or, The Horrors of St. Domingo* (1808) draws on her personal observations of mulatto women during the Haitian Revolution to rewrite the seduction plot, the dominant story line in early national US fiction. Through her comparisons of different classes and races of women in the Americas, Sansay expands the range of stories available to women by rejecting the novel's predictable conclusions—death or marriage—as she envisions single women joining together in a supportive, homosocial community.

Chapter 4 argues that the anonymously published *The Woman of Colour* (1808) employs a postcolonial strategy of "writing back" through a fictional Caribbean woman of color, Olivia Fairfield, who critiques British marriage practices. In doing so, Olivia posits an authentic reserve of domesticity for herself and others in a distinctly regional but morally equal Caribbean domestic sphere. Such a move not only revises British nationalist claims to moral virtue as expressed in the ideology of domesticity, but also writes back against some of the most important literary styles and colonizing themes of the sentimental novel.

While Olivia Fairfield claims the Caribbean as a legitimate site for domesticity, chapter 5 returns to the new United States and its concern to identify a romantic practice representative of the nation and its values. Where many early nationalist writers embraced Yankee bundling—a courtship practice in which parents permit an unmarried couple to share a bed for the night—the pseudonymous picaresque novel, *The Life and Adventures of Obadiah Benjamin Franklin Bloomfield, M.D.* (1818), dispatches the comparative mode in favor of a heteroglossic revelry in the diversity of romantic discourse vying for attention in its present moment. The novel's protagonist, Obadiah, humorously incorporates nearly every romantic discourse and practice in existence, from comparative marriage rites to bundling, adultery, and companionate marriage, highlighting the contradictions in choosing a single national romantic tradition to represent the nation's extensive marital diversity.

As Joseph Allen Boone explains, marriage, especially as it has been idealized in fiction, has come to be the relationship goal that defines a "fully experienced life."[44] It is no wonder, then, that many gay couples in the United States are rallying for what one activist group calls "the freedom to marry."[45] Even as contemporary authors such as Jeffrey Eugenides reject the marriage plot as no longer representative of reality, this plot functions as a central political goal for many monogamous gay couples and LGBT activists hoping to gain state and federal recognition in the twenty-first century. As "Why Marriage Matters," a public-education campaign for gaining same-sex marriage recognition, argues, "Marriage says 'we are family' in a way that no other word does."[46] The book's epilogue connects contemporary US debates about same-sex marriage and the definitions, terms, and rights associated with marriage with this longer history of marital diversity in the Anglo-American novel. Rediscovering the literary history of marital diversity allows us to map the competing rhetorical and discursive strategies currently employed in same-sex marriage debates and the rapid evolution of public opinion surrounding this issue onto a much longer history of controversies surrounding the meanings of marriage.

1

WHY MARRIAGE MATTERED THEN

IN "WHY COMPARE?" R. Radhakrishnan argues that "wanting to learn from 'other' experiences . . . is and should be the real motive behind any comparative endeavor and not just the imperative to hector, proselytize, or hierarchize difference in the name of a dominant 'superior' identity."[1] For most cultural comparison produced in eighteenth-century Britain, however, this was decidedly not the goal. This chapter begins by exploring the intellectual and cultural work of comparing marriage practices and women's status in marriage in texts as varied as *Hymen: An Accurate Description of the Ceremonies Used in Marriage, by Every Nation in the Known World* (1760) and *The Origin of the Distinction of Ranks* (1771). Despite their different audiences and purposes, these texts use differences in marriage customs as a metric for evaluating a group's "civilized" status. And in Britain, where individuals might contract marriages based on affection rather than parental prerogative, the ideal of companionate marriage came to be valued as more free and more personally fulfilling than other marriage practices.

However, by their very nature comparisons have the potential to denaturalize customs and social norms introducing other possibilities for organizing sociality. As quickly as "Uxorious" imagines British marriage as the most enlightened of "the ceremonies used in marriage by every nation in the known world," in *The Female American* (1767), novelist "Unca Eliza Winkfield" (pseudonym) shifts the terms of debate for claims of British women's progress through companionate marriage. Comparing the dull and "commonly domestick" nature of most women's lives with Native American women's mobility and romantic autonomy, *The Female American* undercuts the imperialist rhetoric of "Uxorious" and Millar.

This chapter investigates comparative analyses of courtship traditions in three Enlightenment genres: popular "marriage-rites" compilations; Scottish Enlightenment stadial theory; and an early transatlantic Anglophone novel. By highlighting Enlightenment investments in marital comparison, this chapter illuminates the disruptive potential that reports of indigenous American courtship practices had for claims of British women's supposedly superior status vis-à-vis marriage. This disruptive power is most evident, though, in *The Female American,* a novel in which hybrid points of view and playful narrative techniques dislodge British claims for progressive forms of marital liberty.

Marriage-Rites Anthologies: National and Imperial Propaganda

In "'Matrimonial Ceremonies Displayed': Popular Ethnography and Enlightened Imperialism," Lisa O'Connell outlines the history of the nonfiction marriage-rites genre beginning in 1680 with Louis de Gaya's *Cérémonies nuptiales de toutes les nations,* which was translated into English in 1685, and again in 1687 as *Matrimonial Customs; or, The Various Ceremonies, and Divers Ways of Celebrating Weddings, Practised amongst All the Nations, in the Whole World.*[2] Compiled from various travelers' accounts of courtship and marriage traditions, these texts combine the exotic and erotic with great success. As these anthologies adapt to the changing tastes and demographics of eighteenth-century readers, they shift from the titillating anecdotes and quasi-pornographic addendums of Thomas Brown's *Marriage Ceremonies* (1697) to the didactic, nationalist, and pro-imperial comparative agendas that emerge in the mid- to late eighteenth century. For instance, Thomas Salmon's *Critical Essays Concerning Marriage* (1724) capitalizes on an expanding demographic of female readers by including sections on marital advice and moral essays in the vein of popular conduct books. Moreover, it notably shifts the categories of comparison from religious groups (Christians, Jews, Muslims, and so on) to ethnic groups and larger geopolitical entities across Europe, Asia, Africa, and America. Such a move emphasizes the way that women's status and condition were being used as a comparative tool for evaluating differences between nation-states, a concept emerging precisely at this time.[3] Marriage-rites volumes continue to be popular into the Victorian era with new titles such as Lorenzo Niles Fowler's *Marriage: Its History and Ceremonies; with a Phrenological and Physiological Exposition of the Functions and Qualifications for Happy Marriages* (1847) appearing alongside continually popular late nineteenth-century reissues of Thomas Brown's *Matrimonial Ceremonies Displayed* (1886).

Coinciding with British legal reformations such as Hardwicke's Marriage Bill of 1753, mid-century marriage-rites anthologies such as *Hymen: An Accurate Description of the Ceremonies Used in Marriage, by Every Nation in the Known World* (1760) assure British women that their courtship customs (and the recent legal changes regulating marriage) secure them more advanced institutions and more personally satisfying intimate relations than anywhere else in the world.[4] Dedicated to the "Ladies of Great Britain and Ireland" by "Uxorious," *Hymen* organizes its separate chapters on marriage customs somewhat haphazardly, beginning with Jews and moving on to Romans, Peruvians, Caribes, [East] Indians, Floridians, "inhabitants of Hudson's-bay, Mississippi, and Canada," Mexicans, Indians in New Mexico, Nicaraguans, Brazilians, Americans, "Savages of Darien," and "New Grenada," Bramins, Chinese, Persians, Japanese, Greeks, English, Mahometans, and Hottentots.[5] As a compilation of traveler's sketches and other reports, *Hymen* essentially aims for the fascinating marital anecdote. The connecting tissue between these comparisons is puzzling, however. Why, for instance, are East Indians wedged between Caribes and Floridians? The relation is not simply alphabetical—for example, the English come much later in the anthology. Perhaps unsurprisingly, the work expresses no interest in or recognition of the fact that in any given place, customs change over time. Even the chapter on England, where one might expect more depth, captures no sense of the major recent changes in legal requirements to marry such as a licensed officiate, witnesses, and parental approval attending the Marriage Act of 1753. The only historical changes to English marriage customs that "Uxorious" mentions are changes between Catholic services and post-Reformation Anglican practices, located safely in the past.

A cursory reading of *Hymen* reveals the author's recurring interest in incest taboos, premarital sexual contact, polygamy, the exchange of gifts, curious ceremonial proceedings, regulations on separation and divorce, and dealings with adultery. For instance, "early marriages are not customary among the Floridians who dwell near Panuco, yet we are assured they are scarce maids by ten or twelve years of age." Divorces are easily granted among the American Indians of the Hudson's Bay region (no tribal names given): Father Hennepin "tells us, that their marriage is not a civil contract; that the husband and wife do not bind themselves to each for life: that they cohabit as long as they like one another, but separate without the least formality as soon as their harmony is interrupted by domestic broils."[6] Among the "Mahometans," polygamy is universally practiced, but this practice does not, according to "Uxorious," increase the population. The moral judgment lodged in this comparison is fairly obvious: the excesses of sensuality permitted by "Mahometan" polygamy are not, in fact, generative. *Hymen* ends with the most "curious" of all anecdotes, describing a "Hottentot" ceremony in which the priest repeatedly "pisses" on the bride and groom while offering good wishes such as "May you live long and happy together; may you have a son before the end of the year; may this son live to be a comfort to you in your old age; may this son prove to be a man of courage and a good huntsman."[7] By comparison, "Uxorious" describes the English customs of publishing the banns in church, official vows, the exchange of rings, and so on, explaining that "these mutual contracts are essentially necessary to preserve the honor and secure the safety of mankind." *Hymen* strategically compares differences in marriage rites, implicitly noting that binding "contracts" are essential requirements for "civilized" marriages. In his account of English customs, "Uxorious" emphasizes the legal and institutional structures that legitimate English marriage as well as the public nature of the ceremony. Although the chapter on English traditions references curious local practices such as the "breeding woman's oath," in which an unwed mother may swear to a father's identity and he must pay a tax for the child, the bulk of the chapter touts customs "approved by the church or the governors of it."[8]

For "Uxorious," marital diversity is ultimately linked to a narrative of civilization and progress. These comparisons illustrate that "without [women] the human race had never emerged from the rude and savage state." Moreover, woman's "influence has been always the greatest in countries most distinguished for elegance and refinement of taste." In a flourish of national bombast, "Uxorious" claims that "English ladies" are "indulged in liberties which foreigners can hardly give credit to."[9] According to "Uxorious," then, women are responsible for the "polish" that has made civilized countries more advanced; more particularly, all the glory of England's "elegance and refinement" is owing to the "liberties" English men bestow on women.

This rhetoric will sound familiar to readers of Scottish Enlightenment philosophy by Adam Smith, David Hume, William Robertson, and others. For instance, in *The History of Women* (1779), William Alexander explicitly connects women's "liberties" and the national attainment of civility when he argues that "the rank, therefore, and condition, in which we find women in any country, mark out to us with great precision, the exact point in the scale of civil society, to which the people of such country have arrived."[10] In short, women, and the kinds of courtships and marriages women are subject to, become the measuring sticks by which one could calculate any nation's progress toward civility. Eighteenth-century comparisons of marriage rites around the globe not only exoticize culturally specific sexual behaviors, but they also explicitly evaluate and judge others as more or less civilized.[11] At their core, the comparisons inherent in the British marriage-rites genre promote national chauvinism. Representing the customs of others as absurd, these texts attempt to convince British couples to marry, reproduce, and support the status quo.

The Economics of Romance: John Millar's Stadial History

Whereas marriage-rites anthologies target a popular readership, Scottish Enlightenment "stadial" or "conjectural" histories are primarily aimed at academic and learned readers. As with marriage-rites anthologies, though, stadial histories employ a cross-cultural comparative methodology to situate Britons as the most advanced in the various "stages" of human progress. For instance, according to Adam Smith's stadial model, humans progress through four stages of economic development: a hunter-gatherer phase, a shepherding phase, an agricultural phase, and, finally, a commercial phase.[12] In each stage of increasing economic complexity, the Scots also trace supposed advances in institutions, cultural norms, and interpersonal relationships. They explicitly describe manners and feelings as contingent on the national level of economic progress. Not surprisingly, countries with commercial economies such as Great Britain supposedly produce the most advanced and refined manners. National differences in women's status and treatment are key metrics in these economic comparisons. As William Alexander observes, "were their history entirely silent on every other subject, and only mentioned the manner in which they treated their women, we should, from thence, be enabled to form a tolerable judgment of the barbarity, or culture of their manners."[13]

As a former student of Adam Smith, John Millar builds on and extends Smith's four-stage theory of human advancement. Millar's *The Origin of the Distinction of Ranks* (1771) offers the most sophisticated account of women's progress within his larger project to locate the origins of social and political authority or "rank."[14] Millar argues that economically advanced societies offer women the most respect as well as the most room for determining their own personal happiness in marriage. Unlike Adam Smith, who barely mentions gender differences, or Lord Kames, who segregates women's history to a separate section of his *Sketches of the History of Man* (1774), Millar grounds his theory of the origins of rank in heterosexual relationships. As Carol Pateman and others have shown, contract theorists such as John Locke and Thomas Hobbes—who fantasize a "state of nature" as a space for imagining the rise of political institutions—erase gender inequalities in their fantasies of liberal individuals who "contract" to work together, thus creating governments. They ignore and erase women's agency in the contracting process and presume masculine authority—patriarchy—as a baseline.[15] Millar, fascinatingly, does not ignore the question of how men came to hold their supposedly universal right to govern women and families. However his account is not ideologically neutral.[16] He confronts but, finally, dodges the contradictions inherent in patriarchal power when he grapples with reports of the matrilineal kin networks and marriage practices of the Haudenosaunee (Iroquois) in what will become New York, Ontario, and Quebec. Ultimately, Millar cannot reconcile nonpatriarchal Haudenosaunee marriage and family structures in his stadial theories of women's "progress," which he tracks through supposedly increasing romantic attachments between heterosexual couples across the four stages of economic development.[17] Millar's inability to account for matrilineal Haudenosaunee social structures signals the propagandistic nationalism inherent in his comparative methodology; however, it also highlights the ways comparative analysis can undermine the very hierarchies it is summoned to establish.

Plotting a steady increase in sexual intimacy from the supposed animal lust of the "rudest" economic stage to the companionate-marriage ideal of his own British commercial society, Millar theorizes psychological, emotional, and sexual development occurring alongside economic development. Millar notes that women's status is dependent on three criteria: first, the ease of sexual gratification; second, the value of women's work; and third, the leisure time available for courting. In the hunting stage, there is no time for romance: "When men are in danger of perishing for hunger . . . when they are unable to shelter themselves from beasts of prey, or from enemies of their own kind . . . their constitution would surely be ill adapted to their circumstances, were they endowed with a refined taste of pleasure, and capable of feeling the delicate distresses and enjoyments of love, accompanied with all those elegant sentiments, which, in a civilized and enlightened age, are naturally derived from that passion. Dispositions of this nature would be altogether misplaced in the breast of a savage."[18] For Millar, love is limited by the social and economic conditions in which it takes shape. When subsistence proves difficult, sex is simply an animal instinct, not an emotional commitment. Men in this stage are supposedly severe toward women because they are not emotionally invested.

Moreover, there is no need for romance when men have immediate and unlimited sexual access to women. While this description might imply that so-called savage societies are one prolonged orgiastic experience, Millar reluctantly admits, "It is true, that, even in early ages, some sort of marriage, or permanent union between persons of different sexes, has been almost universally established." However, he points out that even "inferior animals" act on a similar principle in preserving their young. In Millar's analysis, marriage among "rude people" is lacking in the most essential point: mutual affection. The male never marries from "particular inclination;" he "discovers no preference" and allows his parents to conduct the matter "without concerning himself." Unlike the depth of feeling shared by partners in a companionate marriage, "savage" marriage is "completed, on both sides, with the most perfect indifference."[19] Marriage and family ought to be the products of choice, Millar urges. Of course, mutual affection and choice are only possible in the commercial stage of development.

Millar continues his description of advances in women's status in the middle two of the four stages. In the pastoral stage, new restrictions on heterosocial activity increase the value of women more generally. Instead of being interchangeable objects of desire, women present opportunities for male choice; they inspire "inclination and sentiment."[20] Moreover, increased wealth introduces distinctions of rank that lead to rivalries and jealousies, especially with regard to the distribution of women. In the later agricultural age, chivalry becomes the new standard of behavior toward women: "The sincere and faithful passion, which commonly occupied the heart of every warrior, and which he professed upon all occasions, was naturally productive of the utmost purity of manners, and of great respect and veneration for the female sex." Ironically, Millar identifies this as the high point in women's status, finding a connection between delicate behavior toward women and advances in the arts such as bards, wandering minstrels, the poetry of Spenser, and long prose romances. Although these high standards gradually change, the legacy of chivalry "has given an air of refinement to the intercourse of the sexes, which contributes to heighten the elegant pleasures of society, and may therefore be considered as a valuable improvement in society."[21] Millar argues that women's status improves when men have restricted sexual access to women. Men respect and value women when society creates "artificial" social barriers such as modesty and reserve between the sexes.[22] Chastity, then, is a sign of progress; but it is only possible when the right social and economic conditions—such as restrictions on heterosocial contact and increased leisure time for courting—occur in later stages of economic development: "In consequence of these improvements the virtue of chastity begins to be recognized; for when love becomes a passion, instead of being a mere sensual appetite, it is natural to think that those affections which are not dissipated by variety of enjoyment, will be the purest and the strongest."[23] Affection and emotional commitment are the result of postponed sexual fulfillment made possible in economically advanced shepherding societies.

Sexual access and leisure time for courting are not the only measures of women's status, however; the value of women's work is another significant factor. Millar suggests that in hunting societies, men value skills useful in battle or the chase; in this, women cannot easily contribute. Since women cannot compete with men's superior strength and courage, "it falls upon them to manage all the inferior concerns of the household, and to perform such domestic offices . . . which, however useful, . . . are naturally regarded as mean and servile." Women are little better than servants forced to endure hard labor: "digging roots, drawing water, carrying wood, milking cattle, dressing the victuals, and rearing the children."[24] David Smits describes this rhetoric as the "squaw drudge" stereotype, a common European misinterpretation of the valuation of gendered labor in many American Indian communities.[25] Millar extends the typical "squaw drudge" stereotype, making marriage in the supposed early stages of human development not an opportunity for companionship, but the vehicle for gaining just such a laborer: "To marry a wife must there be the same thing as to purchase a female servant."[26] In his discussion of hunter-gatherer modes of marriage, Millar ignores how capitalism allowed supposedly civilized men to openly purchase multiple women's labor without any emotional or long-term financial commitment whatsoever.

From the feudal conditions of the agricultural age, Millar proceeds to his contemporary moment: commerce and companionate marriage. Despite an increase in heterosocial contact that makes women more accessible than in the days of chivalry, Millar suggests that women in the commercial stage are better off because they earn new respect as skilled managers of domestic affairs.[27] When war and military skill are less valuable than trade and politeness, Millar theorizes that men have a new appreciation for domesticity as well as more time to spend at home. Millar notes that women living in commercial economies are increasingly regarded for "their useful or agreeable talents," which extend beyond household duties to include domestic *affections*: "In this situation, the women become, neither the slaves, nor the idols of the other sex, but the friends and companions."[28] Here the narrative sounds much like the standard courtship novel of the day. Essentially, Millar argues that men and women must have time to appreciate and to please one another before marrying. This time is set apart and ritualized through particular customs of courtship, time that ideally produces a mutual preference and equal affection.

Millar identifies companionate marriage as a measure not only of women's progress, but also of social and national progress; indeed, it becomes the ultimate symbol of both. More insidiously, though, Millar describes how domestic affections can be used as tools for controlling women:

> [Women] learn to suit their behavior to the circumstances in which they are placed, and to that particular standard of propriety and excellence set before them. Being respected on account of their diligence and proficiency in the various branches of domestic economy, they naturally endeavor to improve and extend those valuable qualifications. They are taught to apply with assiduity to those occupations which fall under their province, and to look upon idleness as the greatest blemish in female character. . . . As their attention is principally bestowed upon the members of their own family, they are led, in a particular manner, to improve those feelings of the heart which are excited by these tender connections, and they are trained up in the practice of all the domestic virtues.[29]

Millar clearly understands that women in commercial societies are *trained* to invest their time, energy, and emotions toward domestic relations.[30] He subtly suggests that women are best suited for domestic tasks and that the best way to ensure they fulfill such tasks/roles is to affirm "useful" feminine characteristics. Millar sees male politeness (affirming domestic work or "feminine" behaviors) as an ideological tool helpful for controlling women.[31]

Millar rather astoundingly recognizes that gender is culturally constructed. Differences in women's status, he argues, are the result of specific economic circumstances and cultural values. However, Millar retreats from the notion that gender is only a cultural by-product: "Possessed of peculiar delicacy, and sensibility, *whether derived from original constitution, or from her way of life,* [woman] is capable of securing the esteem and affection of her husband, by dividing his cares, by sharing his joys, and by soothing his misfortunes."[32] Ultimately, he offers a narrative where women gain increased social status via the rise of romantic love. His account of women's progress makes companionate marriage and domestic affections the ultimate sign of human development. More-over, he argues that women in his own commercial England benefit from these supposedly more advanced heterosexual relations. Having traced a steady increase in romantic affection and an increasing investment in women's domestic affections through the four stages of economic devel-opment, Millar must now imagine how it was that men came to hold power in the first place. To do so, Millar wrestles with protoethnographic reports of powerful Haudenosaunee (Iroquois) women—reports he will not easily reconcile with his patriarchal theories of development.

In order to show how distinctions of rank evolve into recognizable institutions such as the state, Millar begins by describing how men gain authority over women and establish patriarchy.[33] To show how patriar-chy was established, however, one has to imagine and characterize a state prior to patriarchy when it was possible for women to hold power. Millar looks to Haudenosaunee gender relations to establish a historical prec-edent for such a prepatriarchal "past." As Millar grapples with reports of Haudenosaunee women's public participation in their communities, though, he experiences an epistemological and narrative crisis. He cannot reconcile the data on Haudenosaunee gender arrangements with his sta-dial framework. For if women could and, in some places, did hold power, how did they lose it? And was that loss of political and social power really compensated for by the relatively recent companionate-marriage ideal? Millar's story of the rise of patriarchy contains a trace of this epis-temological crisis as his comparisons fold back on him.

In a section titled "The influence acquired by the mother of a family before marriage is completely established," Millar addresses the challenge of solidifying patriarchy prior to the institutionalization of "civilized" marriage, that is, before men made women their legal property. Millar's task proves difficult; he must simultaneously explain away Haudeno-saunee women's power and convince English women that they have the best marital arrangements. He does this, in part, by making contempo-rary Haudenosaunee women's power seem primitive, part of an untena-ble past. The custom of matrilineal genealogy, Millar notes, is as common "among the ancient inhabitants of Attica; as it [is] at present among sev-eral tribes of the natives of North America, and of the Indians upon the coast of Malabar. In this situation the mother of a numerous family, who lives at a distance from her other relations, will often be raised to a degree of rank and dignity to which, from her sex, she would not otherwise be entitled."[34] Millar clearly engages in what the anthropologist Johannes Fabian calls a denial of coevalness, a view of time that locates supposedly primitive peoples in a hypothetical past not equally living in the present alongside "modern" peoples. For Millar, this is a time—both "at present" and among the "ancient[s]"—when "savage" women possess(ed) power in their communities and over their families. He concludes: "In a country where children have no acquaintance with their father, and are not indebted to him for subsistence and protection, they can hardly fail, during a considerable part of their life, to regard their mother as the principal person in the family. This is in all probability the source of that influence which appears to have been possessed by women in several rude and barbarous parts of the world." Although Britons exist in a present that excludes matrilineal kin structures, the difficulty is that other communities also live in this present moment, and they *do* allow women to head households. As Millar acknowledges, in his contemporary moment Haudenosaunee people trace their genealogies through the mother's line and grant women voting rights in tribal assemblies. "The North American tribes," Millar observes, "are accustomed to admit their women into their public councils, and even to allow them the privilege of being first called to give their opinion upon every subject of deliberation." Millar downplays this authority by claiming a perceived lack of emotional fulfillment on the part of Haudenosaunee women. He reassures his readers that "the women of North America do not arrive at this [political] influence . . . till after a certain age, . . . before this period they are commonly treated as the slaves of men; and that there is no country in the world where the female sex is in general more neglected and despised." Here, again, is the rhetoric of the "squaw drudge," the emotionally unfulfilled "slaves of men." As I show in greater detail in the next chapter, this stereotype is quite inaccurate. Given the Enlightenment investment in companionate marriage, this last point proves most damning of all, for emotional affection supposedly marks the great divide between utilitarian "savage" sex and affectionate "civilized" marriage. Still Millar admits that "in a country where marriage is unknown, females are commonly exalted to be the heads of families, or chiefs, and thus acquire an authority, which notwithstanding their inferiority in strength, may extend to the direction of war, as well as other transactions."[35] This level of female authority proves difficult for Millar to reconcile. Its attractiveness to women readers can only be reduced by claiming that mutual affection—women's emotional companionship— somehow outweighs women's political and familial authority.

Millar never effectively describes how patriarchal marriage becomes institutionalized in most locations around the world, but at least part of his problem has to do with the strange temporality at work in the stadial schema. Millar has to describe how patriarchy has already been established in certain locations and how it *will* happen in other locations—his historical analysis must simultaneously report the past and prescribe the future, equally universal and particular in its parameters. Having faced a time prior to patriarchy that was still in existence in certain "underdeveloped" cultures, Millar seems unable to describe how men claimed and, in some cases, will claim their power. This is an absolutely crucial evasion.

Millar turns to ancient Greek myth, the moment when the women of Attica lost their right to speak in public deliberations, to locate the origins of patriarchy. Firmly rooted in the past, this particular example also suggests a potential future event whereby Haudenosaunee women's political status might conform to "civilized" patriarchal standards. Millar reports that after the construction of Athens was complete, there was a contest between the gods Minerva and Neptune for the honor of naming the city. A public assembly was called and the women supported Minerva, while the men supported Neptune. Ultimately, the women won by a single vote. Shortly thereafter, the city was hit by a forceful sea storm and the citizens feared that Neptune was seeking revenge. "To appease him," Millar notes, "they resolved to punish the female sex, by whom the offence was committed, and determined that no woman should for the future be admitted into the public assemblies, nor any child be allowed to bear the name of its mother."[36] In this account, Greek women's loss of political influence is punishment pure and simple; it is hard to comprehend it as an act of friendship or an inevitable move toward civility.[37] According to this legend, it was during the same time that "marriage was first established among the Athenians" with the result that "children were no longer accustomed to bear the name of their mother, but that of their father, who, from his superior strength and military talents, became the head and governor of the family; and as the influence of women was thereby greatly diminished, it was to be expected that they should, in a little time, be entirely excluded from those great assemblies which deliberated upon public affairs."[38] As men assume the role of head of household, Millar conjectures, their domestic authority would naturally transfer to the public arena as well. Millar fantastically declares that women's loss of political power "was to be expected" as a natural consequence of their diminished social and familial influence. In the end, Millar can only suggest that what women lose in political power they make up in romantic love and male companionship, although this "restoration" does not take place until the economy advances to the commercial stage. His teleology suggests that women's reward for becoming demure domestic partners is, eventually, companionate marriage; however, by his own account, there is a long period of suffering and degradation between.

What I find so odd in Millar's account is how this flimsy fable—so particular in its setting and mythological references—becomes the crux for all of the other descriptions of power and rank in Millar's book. He seems to hope beyond hope that his readers have forgotten about contemporary Haudenosaunee women selecting chiefs, or at least, that they agree that romance outweighs women's political participation. Millar quickly moves on to explain how this initial "distinction of rank" leads to more complex iterations such as the authority of the father, the chief, and the sovereign. From here, women are once again relegated to a subplot in the larger story of power and authority. Yet Millar, more than any other conjectural historian, seems haunted by the task of accounting for the disruptive potential of Haudenosaunee gender and marriage traditions. Millar's comparisons make the myth of women's progress through companionate marriage visible, allowing readers to question their assumptions about its real benefits for women.

Debunking Companionate Marriage as Women's Progress

The anonymously published *The Female American; or, The Adventures of Unca Eliza Winkfield* (1767) combines familiar themes of transatlantic Anglophone fiction—cross-cultural contact and Atlantic travel—with a female robinsonade plot.[39] Written in the first-person perspective of Unca Eliza Winkfield, a biracial Native American–Caucasian woman, *The Female American* brings together a perplexing number of genres and intertextual referents. Unca Eliza, a self-proclaimed "female American," is the child of parents involved in a Pocahontas-style romance. She eventually goes to England to be educated and Christianized, is later abandoned on a desert island à la Robinson Crusoe, and eventually converts a neighboring group of American Indians, establishing herself as a prophet and leader of this utopian Christian community. In a complicated series of events, Unca Eliza's cousin hears of her fate and determines to rescue her. When he finally finds her, Cousin Winkfield marries Unca Eliza and takes over her missionary work. The novel ends with several new narrators giving an account of her discovery and rescue.

Previous scholarship on *The Female American* tends to focus on the novel's robinsonade qualities and its obviously fictional strategies for surviving and thriving in the Americas. Although this point is often overlooked, Unca Eliza's adventures are predicated on her single status and her repeated rejection of marriage offers. Although Unca Eliza does finally marry her cousin, contained by the gravitational pull of what Rachel Blau DuPlessis calls the "conventional" romance ending,[40] the novel challenges the conventionality of a typical companionate-marriage ending by illustrating Unca Eliza's apathy toward married life. If marriage typically provides a heroine with a happy end to her story, and if it also serves as evidence of national progress, what are readers to make of Unca Eliza's continued indifference to marriage, her rejection of all ties to England, and her continued career as a missionary and translator even after marriage? Unca Eliza's life story is more than a robinsonade; her adventures challenge the ideological claim that companionate marriage was a form of progress for women.

Identifying as both English and American Indian, our strong-willed heroine begins by contrasting her freedoms to speak, to move, and to choose her own destiny with the standard lot of women: "The lives of women being commonly domestick, the occurrences of them are generally pretty nearly of the same kind; whilst those of men, frequently more vagrant, subject them often to experience greater vicissitudes, many times wonderful and strange. Though a woman, it has been my lot to have experienced much of the latter; for so wonderful, strange, and uncommon have been the events of my life, that true history, perhaps, never recorded any that were more so."[41] On the first page, Unca Eliza sets herself apart from ordinary women—her story stands out precisely because it is unlike other women's stories. This difference can be located in her biracial, bicultural heritage; in her Atlantic travels; as well as in her desire to remain single. As the child of a white Virginia colonist and a Native American "princess" (whose tribal designation is never named), Unca Eliza informs us early on of her mother's status, power, and romantic intensity. Pocahontas-like, Unca Eliza's mother, Unca, rescues her father and falls deeply in love with him. However, Unca's sister also instantly falls in love with Unca Eliza's father and just misses rescuing him herself. This jealous aunt tries various means to convince Unca Eliza's father to choose her over her sister; through this portrait of the two sisters, readers glimpse a world of relatively autonomous, passionate Native women. While one sister acts with kindness and love, the other is jealous to the point of murder. Yet each controls her own romantic destiny, operating outside parental control. This fictional glimpse of Virginia Native women's relative romantic freedom offers a compelling contrast to the typical pleasures and frustrations of courtship plots.

Unca Eliza's unusual upbringing precludes the kind of feminine domesticity that makes the lives of women "pretty nearly of the same kind." For instance, in England Unca Eliza plays up her unique heritage through her external appearance: "My tawny complexion, and the oddity of my dress, attracted every one's attention, for my mother used to dress me in a kind of mixed habit, neither perfectly in the Indian, nor yet in the European taste."[42] Every sign leads one to understand her as a blend of identities, neither English nor Indian, but something new: a female American. Even Unca Eliza's name suggests hybridity; she is named for her Native princess mother and the reigning Queen Elizabeth. She also notes how her class position as an indigenous princess garners her much attention in England. Because of her high-ranking status, our heroine is *not* dismissed as a "savage"; rather, her abundant display of diamonds and entourage of Native slaves makes her hybrid identity more appealing to her English acquaintances. In Unca Eliza's experience, royalty status overrides racial difference.[43] Finally, Unca Eliza's education is another factor in her exceptional history. While staying with her Uncle Winkfield, an Anglican minister, she and her female cousins receive the same education as her male cousin. Most unusually, she learns Greek, Latin, Christian theology, and "other polite literature; whilst my good aunt took care of the female part of my education." This is a thoroughly progressive education and quite remarkable for any woman in this period. Despite her desire to remain single, Unca Eliza is nevertheless courted. She relays her atypical point of view on the routine events of courtship through her unabashedly confident and playful narrative voice. For instance, when she describes her potential eligibility on the English marriage market, Unca Eliza coquettishly acknowledges her potential lovers' money-grubbing motives. She writes, "Tawny as I was, with my lank black hair, I yet had my admirers, or such they pretended to be; though perhaps my fortune tempted them more than my person, at least I thought so, and accordingly diverted myself at their expense; for none touched my heart." This is a woman who understands the game of the marriage market as distinct from the rhetoric of companionship; she acknowledges her strengths and weaknesses from the perspective of her English suitors, maintaining an absolute independence throughout. When her cousin woos her, she coyly refuses, saying, "I would never marry any man who could not use a bow and arrow as well as I could." While this is perhaps simply an avoidance strategy, the quip also suggests that Cousin Winkfield does not live up to Unca Eliza's culturally distinct gender expectations. When he persists, she laughingly answers him in "the Indian language, of which he was entirely ignorant; and so by degrees wearied him into silence on that head."[44]

Unca Eliza knowingly deploys her Native language to block her cousin's courtship. Still, one senses that it is actually Unca Eliza who is wearied by her cousin's romantic insinuations since she so clearly makes known her preference to remain single. Unca Eliza's refusal to translate leaves Cousin Winkfield speechless. In his momentary silence, he faces the epistemological impossibility of knowing all there is to this mixed-race female American. Unca Eliza's untranslated Native speech disrupts the plot's romantic drive, making possible the robinsonade adventures that follow; at this moment, her Native tongue enables her to avoid becoming "pretty nearly of the same kind."

The most overt assault on Unca Eliza's independence and her most overt rejection of marriage up to this point occurs when a ship captain threatens to abandon her on a deserted island unless she marries his son (whereby her person and her inheritance would become the property of another). She flatly refuses this proposition and exerts her utmost strength to retain control over her own destiny. In a bloody battle between her Native slaves and the ship's crew, she loses; like Robinson Crusoe, she finds herself alone and stranded on what appears to be an empty island. *The Female American* dodges its audience's likely suspicion that a single young woman would not be able to survive on her own by providing Unca Eliza with a previous islander's survival guide. Detailing how to gather and store water, how to create an oil lamp and fuel it, as well as how to hunt and gather food, the survival guide is an especially contrived means of granting Eliza independence. Ironically, this solution to Unca Eliza's presumed feminine weakness undermines her thoroughly independent personality and her self-professed archery skills. For on the island, Unca Eliza suddenly abandons her bow and arrows, remembers her distressing femininity, and continually complains of her utter inability to survive alone in the wild. With her guidebook in hand, though, Unca Eliza settles more comfortably into her solitary life and begins to explore and confidently assert her presence on the island. Like Crusoe, Unca Eliza might eventually wish to declare, "How like a King I look'd . . . the whole Country was my own meer property," as she learns to domesticate the island's population of goats or writes a natural history of an unusual species of sloth-like animal she discovers.[45] However, Unca Eliza aims higher than Crusoe's kingly ambitions; she literally makes herself a god.

The enterprising Unca Eliza soon concocts a plan to Christianize the neighboring Native peoples who visit "her" island. In a supreme example of Unca Eliza's authoritative voice, she enters a hollowed-out statue and speaks to the visiting group as if she is one of their gods, though she claims her motive is to convert them. Of course, there are a number of problems with this strategy. First, Unca Eliza speaks as God—a blasphemous and hubristic move even when motivated by good intentions. Second, she speaks as God by talking through an idol—certainly a questionable conversion tactic. Finally, Unca Eliza seemingly appropriates the rhetoric of white imperialist domination—she will "rescue" the Indians from their false worship—in the guise of her missionary work. She draws on the rhetoric of contemporary missionary groups such as the Society for the Propagation of the Gospel to justify her conquest of others.[46]

But Unca Eliza does *not* need rescuing by white men. She assumes that role herself when she actively "saves" others by converting them to Christianity. With her godlike voice, Unca Eliza declares: "By keeping them ignorant who I was, or how I came to them, I might preserve a superiority over them, sufficient to keep them in awe, and to excite their obedience: yet I determined to speak no untruth."[47] Unca Eliza clearly prefers to keep the upper hand in all of her relationships. To ensure her dominance, Unca Eliza, still speaking from the statue, commands:

> A person shall come to you, like yourselves, and that you may be the less fearful or suspicious, that person shall be a woman, who shall live among you as you do.
>
> . . . You must be sure to show the greatest respect to her, do every thing that she shall command you, never ask who she is, from whence she comes, or when, or whether she will leave you. Never hinder her from coming to this island when she pleases, nor follow her hither without her leave. You must all believe, and do as she shall instruct you, and never presume to come to this island without her leave, or do anything she forbids.[48]

This makes Robinson Crusoe's capture and enslavement of Friday seem rather paltry by comparison. Unca Eliza manages to extract complete submission and willing obedience from the entire population she intends to convert; she asks not simply for religious obedience, but absolute dominion over every aspect of their lives. Furthermore, Unca Eliza uses her own hybrid subjectivity—her knowledge of Native languages, customs, and beliefs as well as her English education and Christian beliefs—to effect this submission.[49] She makes her entrance into their community more comfortable by suggesting her "likeness" to her new converts (she looks like them and speaks their language) but, of course, her claim to authority resides in her difference from them.

Unca Eliza's fantasy of female authority is legitimated by her English background: her father's cultural patrimony, her uncle's religious instruction, and the Christian imagery of God the Father. Indeed, she often imagines what her uncle would say as she preaches to her potential converts—a haunting instance of colonial mimicry. Unca Eliza straight-forwardly borrows Christian theology in what is certainly an imperialist grab for power. She claims this superiority through a dual sense of priv-ilege as a part-European Christian. Her missionary work is a caution against reading this novel as an exuberant expression of early feminism or a strictly anticolonial assertion of indigenous agency; it is neither. Still, this Christian prophetess would not be so successful without her Native language skills and cultural knowledge. Her hybrid identity enables Unca Eliza's unique relationship to Christianity and to other Native peoples.

Initially, Unca Eliza's curious and potentially threatening assumption of missionizing colonial authority seems contained by the novel's con-clusion. Unca Eliza is "rescued" by her obstinate lover, Cousin Wink-field, who determines not only to stay with Unca Eliza and take over her missionary practice, but to finally make her a wife as well. Before Unca Eliza submits to this "commonly domestick" fate, however, she of-fers up a characteristic display of spunk. Having successfully begun the work of converting her Native neighbors and having established herself as a member of their community, Unca Eliza is quite surprised to see her Cousin Winkfield and a number of sailors on "her" old island. When she realizes they are looking for her, she decides to play a trick on them using a familiar tool, the hollowed-out statue of the sun idol. She explains, "The joy of finding my cousin raised my spirits, and I was determined to indulge an adventure which promised much pleasure." Speaking to the search party from inside the statue, Unca Eliza inquires after her uncle. The crew, including her cousin, are so stunned by the seemingly magical address that they fear it is the voice of an evil spirit. Unca Eliza revels in the hoax: "I could not help being much diverted at their fears; but unwill-ing to discover myself, I however determined to dissipate their terrors."[50] So she sings a hymn particular to her family, knowing that her cousin will recognize it and that the religious nature of the song would calm the crew's anxieties about evil spirits.

Although she claims that she hopes to "dissipate their terrors," Unca Eliza actually transforms her uncle's hymn into a tool for exposing the superstitions of Europeans. Unca Eliza has previously used Christian rhetoric to assert her power over others, but, in this instance, she does not attempt to govern the sailors. She only wants to mischievously resist her cousin's rescue attempts. This difference reflects Unca Eliza's recognition of a hierarchy of power that moves from the Winkfields (English, Christian, male), to the hybrid Unca Eliza (part-English, Christian, female), to the indigenous population ("native," "heathen"). In the short moment before she reveals herself, Unca Eliza retains a sense of power and control over her own fate. When she finally shows herself, the crew runs back to the ship and Cousin Winkfield is left standing alone and, again, speechless. In this scene, Unca Eliza briefly obtains the apex of her potential powers, manipulating both European and indigenous superstitions.

Almost as if in retaliation for Unca Eliza's presumption, her first-person narration is abruptly interpolated by the dramatic dialogue of others, a narrative intrusion that weakens Unca Eliza's control over the story. After their initial reunion, Cousin Winkfield's voice commands a significant portion of the narrative. He questions Unca Eliza while she relates how she survived on the desolate island. Unca Eliza's authority over her own story, her ability to portray herself in first-person narration, slips away. When her cousin again declares his love for her, Unca Eliza uncomfortably attempts to dissuade him from staying with her. This time her words lack the power they once commanded; Winkfield announces: "It seems . . . as if providence . . . designs that I shall carry my resolution to teach the Indians into practice, and spend my days with my dear Unca, whether she will or no." Unca Eliza has no choice at all; she has fallen from godlike power to become a mere wife. She observes, "Though I loved him as a friend and relation, I had never considered him as a lover; nor any other person. It appeared to me, indeed, as if it must be as he would have it, yet the reflection gave me no pleasure." After holding out for two months, Unca Eliza marries her cousin and turns her missionary efforts over to her properly ordained husband: "From the time of my cousin's settling here, or rather my husband, as I must now for the future call him, the Indians were properly baptized, married, and many of them, at their earnest desire, admitted to the Lord's supper. My husband and I spent much of our time in teaching the Christian religion to the children; he the boys and I the girls."[51] Her telling admission that she works as a *translator* for her husband—a role she explicitly refused earlier in the story—suggests her fall from power after marriage. Instead of speaking for herself, she must now speak the words of others. At this point, Unca Eliza's story is almost entirely overrun as first her cousin tells of how he learned of her desertion on the island, and then other characters interrupt Winkfield's narration to share their parts in the adventure. These narrative interruptions suggest that now that she is rescued, Unca Eliza's voice is no longer necessary to the story. Official white male voices from ship captains to ordained ministers dominate the novel's conclusion.

As many eighteenth-century courtship novels do, *The Female American* provides readers with a marriage. But Unca Eliza's story allows us to see that marriage may not be the happy ending readers expect. We are invited to recognize that for this heroine, at least, marriage is not the goal or reward. Indeed, Unca Eliza expresses "no pleasure" in this most important new relationship. The novel's female robinsonade plot offers a fleeting alternative to the usual woman's story, one that capitalizes on the hybrid vantage point of a transatlantic mixed-race Native woman. Unca Eliza's earlier independence—the result of her status as a single, "female American"—serves as a critique of the supposed privileges of English companionate marriage. Comparing Unca Eliza's mother's and aunt's stories of Native women's passionate, intimate, and autonomously formed romantic relations with Unca Eliza's evident loss of power as she reluctantly marries her English cousin demonstrates how the narrative force of the happily-ever-after ending functions as a kind of trap in which Unca Eliza must conform herself to the "commonly domestick" lives of women.

Yet even as Unca Eliza's marriage reads as a defeat, her spirited resistance and playful determination to avoid the common lot of women stands in opposition to the eighteenth-century novel's powerful mythos of courtship. For one thing, she continues to work after marriage, extending the missionary inroads she set in motion by translating for her husband and instructing Native girls. As a translator, Unca Eliza has to the opportunity to insert her own agenda, to conspire, and to transform her cousin's missionary work.[52] Just as she previously used her Native language skills and cultural knowledge as a form of resistance to her cousin's patriarchal expectations during courtship, Unca Eliza may use her Native language to undermine the patriarchal structures of Christianity in this new "praying" island. Moreover, when Unca Eliza and her missionary friends determine to sever all ties with England in an attempt to prevent the inevitable influx of violence and corruption that accompanies colonization, the resulting isolation could possibly engender more creative and flexible local interpretations of community governance, syncretic religious practice, and gender performance.

While *Hymen* bombastically declares that "English ladies" are "indulged in liberties which foreigners can hardly give credit to,"[53] Unca Eliza prefers the liberties of her single life as a Christian missionary among Native peoples to the supposed "liberties" of English ladies. Even after marriage, Unca Eliza's island setting enables a new kind of gender dynamic, which she obviously prefers to England. If anyone could bring such a utopian gender revision to fruition, Unca Eliza is a likely candidate. Finally, given her own surprisingly gender-neutral education, one wonders what instruction Unca Eliza would likely provide to Native women. How would our hybrid heroine "world" this space and how would the indigenous inhabitants reject, revise, and/or create that world with her? I do not claim that Unca Eliza is anticolonial, nor that *The Female American* offers a working model for just social relations. Still, simply imagining such questions indicates how far this woman-centered novel moves beyond the popular courtship plot of its day.

Marriage-rites anthologies and stadial histories assure readers that companionate marriage is not only the best relation in which to experience marriage, but it is also a powerful sign of progress for women and for the nation. These texts use comparisons to measure women's "liberties" in marriage and rank global marriage traditions, reiterating Britain's supposedly superior status through these "objective" comparisons. Written in the age of sensibility, texts such as *Hymen* and *The Origin of the Distinction of Ranks* prioritize emotional companionship within marriage as the ultimate measure of civilization; however, they do not attempt to account for the many ways women experience satisfaction in sexual and nonsexual relationships inside and outside of marriage. Moreover, these male-authored texts make little room for women's own voices in their collections of anecdotes and theories.

The Female American is, of course, fiction and does not accurately or comprehensively represent a biracial indigenous woman's experiences; however, the novel proves a more flexible genre in terms of including a Native woman's perspective and communicating a multiplicity of cultural responses to marriage. From Unca Eliza's perspective, British marriage is no guarantor of civilization or happiness. Indeed, she rightly understands the English game of courtship as a strategy for acquiring wealth. While this novel rejects the happily-ever-after ending and the reader's emotional investment in that ending, our emotional dissatisfaction with Unca Eliza's capitulation to her cousin's marriage proposal ironically testifies to the genre's capacious representational strategies for imagining different socialities. As a form of protest, Unca Eliza's unhappy "happy ending" contests the real restrictions of British marriage from a "wonderful, strange, and uncommon" point of view.[54]

2

COMPARING RIGHTS, COMPARING STORIES

FEMINISTS HAVE LONG BEEN fascinated by Haudenosaunee (Iroquois) gender traditions. In *Sisters in Spirit,* Sally Roesch Wagner names the Haudenosaunee as one model for the gender reforms demanded by the 1848 Seneca Falls Convention and the US women's suffrage movement.[1] Wagner makes her case most clearly through the work of Matilda Joslyn Gage. Less familiar than her suffragist peers Elizabeth Cady Stanton and Susan B. Anthony, Gage "introduced readers to the Six Nations of the Iroquois Confederacy in articles [for] the newspaper she edited" and "her magnum opus" *Woman, Church, and State* (1893).[2] As an adopted member of the Wolf Clan of the Mohawk nation, Gage was working on a book about the Haudenosaunee at her death in 1898.

Gage, however, proves only one link in a longer line of early American women interested in Haudenosaunee gender arrangements. Gage's chapter, "Preceding Causes," in the massive *History of Woman Suffrage* (1881–1922), specifically cites Abigail Adams's famous "Remember the Ladies" letter of March 31, 1776, as a culminating point in the US movement toward women's rights. In the letter to her husband, John, Adams playfully turns revolutionary rhetoric to a new purpose when she warns, "We [women] are determined to foment a rebellion, and will not hold ourselves bound by any laws in which we have no voice or representation." After issuing this threat, Adams restores the power to change women's position to "Men of sense" who "in all Ages abhor those customs which treat us only as the vassals of your Sex. Regard us then as Beings placed by providence under your protection and in immitation [*sic*] of the Supreem [*sic*] Being make use of that power only for our happiness."[3] Gage would not have known that some of Adams's best lines, including the previous quotes, are only slightly revised from British sentimental novelist Frances Brooke's *The History of Emily Montague* (1769)—a novel that builds its most provocative claims for women's rights through comparisons with Wendat (Huron) and Haudenosaunee gender practices. Gage, who once proclaimed, "Never was justice more perfect, never civilization higher than under the [Haudenosaunee] Matriarchate," would probably not have been surprised, though.[4]

"We Are the Savages": Unsettling Claims for
British Women's Progress

Before Gage and the suffragists and, indeed, before Abigail Adams, novelist France Brooke turned to Haudenosaunee and Wendat peoples to imagine a more egalitarian world. Locating Brooke within long-standing debates about the extent of Native women's agency, this chapter traces a surprising intersection between the discourse of companionate marriage idealized in the marriage plot, early American calls for women's rights, and an emerging anthropological interest in Wendat and Haudenosaunee marriage and courtship practices. Often described as the first Canadian novel, *Emily Montague* is based on British author Frances Brooke's firsthand observations during a stay in Quebec, Canada, while her husband served as an army chaplain just after the Seven Years' War. The novel deeply dialogues with existing protoethnographic regional travel accounts, missionary records, and regional histories of lower Canada to generate a new British social analysis of the formerly French colonial population as well as the significant Native populations occupying their traditional homelands. Intersections between the marriage plot and cross-cultural descriptions of various Canadian marriage traditions comprise the central concerns of *Emily Montague*.

Written as an epistolary novel, the text is composed of multiple British settler perspectives, from Edward Rivers, the sentimental primary protagonist, a former British soldier, and recent immigrant to Quebec, to the more conservative Captain Fermor and his coquettish daughter Arabella Fermor. The many first-person perspectives utilized in the epistolary format make this novel a rich source for competing British attitudes toward the occupation and settlement of a former European rival's colonial territory. The novel begins when Edward Rivers decides to farm his allotment of Canadian land, his payment for military service, rather than live on his mother's meager income. As an aspiring permanent settler, Edward writes to family and friends in Britain about his Canadian adventures and the social customs of various groups of locals. In the tradition of the courtship novel, the plot revolves around Edward's romantic interest in the delectably sensible Emily Montague, while the coquettish Arabella Fermor falls for Fitzgerald, another British soldier. The pairs of lovers eventually marry, return to England, and meet up with their old friends. They live near one another in a utopian agrarian English setting, significantly not in Canada. While the majority of the novel is taken up with discussions of love, marriage, and the essential qualities necessary in a potential spouse, there are also significant descriptions of Canadian scenery, weather, social events, and local inhabitants. As Brooke's biographer, Lorraine McMullen, notes, Brooke's novel was often recommended as required reading for anyone traveling to Canada and most remembered for its extensive commentary on customs and manners, including local indigenous marriage practices.[5]

I argue that Brooke's novel employs a comparative marriage plot to explore the advantages that Haudenosaunee and Wendat women had relative to British women's supposedly advanced status via companionate marriage. However, in many ways this argument requires reading against the grain, for Brooke's characters continue to promote racist colonial evaluations of Native women's political and romantic relations. Brooke's primary aim is a critique of eighteenth-century British patriarchy, a critique that resonated with contemporary readers such as Abigail Adams. But she is only able to launch this critique via comparative analyses of social and romantic relations in lower Canada. Because Brooke's comparisons of Native gender practices become the means of critiquing British patriarchy, these reports implicitly unsettle the hierarchical comparisons of women's status that I traced in the previous chapter. To recognize precisely how far Haudenosaunee gender practices unsettle British claims for women's progress, though, readers must move beyond the text and attend to Haudenosaunee accounts of gender and romance. These accounts fundamentally challenge the primary features and concerns of the typical British marriage plot.

In *When Did Indians Become Straight?* Mark Rifkin argues that Native American kinship structures disrupt, or "queer," hegemonic, normative forms of heterosexuality exemplified by the nuclear family. According to Rifkin, "official and popular narratives from the early Republic onward demeaned and dismissed the kinds of social relations around which Native communities were structured, denying the possibility of interpreting countervailing cultural patterns as principles of geopolitical organization."[6] In this regard, *Emily Montague* walks a fine line, by turns dismissive of Native social relations, and, then again, earnestly admiring of certain aspects of gender performance. These contradictory and, at times, competing representations are partly the result of the multiple first-person points of view contained in Brooke's epistolary novel, but ultimately the novel trumpets the companionate-marriage ideals of eighteenth-century Britain. Exploring the sites where Brooke's characters admire Native gender systems as progressive does not excuse the novel's colonialism or its hegemonic promotion of the companionate-marriage ideal. Nevertheless, such sites mark the unsettling, or in Rifkin's term, the "queering," potential of Native gender, sexuality, and family structures.

After a visit to the Wendat village of Lorette near Quebec City, Brooke's protagonist, Edward Rivers, notes that Wendat women "have a great share in the Huron government; the chief is chose [sic] by the matrons [clan mothers]." Edward teasingly continues, "I am pleased with this last regulation, as women are, beyond all doubt, the best judges of the merit of men; and I should be extremely pleased to see it adopted in England."[7] Brooke most likely culls these observations from historic reports such as the seventeenth-century *Jesuit Relations,* Father Joseph-François Lafitau's study of the Haudenosaunee, *Customs of the American Indians as Compared with Customs of Primitive Times* (1724), and Pierre François Xavier de Charlevoix's *History of New France* (1744). Although Rivers specifically names the Wendat, his remark on Wendat women's ability to nominate chiefs does not appear in the *Jesuit Relations.*[8] Rivers's descriptions of Native women's political roles more closely resemble information from Lafitau's reports of Haudenosaunee gender arrangements.[9] This does not mean that such a statement is incorrect, only that it is difficult for Brooke and her sources to parse the differences in customs between the neighboring nations. At this historical remove, it is difficult to make refined distinctions; Brooke, of course, is not particularly interested in cultural or historical accuracy. Her character, Edward, primarily uses the fact of Wendat and/or Haudenosaunee women's political participation to launch a critique of British gender norms—a critique that we have already observed and that contemporary readers such as Abigail Adams found compelling.

Edward's observation that women "have a great share in the Huron government" leads directly to his radical reassessment of British gender progress. In a line that Abigail Adams will revise, Edward declares, "In the true sense of the word, *we* [British men] are the savages, who so impolitely deprive you of the common rights of citizenship. . . . By the way, I don't think you are obliged in conscience to obey laws you have had no share in making."[10] Edward's remarkable reversal of the term *savage* precisely overturns Enlightenment discourses linking economics, social civility, and the prioritizing of affectionate marriage relations traced in the previous chapter. To summarize that argument, marriage-rites anthologies and stadial histories both situate nationalist claims for British women's superior progress within social and economic structures that value companionship in marriage. Using a comparative framework, these texts argue that British women's "right" to marry for love conferred on them a supposedly more advanced status. However, Edward's comparison reveals that when it comes to political participation, Wendat women have a distinct advantage. Even more than this, Rivers's claim that "*we are the savages*" challenges the telos of British women's progress so painstakingly constructed in marriage-rites anthologies and stadial histories.

If one weighs the many arenas in which women could exercise agency —a term I use to describe women's ability to make significant decisions in their communities and personal lives—it is clear that Wendat and Haudenosaunee women express their agency within a wider terrain than do British women in this same period. As I trace in more detail below, Brooke's spunky narrator, Arabella Fermor, narrows these different expressions of Native and British women's agency to two options: Native women's right to choose a chief and British women's right to choose a husband. However, in polarizing political and romantic "rights," Arabella misrepresents both Native and British marriage customs. Arabella claims that indigenous women are "slaves" in a tyrannical system of arranged marriages, while England is the land of "liberty": "there is no true freedom any where else. They may talk of the privilege of chusing a chief; but what is that to the dear English privilege of chusing a husband?"[11] Although Arabella describes England as the seat of liberty, British women in this period were legally "feme coverts," covered by their husband's legal identity.[12] Children were the property of their fathers. Married women could not own property or keep income independently of their husbands without special provisions in the marriage contract. Women's very bodies belonged to their husbands, who possessed the legal right to physically discipline and even rape their wives.[13]

With this reality sharply in focus, it is not surprising to find women readers of Anglophone novels attracted to the illusion of control offered by the marriage plot's emphasis on spousal choice. As Cathy Davidson suggests, "by reading about a female character's good or bad decisions in sexual and marital matters, the early American woman could vicariously enact her own courtship and marriage fantasies. She could, at least in those fantasies, view her life as largely the consequence of her own choices and not merely as the product of the power of others in her life."[14] Historians note that in reality women had much less claim to choose their own spouses than courtship novels suggest.[15] For instance, David Lemmings and Paul Langford argue that elite British marriages continued to reflect patriarchal and economic motives as these marriages were frequently made to establish advantageous family alliances and pool significant resources such as land and wealth.[16] Because men primarily proposed marriage, women had the "choice" of simply saying yes or no to a suitor's proposal, weighing the likelihood that another such "choice" may not recur. If, then, courtship is the primary arena in which British women exercise agency, it is little wonder that they are both startled by and dismissive of indigenous women's agency beyond marriage.

The Direction of the Sky: A Tradition of Gender Balance

In 1769, when Brooke published *Emily Montague,* the Native populations around the Saint Lawrence River and along the border of what is now upstate New York were experiencing major changes. Missionary efforts and new trade relationships brought tremendous culture change, while disease and near-constant warfare led to severe Native population losses. The once-mighty confederacy of the Wendat was effectively destroyed by the neighboring Haudenosaunee in a series of mid-seventeenth-century conflicts known alternately as the Beaver Wars or the Mourning Wars.[17] The Haudenosaunee—a league of six nations that includes the Mohawk, Cayuga, Oneida, Onondaga, Seneca, and Tuscarora—scattered some Wendats to Ohio country, where they reorganized as the Wyandotte; others were adopted by the Haudenosaunee; and a smaller group moved just outside Quebec City to the village of Lorette. Known today as Wendake, this village reservation remains the home of the federally recognized Huron-Wendat First Nations. At the close of the Seven Years' War in 1763, the formerly French Quebec territory came under British control, leaving the sovereign Haudenosaunee nations uncomfortably situated between two massive British territories. This border territory would be even more hotly contested after the American Revolution, when the Haudenosaunee continued their claims for control over lands located between British Canada and the newly formed United States. These disputes continue today.[18]

The Wendat and Haudenosaunee are part of the Iroquoian language group, sharing a number of cultural and social features. Both the Wendat and Haudenosaunee are matrilineal, tracing family lines through the mother's clan; both subsisted largely by means of agriculture, which was primarily women's work; both lived in longhouses containing large extended families; and although there is still some doubt, it seems likely that both granted clan mothers the power to nominate chiefs to the larger village and national councils.[19] Although social, political, and family life was divided along gender lines, Wendat and Haudenosaunee women were not less valued than men.

In contrast to Arabella's claims for Native women's "slave" status, eighteenth-century Jesuit missionary Joseph-François Lafitau offers perhaps the most famous and controversial assessment of Haudenosaunee gender in his one-thousand-page study of Native American political, social, and religious practices, *Customs of the American Indians* (1724). Living for five years with the Haudenosaunee at Kahnawake (also known as the Sault Saint Louis mission) outside of Montreal, Lafitau concludes that the Haudenosaunee are a "gynocracy":

> Nothing is more real, however, than the women's superiority. It is they who really maintain the tribe, the nobility of blood, the genealogical tree, the order of generations, and conservation of the families. In them resides all real authority: the land, fields, and all their harvest belong to them; they are the soul of the councils, the arbiters of peace and of war; they hold the taxes and the public treasure. It is to them that the slaves [captives] are entrusted; they arrange marriages; the children are under their authority, and the order of succession is founded on their blood. . . . And, although the chiefs are chosen among [the men], they are purely honorary. The Council of Elders which transacts all the business does not work for itself. It seems that they serve only to represent and aid the women in the matters in which decorum does not permit the latter to appear or act.[20]

Centuries of scholarly commentary on this particular passage attempts to prove that Lafitau exaggerated women's power or that he is simply wrong.[21] Elizabeth Tooker has been most vocal in countering claims for Haudenosaunee women's political influence, naming it simply "indirect" at best.[22] Nancy Shoemaker concludes that "Iroquois women probably had more influence in the private sphere than in the public."[23] However, Jan Noel argues that recent reassessments of gender in Iroquoia lead us closer to Lafitau's conclusion: not gynocracy exactly, but certainly an unusually egalitarian society.[24]

Haudenosaunee gender balance is the core theme in two valuable new studies by Barbara Mann (Ohio Bear Clan Seneca) and Roland Viau. In *Femmes de personne,* Roland Viau describes Iroquoia as "the human society which, from an anthropological point of view, appears to have come the closest to the definition of a matriarchy."[25] Viau maintains that

Haudenosaunee culture was *not* matriarchal; rather, elders of both sexes held the most authority. Noting the central role of Sky Woman in the creation myth, the importance of the women's agricultural work and celebrations of the Three Sisters (corn, beans, and squash that women grew), the frequent practice of marrying younger grooms to older brides, and the preference for female infants, Viau confirms the remarkable position of Haudenosaunee women. Similarly, Barbara Mann argues, in "'They Are the Soul of the Councils,'" that the tradition of gender balance is officially encoded in the Haudenosaunee League's Great Law of Peace, granting women power as "*sole* counselors at the local, or 'grassroots,' level of government; women as the *sole* keepers of peace and war; women as the *sole* keepers of Mother Earth; women as the *sole* keepers of lineages and 'names.'"[26] Whereas Viau shies away from claims of matriarchy, criticizing some feminists for going too far, Mann expresses no such qualms. Mann's definition of matriarchy aligns with Heide Goettner-Abendroth's understanding that "widespread misconceptions notwithstanding . . . in matriarchies women's power is counterbalanced by men's power, so that neither gender dominates the other. The governing principle of these societies is balance, rather than domination."[27] Balance is not a duality, Mann notes. In the Haudenosaunee concept of "The Direction of the Sky . . . the base number of woodlands cultures is TWO. Everything that exists, exists by halves, at once independent yet interdependent."[28] The sky is divided by halves, east and west, representing the beginning and end of the day; but to be a whole, both halves must be present. Similarly, a healthy, functioning community needs men and women, hunters and growers, complementing one another with their knowledge and skills.

These reciprocal relationships operate quite differently from typical patriarchal divisions of gendered labor into male/public and female/private spheres. Anthropologists have shorthanded the traditional Haudenosaunee division of labor into the women's space of the "clearings"—comprising the village organized by female-headed households and the agricultural fields that women planted and reaped—and the men's space of the "forest," where hunting, trading, and war occurred.[29] Such a binary oversimplifies complementary divisions of labor where men built houses and helped to clear the fields and women often went into the forest as active participants in hunting and trading parties. Moreover, pre-reservation-era conceptions of space are not gendered in the same ways as the emerging "separate spheres" doctrine.[30] As John Mohawk (Seneca) claims, "Women participated as equals in public political life, but they also had the power to make [war] demands such as instructing warriors to seek captives to replace lost loved ones."[31] Unlike British men in this same period, Haudenosaunee men were not more valued than women, nor given more freedoms, nor permitted more opportunities for making decisions. We may never know just how much eighteenth-century Haudenosaunee women participated in social and political decision making or how their labor translated into community authority. What we do know is that Haudenosaunee gender traditions inspired early American suffragettes' visions of a nonpatriarchal society where women might be valued as contributing citizens, not simply as marriage partners or mothers. For some, this vision may have seemed threatening, uncoupling British companionate-marriage relations from notions of progress.

To recognize real differences in British and Haudenosaunee women's agency, one should begin with the longhouse. As both the source of the name *Haudenosaunee,* meaning "the People of the Longhouse," and also the symbol for the political structure organizing relations between the six nations of the league, the longhouse plays an important role in conceptions of Haudenosaunee identity. Up until the early nineteenth century, Haudenosaunee families lived in multigenerational households with the husband usually relocating to his wife's longhouse. Because his happiness depended on maintaining good relations with his wife's family, a new husband usually worked to please both his bride and her family. The "matron," or female head of house, owned and oversaw the longhouse, while each person living there owned his or her own personal property. Longhouses frequently contained more than fifty individuals; a family could include a female head of house and her husband, her sisters and their husbands and children, her daughters and their spouses and children, and any unmarried sons. As a rule, one would not marry within one's clan; moreover, marriage did not change a husband's or wife's clan membership, arguably more fundamental to an individual's sense of social identity than marriage. Children always belong to the mother's clan; thus, maternal uncles, not fathers (who belonged to a different clan), were primarily responsible for helping their sisters' children learn the rituals and roles required of them. Finally, a Haudenosaunee woman's body was always her own. She was never her husband's property, "covered" by his identity. Before the adoption of the early nineteenth-century Seneca prophet Handsome Lake's "Good Message," which I address in more detail later in this chapter, divorce was easily accomplished and most marriages included a roughly one-year trial period during which either partner could decide to end the marriage.[32] All property acquired during this trial period belonged to the wife, as did any children. Although cou-

ples were less likely to divorce after children were born, the process simply required the husband to return to his mother's or sister's household.

Outside of the longhouse, Haudenosaunee women were keepers of
Mother Earth, supervising agricultural lands, food production, and distribution. As Judith Brown argues, Haudenosaunee women did not simply
"work" the fields; rather, they held the land in trust for future generations;
they possessed the particular reproductive and spiritual powers necessary
to cultivate crops; they maintained contact with the spirit realm through
seasonal ceremonies that established a sustainable and spiritually meaningful agricultural life; they controlled the food stores and prepared food
for family, visitors, war parties, and all public ceremonies; and they reserved
the seed for the next year's crops.[33] Women shared agricultural work across
families and across generations; men balanced these activities by clearing
fields and harvesting crops, as well as fishing and hunting. The female head
of household controlled the distribution of food to the entire longhouse, dividing and sharing resources, including any male contributions from hunting. Brown argues that as distributers of food, Haudenosaunee women held
considerable power in their families and communities. For instance, war
parties would not receive supplies without women's support. Thus, wom-
en's powers balanced the powers held by men.

Haudenosaunee women exercised agency in social and political life as
well. Contemporary Mohawk leader Tom Porter confirms that clan mothers confer names to individuals at various stages in their lives, select male
chiefs within their clans to sit on the grand council, and have the power to
"dehorn" a chief if he does not appropriately fulfill his duties.[34] Women also
serve as faithkeepers, and traditionally clans appointed an equal number of
male and female faithkeepers to lead important ceremonies. Although scholars disagree about the extent of women's participation in Haudenosaunee
politics, there is historical evidence to support claims that women participated in treaty agreements and war deliberations. For example, in 1791,
Thomas Proctor, US commissioner to the Indians, requested Haudenosaunee
support in diplomatic relations with the Shawnee and Miamis, who were
reportedly disturbing white settlements in the Ohio country. Proctor's negotiations were not going well, but on May 15, he reports that the Haudenosaunee women at the deliberations remind him that they have a say:

> Early this morning the leaders of the Indian women resorted to my hut,
> (present a number of chiefs.) Having heard the general conversation that
> took place between me and the Young King [Cornplanter] the evening be-
> fore, [they] addressed me in the following manner: "Brother: . . . you ought

to hear and listen to what we women shall speak, as well as to the sachems; for we are the owners of this land and it is ours; for it is we that plant it for our and for their use. Hear us, therefore, for we speak of things that concern us and our children, and you must not think hard of us while our men shall say more to you; for we have told them."[35]

Proctor's report indicates that Haudenosaunee women used a male speaker to represent their deliberations to the white male audience, but that they confidently asserted their interest in and authority to speak as guardians/ owners of the land and as mothers of the nation. Haudenosaunee women also expressed agency when making decisions regarding the fate of captives and prisoners of war. As Daniel Richter and Gordon Sayre have observed, women possessed life-or-death power over captives when they decided whom to adopt and whom to torture in the mourning ceremonies for lost family members.[36] Moreover, adopted women captives were potentially more valuable than male captives as the family line is sustained through women. Certainly, the captivities of Eunice Williams and Mary Jemison demonstrate that some white captive women preferred to remain with their adopted Haudenosaunee families rather than return to a more restrictive colonial society.[37]

This picture of Haudenosaunee gender balance is far removed from the stereotyped "slave" status that Arabella claims Native women were subject to through their system of arranged marriages. But even acknowledging Haudenosaunee women's significant political, social, and family authority, how did they experience the quotidian practical and emotional aspects of married life? To ask such a question is to face the abysmal lack of primary source materials one would need to formulate an answer.

What's Love Got to Do with It?

Few historical sources remain neutral when it comes to Native romantic relations. Like the colonizing descriptions of "savage" sexual relations John Millar describes in his stadial theories of romance outlined in the previous chapter, in *Emily Montague* Edward Rivers claims Wendats are "strangers to the softer passions, love being with them on the same footing as amongst their fellow-tenants of the woods."[38] Although Brooke's characters acknowledge Native women's political agency, they adamantly deny any progressive position for Native women in romantic relations. Edward's observation is only one in a long line of negative assessments of Native romantic inclinations.

In *The History of America* (1777), Scottish historian William Robertson similarly sought evidence of American Indian romantic love and expressed doubts about its existence in his accounts of Native American marriage practices. Drawing on data from a variety of colonial reports, Robertson concludes that "to despise and degrade the female sex, is the characteristic of the savage state in every part of the globe." Robertson ties this supposedly degrading treatment of women to a lack of romantic love and companionship as he observes that it is "not by a studied display of tenderness and attachment, that the American [Indian] endeavours to gain the heart of the woman whom he wishes to marry."[39] Given Robertson's stereotypically conventional depictions of American Indian gender and sexuality, it may surprise readers to discover that he sent out a questionnaire to North and South American colonial officials, naturalists, and missionaries to gather firsthand information for his history. On the topic of American Indian gender and sexuality, he asks:

> Are the Indians defective in the animal passion for their females? Have their songs and dances any reference to love and the commerce between the sexes, or are they not rather martial and formal? Does their common discourse relate much to love and the passion between the sexes? Does polygamy take place among the Indians of North America? Are their marriages permanent or if dissolved how are the offspring disposed of? What is the character of the Indian women with regard to chastity, both before and after marriage? How are the Indian women treated by their husbands? What is the state of parental tenderness and affection, and what the returns of filial duty and love compared with other nations?[40]

By my count, leading questions about both Indian and British colonial women, human reproduction, and families account for approximately 20 percent of the total number of questions Robertson asks in his first set of queries. He is concerned with confirming European hypotheses about "defective" "animal passions" or the reportedly martial nature of songs; he does not seem interested in reports of matrilineal kin structures or women's political participation. Rather typically, Robertson prioritizes questions about romantic affection and marriage relations as a primary category for evaluating a people's civility. Despite differences in reports from his respondents, Robertson concludes that overall, Native women are socially denigrated.[41]

Even earlier accounts of American Indian divisions of labor inevitably report a perceived imbalance of work as evidence of Native women's oppression. For instance, Samuel Champlain describes Wendat women as having "almost the whole care of the house and the work," serving "as mules to carry the baggage, with a thousand other kinds of duties . . . they are required to carry out. As to the men, they do nothing but hunt deer, and other animals, fish, build lodges, and go on the warpath."[42] These "drudge" descriptions frequently comment on a seeming lack of affection between spouses. And it is to the realm of romance that Brooke and other observers turn when dismissing Native women's political agency.

Brooke's Edward Rivers both confirms the "squaw drudge" stereotype and actively collects ethnographic information on romantic love among the Wendat at Lorette:

> Every one must have heard of the war dance, and their songs are almost all on the same subject: on the most diligent enquiry, I find but one love song in their language, which is short and simple, tho' perhaps not inexpressive: "I love you, / I love you dearly, / I love you all day long." An old Indian told me, they had also songs of friendship, but I could never procure a translation of one of them: on my pressing this Indian to translate one into French for me, he told me with a haughty air, the Indians were not us'd to make translations, and that if I chose to understand their songs I must learn their language.[43]

Seen through Edward's colonizing gaze, this song renders Wendat love simple, even quaint. Still, Edward must acknowledge the limits of his knowledge when his "old Indian" informant rejects Edward's authority to represent Wendat emotional life. I return to the issue of control over the dissemination of cultural knowledge in the final section of this chapter.

If this scene briefly invites readers to question how reliable European reports of Wendat culture really are, such a critique is quickly dismissed in favor of clichéd and overconfident cultural assessments. Edward quickly returns from this failure of translation to consider Wendat women's bodies—a subject for which he needs no translator—and their unprecedented "empire" after marriage:

> The Indian women are tall and well shaped; have good eyes, and before marriage are, except their color, and their coarse greasy black hair, very far from being disagreeable; but the laborious life they afterwards lead is extremely unfavorable to beauty; they become coarse and masculine, and lose in a year or two the power as well as the desire of pleasing. To compensate however for the loss of their charms, they acquire a new empire in marrying; are consulted in all the affairs of state, chuse a chief on every vacancy of the throne, are sovereign arbiters of peace and war, as well as of the fate of those unhappy captives that have the misfortune to fall into their hands, who are adopted as children, or put to the most cruel death, as the wives of the conquerors smile or frown.[44]

Edward posits Wendat women's "empire" after marriage as a substitute for their loss of more feminine "charms." In this representation, an "empire" in politics is small compensation for the laborious lives Native women must endure. Whereas British women hope for a happy and satisfying marriage to men who might possibly grant them some degree of respect, Brooke's novel shows that indigenous women's agency is unrelated to romantic satisfaction; Native women have an important role in the community with or without romantic love. Their agency is not so precariously linked to marriage, happy or not.

Strangely, then, Brooke's novel tenaciously upholds the marriage plot with its ideals of companionate marriage as preferable to Native women's agency. Brooke's Arabella Fermor makes her allegiance to the marriage plot explicit in a fascinating encounter with what I take to be a group of traveling Mohawk women: "I was sitting after dinner with a book . . . near the beach . . . where I saw a canoe of savages making to the shore; there were six women, and two or three children without a man amongst them."[45] As she dines, dances, and exchanges gifts with the women, Arabella describes a strong sense of intimacy with her new friends. She tells her correspondent that "I will marry a savage, and turn squaw . . . never was anything so delightful as their lives; they talk of French husbands, but commend me to an Indian one, who lets his wife ramble five hundred miles, without asking where she is going." Arabella envies the freedom of movement described by her companions; quickly, though, she revises her wish to be a Native woman when she discovers the Haudenosaunee practice of arranged marriage: "I declare off at once; I will not be a squaw; . . . in the most essential point, they are slaves: the mothers marry their children without ever consulting their inclinations, and they are obliged to submit to this foolish tyranny. Dear England! where liberty appears, not as here among these odious savages, wild and ferocious like themselves, but lovely, smiling, led by the hand of the Graces. There is no true freedom anywhere else. They may talk of the privilege of chusing a chief; but what is that to the dear English privilege of chusing a husband?"[46] Arabella's raw response is laden with British patriotism as she faces what she perceives as a threat to the most important—indeed, the only—form of self-expression a heroine is permitted.

Although Arabella may wish to represent her choice of a husband as a right—a right she believes Native women are denied—in actuality British women had very little right to expect that they could control the terms of their marriage. Arabella's fantasy of control is a result of the structural mechanics of the marriage plot rather than a reality for most

eighteenth-century British women. As any Jane Austen heroine could remind her, British women really had the right to refuse, not to choose, a
husband. For instance, Lord Kames flatly states, "With respect to matrimony, it is the privilege of the male, as superior and protector, to make a
choice; the female preferred has no privilege but barely to consent or to
refuse."[47] This puts British women's "choice" much closer to the arranged
marriages of Haudenosaunee women than Arabella might like to admit.

Early eighteenth-century changes in British attitudes toward "mercenary" arranged marriage go far to explain Arabella's visceral reaction to
the "tyranny" of Haudenosaunee arranged marriages.[48] As Jodi Wyett
argues, "Since Arabella, paradoxically, sees choice in marriage as the sole
potential choice for English women, she cannot reconcile Native subjectivity to her ideal of female free will, which is dependent on a companionate marriage."[49] Although Arabella understands Haudenosaunee arranged marriage practices as limiting a woman's personal freedom, John
Mohawk (Seneca) keenly observes that "during the seventeenth century,
most cultures of the world practiced some form of arranged marriages,
and Seneca custom allocated to women privileges that most traditional
European societies reserved to men."[50] That is, most Haudenosaunee
marriages in this period were arranged by the elderly matrons of the families, as opposed to the patriarchal custom of European fathers arranging
their children's marriages based on financial or status considerations. Although Arabella cannot move beyond marriage to see the wider exercise
of agency that local indigenous women possess, she also refuses to see
the limitations British women faced in their "right" to choose a husband.

Almost one hundred years later, Lewis Henry Morgan reiterates
Brooke's assessment of "tyrannical" Haudenosaunee arranged marriages in
his widely influential anthropological study, *League of the Iroquois* (1851).
Morgan reaches his surprising conclusion despite the fact that he drew
on reputable local sources, particularly his partnership with Ely Parker,
a young Seneca man who later became the first American Indian to hold
the office of commissioner of Indian affairs. Morgan argues that Haudenosaunee "marriage was not founded upon the affections, which constitute the only legitimate basis of this relation in civilized society, but was
regulated exclusively as a matter of physical necessity. It was not even
a contract between the parties to be married, but substantially between
their mothers, acting oftentimes under the suggestions of the matrons
[clan mothers] and wise-men of the tribes to which the parties respec-
tively belonged."[51] Morgan extends this misrepresentation of Haudenosaunee marriage to make wider claims for Haudenosaunee women's

supposed oppression: "The Indian regarded woman as the inferior, the dependent, and the servant of man, and from nurture and habit, she actually considered herself to be so."[52] If Morgan, like so many others, sees Native women's labor as evidence for the truth of the "squaw drudge" stereotype, at least one historical source makes the opposite claim: Native women's labor is a source of independence and marital affection. Surprisingly, in his 1838 report on the Seneca, Indian agent Henry Dearborn does just this: women's "duties are not arbitrarily imposed and exacted, but are considered as belonging to the females as not only indispensable but proper in all respects, and they therefore cheerfully perform them. . . . In fact the wife is more useful and important to the husband than he is to her. *She lives with him from love.* For she can obtain her own means of support better than he can."[53] In his journal, Dearborn offers a rare perspective on Native romantic relations. He claims that Seneca women's labor leaves them economically independent and, thus, their marriages are more genuinely affectionate than in societies where women must marry for economic support. In Dearborn's assessment, love must be the sustaining source for fiercely independent Haudenosaunee relationships. In drawing together Morgan's and Dearborn's comments, I am not advocating that Native peoples' romantic relations should mirror Western conventions or, for that matter, that they ought to drastically depart from them. Rather, I am interested in asking how and why these sources produce such differing analyses of Haudenosaunee romance and what we ought to make of those differences.

Brooke, Robertson, and Morgan describe Native American marriage customs as loveless and tyrannical, oppressive toward Native women, frozen in a less developed stage of human history—what Johannes Fabian calls "a denial of coevalness."[54] Dearborn's assessment of women's labor, however, recognizes a community value in women's labor as well as the ways that labor creates a powerful form of economic self-sustainability and independence. Taken together, these perceptions of women's labor enable Dearborn to credit Seneca women with deep romantic affections. In Dearborn's account, Seneca love is different from Anglo-American romantic traditions because it is produced from unique Haudenosaunee economic, social, and kin relations. This may mean that, in this period, Haudenosaunee women's self-worth is less dependent on a husband's protection and affection, but it does not mean that her affections are less real.

As Elizabeth Povinelli observes in *The Empire of Love,* conceptions of personal liberty are deeply embedded in liberal forms of heterosexual coupledom, a private relationship conceived to be fundamentally sepa-rate from public/state control. The inverse of this liberal sexual logic is "the genealogically determined collective" trapped in a web of genealog-ical inheritances such as kinship, tribalism, and patriarchy.[55] Whereas in liberalism the conjugal couple represents the achievement of maturity as one breaks with one's birth family to pursue a separate and distinct household, Native peoples are understood as slaves to unchanging tradi-tion, bound to clans and elders who limit their personal freedom. If we recognize, then, that the demand for heterosexual romance (or the insist-ence on the companionate-marriage ideal) is both a claim for "civiliza-tion" and a liberal fantasy of individual freedom, then we must also rec-ognize that denying or denigrating indigenous forms of social and sexual relations as "less free" is a form of colonizing discourse that pathologizes Native peoples.

When we return to the significant problem of a lack of eighteenth-century Native voices representing Native sexual practices in the existing archival materials, we face a crisis of representation. How do we avoid repathologizing Native peoples in the past? How do we recognize the de-mand for romance and the repeated disavowal of its existence in Brooke, Morgan, and others as the unsettling site of indigenous-settler struggle? As Povinelli argues, instead of seeing liberal and genealogical subjects as opposites, "the intimate event" should be understood as framing the ways that us public discourse addresses indigenous and other alternative social formations. One goal of this chapter is to trace a complex and con-tinually evolving history of Haudenosaunee marriage customs alongside a similarly in-flux tradition of eighteenth-century British marriage prac-tices. Situating these histories side by side shows both groups as dynamic historical agents actively making changes and responding to shifting at-titudes in their respective societies. Such a project requires scholars not only to correct inaccurate assessments such as those made by Brooke and Morgan, but also to do so by turning to local Native communities as the proper authorities on the subject.

Akwesasne Oral Tradition and Haudenosaunee Marriage Customs

Arabella's concerns about the ways arranged marriage might limit per-sonal freedom led me to wonder how Mohawk couples experienced this custom. Such a question is difficult to answer with the limited and obvi-ously biased historical sources available.[56] The Choctaw scholar Devon

Mihesuah advises, "If writers want to find out about what Indian women think, they should ask Indian women. If they want to know about past events and cultures they should do the same thing."[57] Taking Mihesuah's advice, I traveled to Akwesasne Mohawk Reservation,[58] a politically active Haudenosaunee community straddling the New York–Canadian border. The trip was my initiation into what Norman Denzin and Yvonna Lincoln term *decolonizing inquiry*: "a performance of counterhegemonic theories that disrupt the colonial and postcolonial," a scholarship that pursues open-ended, subversive, and emancipatory counternarratives of history.[59] Decolonizing methodologies necessarily involve comparisons of indigenous sources and ways of knowing with continually colonizing archives and epistemologies. As R. Radhakrishnan argues, "comparisons are never neutral . . . behind [them] . . . there always lurks the aggression of a thesis."[60]

If comparisons will inevitably be made, and if the goal of critical comparison is corrective and liberatory narratives of indigenous peoples' worth, then it is time to include indigenous voices and indigenous knowledge in our comparisons. The final sections of this chapter employ a decolonizing strategy to challenge long-standing colonizing claims of observers such as Brooke and Morgan by comparing them with Haudenosaunee political history, individual family stories, and spiritual teachings shared by Mohawk community leaders themselves. At Akwesasne Mohawk Reservation, I asked Faithkeeper Richard Mitchell (Wolf Clan Mohawk), Clan Mother Louise McDonald (Bear Clan Mohawk), and Akwesasne Museum program coordinator Sue Ellen Herne (Bear Clan Mohawk): what did arranged marriage mean in Haudenosaunee communities? What were the reasons for arranging marriages? And what did women think about their arranged marriages? Such a move requires readers to accept Mohawk oral tradition as credible and valuable historical evidence, despite the more than 250-year gap between Brooke and my contemporary Mohawk sources. Given the obviously biased print archive I have traced above, this decolonial turn to Mohawk oral history/tradition is a necessary corrective to previously colonizing histories of Haudenosaunee marriage.[61]

Faithkeeper Richard Mitchell is a middle-aged man, probably in his fifties, with glasses and coal-black hair cut short, but now growing out a bit. His wife greets me outside their comfortable two-story home, introduces me, and announces she has some errands to run. We sit in the kitchen: I at the kitchen table with my tape recorder, Mitchell in a creaky rocking chair in a nearby corner. The afternoon light streams in through the glass sliding doors leading out to the backyard. From this window, Mitchell will later point out Cornwall Island, where he grew up and where he still keeps a garden for growing ceremonial foods. In the background, I hear dogs bark now and then. It is pretty quiet, though, as I sit and listen. The interview takes about an hour and a half. At the end, he invites me to come back. "Next time you come, I'll show you my garden," he says.

In Mitchell's expansive history of the Haudenosaunee from human creation through Handsome Lake's Karihwiio (rendered here in Mohawk) and into the present, I learn how Haudenosaunee marriage traditions have evolved over time. Enlightenment histories present American Indian cultures as part of a less developed past, and today many museums continue this line of thought by displaying Native American peoples and their cultural objects as static or frozen in time. However, Mohawk oral tradition presents Haudenosaunee culture as dynamic and continually changing; marriage traditions are no exception to this. In my interview with Mitchell, for instance, I learn to listen carefully and remain alert for rapid leaps through time. Mitchell moves quickly between centuries, each story marking a particular epoch of time as well as a change in marriage practice: from Skyholder's creation of the first human pair—which Mitchell observed was the original pattern for human marriage—to the Peace Maker's creation of the League of the Iroquois—which gave clan mothers' their official powers—to the prophet Handsome Lake's early nineteenth-century Gaiwiio, or "Good Message"—which significantly revises former marriage customs.[62]

Listening to Mitchell, I was especially struck by changes such as divorce regulations and the formality of ceremonies between pre-Gaiwiio and post-Gaiwiio marriages. The Haudenosaunee scholar John Mohawk notes, for instance, pre-Gaiwiio marriages were "arranged by the elder women of the two families. It was initiated by the young woman's female clan elder, who negotiated the affair and, to seal the offer, left twenty-four wedding bread loaves at the door of the longhouse of the female clan elder of the intended groom. . . . Unless the prospective bridegroom's mother had valid objections to the union, the grandmother then made twenty-four cakes to send to the clan elder of the proposed bride's household. Upon receipt, the young woman was informed of the arrangement."[63] Typically, marriages were formed with a one-year trial period, after which the couple might choose to continue the marriage or end it. This all changed in the dark days of the early nineteenth century, after missionaries, alcohol, and significant land loss threatened the survival of traditional Haudenosaunee life; a Seneca man named Handsome Lake had a vision, during which he received the Gaiwiio, or "Good Message." The prophecy he received adapted traditional Haudenosaunee ways to reservation realities. As Mitchell describes it, the Gaiwiio also affected how couples married:

> [The Code] talks about a revision of the ceremonies, the way we do things; [it] even tells in there that when people get to a certain age, it tells them that what the chiefs and the clan mothers should do is encourage people to get married. And when they get married, it also tells them that's a lifetime thing . . . in a traditional [Longhouse] marriage there's no such thing as divorce. . . . You make that pledge to the Creator [for] as long as you people live, and if something goes wrong sometime—that there's arguments or things like that—then the chiefs will first approach these people and, again, they'll say, "When you got together, and when you got married, these are the things you agreed to: that it's a lifetime thing." So Indian marriages take at least an hour and a half just talking; it's not no ten-minute ceremony.[64]

Like British marriage practices, Haudenosaunee marriage traditions have evolved over time. Handsome Lake's revivalist religion is clearly an early example of what Gerald Vizenor (Anishinaanbe) calls *survivance*, a strategy for maintaining and adapting traditions as needed.[65] Rather than criticize this change as somehow less "authentic," what I took away from Mitchell's incredible rendering of Haudenosaunee history was his powerfully expressed sense of Mohawk people adapting marriage practices from human creation to the present. Instead of representing Mohawk marriage as static, as if there was only one way Haudenosaunee marriages were made, we might situate dynamic changes such as the Gaiwiio alongside significant changes in British marriage practices such as Hardwicke's Marriage Act of 1753. Haudenosaunee culture is equally dynamic and adaptive to peoples' needs and historical circumstances.

Although arranged marriages are no longer practiced among the Haudenosaunee, clan mothers and elders continue to play an important role in preparing couples for the responsibilities of marriage and supporting them afterward. Mitchell explains these changes in marriage practices:

> Today the way people are, it's more or less [based on] affection: where you're going to meet, and you get to like that person, then you marry. In them days, it was the mothers of the children; they would say, "We really think it would be a good selection if you were to marry that one." That's how they used to do long time ago. They didn't have a choice. I even re-

member my grandmother telling stories when I was young how she got married. It was through her parents and my grandfather's parents; they told, they said, "We believe that these two will marry," and that's how they got together when they got married. . . . It was always the mothers [in] them days that will pick.[66]

Obviously, Mitchell's claim that Mohawk couples did not have a choice does not mean that romantic love did not exist inside marriage, but, in Mitchell's description, the couple did not initially choose one another on the basis of emotional compatibility.

What were the criteria for choosing a mate then? Marriage is a formal way to ensure that families (broadly defined) have the resources they need to survive and thrive. In Western societies, marriage is a system for passing wealth and property across generations and tracing ancestry through the father's line. In traditional Haudenosaunee culture, by contrast, no one owned the land, and wealth was typically estimated in food stores or personal tools and resources;[67] it is safe to say that consolidating land and wealth resources was not the primary motive for Haudenosaunee marriage. Rather, these marriages formalized reciprocal duties and divisions of labor between spouses and their families. Marriage also forged alliances between families and clans across villages and within larger communities. When asked what criteria mothers might have used in the process of mate selection, Bear Clan Mother Louise McDonald returns to the significant rule of exogamous clan structures, as we talk in her office at the St. Regis Health Services building:

> The Mohawks have three distinct clans: Bear, Wolf, and Turtle. So a Bear couldn't marry a Bear. When [a woman] went to look for a mate, she had to look to those other clans in order to find a partner. . . . In terms of arranged marriages, I think that's the only place that the law would apply, that you couldn't marry your own clan in those times that you're talking about. So it was strictly looked over and made sure that you weren't choosing somebody from your own side, because it was our whole—not just our political structure, but our spiritual structure—and it greatly affected the whole society. The old ladies [clan mothers and female heads of houses] were vigilant to make sure that young people . . . did not marry within their own clan in order to maintain that structure.[68]

Mitchell and Sue Ellen Herne, the Akwesasne Museum program coordinator, respond to the same question with Haudenosaunee oral tradition. Mitchell relates the origin of Mohawk clans and of the restriction against marrying within your own clan. In her office at the Akwesasne Museum, Herne turns to the Haudenosaunee creation story to illustrate why Sky Woman chose the less attractive but more resourceful suitor as her daughter's companion. All three of my collaborators explain in different ways and through a shared body of oral tradition that with the rule of exogamous clans firmly established, one looks for a stable partner with a demonstrated ability to provide. The decision to choose a mate was primarily about maintaining families in a subsistence economy where both partners contributed to a family's well-being. Thinking about the many personalities living together in a traditional longhouse kinship network, marriage was a relationship that intimately affected upward of fifty family members. Considerations of temperament were obviously important, but just as important were both partners' abilities to contribute to sustaining the extended family. John Mohawk notes that "most traditional societies considered young people too inexperienced to make such important decisions without their elders' assistance."[69]

McDonald, a middle-aged medical professional, greeted me warmly with a hug and a beaming smile. The interview quickly turned to women's roles in the community. "Here in Akwesasne and in any Mohawk community," she explains, "we have more academic women, women in scholarship, than we do men. And women in this building [St. Regis Health Services] alone are more at the helm. . . . We're the caretakers, we're the organizers, we're the food suppliers. We're many things." Concerning her thoughts about the past, McDonald emphasizes that Mohawk women have always had choices when it comes to arranging families. Because women lived in their own birth families with other dominant women around, domestic violence was virtually unknown—"each woman was protected by a kinship of women."[70] Moreover, "sexuality wasn't taboo."[71] Women had opportunities to court multiple potential partners. McDonald notes, "You really had free will. Once a woman chose you, it was an honor for the man to . . . become the father of her children. But there was no judgments; if a woman courted several different men prior to that, it was widely accepted."[72] Although it is difficult to know with certainty if these relationships necessarily led to marriage, McDonald's account suggests—like the images in Lahontan's *Mémoires de l'Amérique Septentrionale ou la Suite des Voyages de Mr. Le Baron de Lahontan* (1703) of a Wendat suitor courting a woman in her bed (see figure 1 in the introduction)—that Mohawk couples before the Gaiwiio may have had more opportunity for emotional and physical intimacy prior to the official arrangement of marriage.

In the post-Gaiwiio era when divorce was discouraged, arranged marriages may have felt more restrictive. Turning to family stories, we can begin to piece together a range of lived experiences of Mohawk customs of arranged marriage, though these family stories do not reach as far back as the eighteenth century. Mitchell's grandparents, for instance, seem not to have experienced any long-term conflicts in their arranged marriage. For most couples, the consequences for rejecting an arranged marriage—being disowned—probably outweighed minor objections. This does not mean that young people did not choose their own paths, as Sue Ellen Herne generously relates in a family story she shared with me. Sitting in her office at the museum, Herne is frequently interrupted by phone calls and managing other projects. She is welcoming and patient as I ask a barrage of questions. She begins with a context that frames her story across generations of women in her family, "This is from my perspective, a couple of generations later. I've heard it from my mother and I've heard it from one of my aunts. It's something that they thought was important to tell, and retell; so I've heard it more than once over the years, and it'll come up, you know, at different settings." From there, Herne locates the story's actors within her family genealogy: "This was my great-aunt who had an arranged marriage, and she was a half sister to my great-grandfather." With these preliminaries established, the story's action unfolds.

So she was supposed to be married to this older man from the community, and she did not particularly like him. She didn't like the idea; she already had a boyfriend, and so, it wasn't something she was happy with. But from what I remember, she did actually get married. And the way I remember hearing it is that the marriage took place, and then she was at [her husband's] home, and—I don't know if this was a joke—but this is how my aunt would always say it: she said they got married and then she sat in a chair for two weeks. In my mind, I see her sitting in a chair for two weeks, . . . she just sat in a chair for two weeks and wouldn't move. And so her boyfriend—she already had this boyfriend—I guess he came to the window. And she went out the window, and they took off. And so I've also heard it that she eloped. So you elope if you're already married! [Laughing] . . .

They ran off and they went to Oka, which is a community nearby. Today it takes an hour and a half to drive there, but this was a long time ago. . . . It was far enough away that she didn't really come back as far as I know. But it was close enough that they knew where she was. [Laughing] And the older man, he never, you know, pursued her or anything. I've never heard anything like that. So as far as I know, they went safely off and lived happily ever after. [Laughing] . . . My grandpa, who would have been her nephew, he would say, "I wonder if [she] will ever come home." And my mother said he always sounded wistful about it. As far as I know, she never did come home. But now she has descendants that live there; she's got grandchildren and great-grandchildren that live there, great-great-grandchildren.[73]

In cases of extreme disagreement, it is good to keep in mind that there is an exit strategy—there is Oka or, in the pre-Gaiwiio period, separation or divorce. In this fascinating family story, the detail I return to is how generations of women continue to tell it. It is an important story, containing as it does, difficult decisions and the lasting consequences of those decisions for the individuals involved and for generations of the family. This story both confirms Mitchell's statement about "no choice" and qualifies it. The stories, looped together, tell—Well, maybe it is better to let them speak for themselves. This is what stories are meant to do. They stay with you; you mull them over. You have to decide for yourself what it means and how to act on that knowledge.

Nineteenth-century commentators such as Lewis Henry Morgan frown on the significant age gaps between spouses found in stories such as Herne's.[74] Listening carefully to Bear Clan Mother McDonald, we gain a decolonized perspective on the motivation for such arrangements. Explaining mate selection through the lens of Mohawk spiritual philosophy, McDonald observes:

In these puberty rites I work with our young women. . . . I remember working with this one niece of mine—because we call them all our nieces and nephews—as she was preparing herself for her fast. The uncles had cut some wood, some of it was fresh and some of it was seasoned and put aside in a barn. And she went and got her wagon. She was loading up this freshly cut wood that was right in front of her and she was going to take it into the woods for her fast, right? And her grandmother and her aunties were telling her, "Don't use that wood. It is freshly cut." But she didn't listen to them. And then I came along and I had to be gentle with her, to take this situation and tell a story with it.

I said to her, "You know, my dear niece, you are going to fast for four days in the woods. You are going to be alone and you are going to have to tend to a fire." I said, "Let me give you a story about selecting your wood. It's like selecting a husband." I said, "You can go and stand next to a young, good-looking man and, you know, take part in his company, but the odds will be against you. He probably won't be in your company for long. That fire won't last because he's going to wonder about the world and he's going to wonder about other women. However, if you take the time and you have patience, and you take your wagon, and walk the extra 150 yards over to the barn where there's wood that's been seasoned and dried and is more mature, that fire will light for you much more quickly and will burn longer. So you have to look at the maturity of your wood and the maturity of your men when you enter that place of relationships and courtship." . . . So she unloaded all that fresh, new wood and walked over to the shed and got the dry, seasoned wood. I thought that was a huge lesson in relationships. . . . Now she's in a relationship two years later, and she's with a wonderful, wonderful young man.

McDonald is a gifted storyteller. She recognizes a teachable moment and intervenes for the benefit of her "niece," but she also carries this story forward as a way to explain the need for patience and maturity in others. The story becomes more than an isolated incident; it is a tool for sharing cultural values. As the best teachers and spiritual advisors do, McDonald goes on to comment on the story:

> For me, [our relationships are] not just founded in romantic love. Because I think our ways are founded more on what the [clan] status of your children will be, founded in the mother. And I always tell our young men to . . . wait for the girl who's preparing herself because she'll be worth waiting for. She'll be a good leader, she'll be a good mother, and she'll also be a good partner. She'll have the skills of life. . . . If you are eager and in a hurry to enter into a relationship with a girl, that's what you're going to get, a girl. But if you wait a while, you are going to get a seasoned woman who is going to step into and carry the weight of a relationship. Because relation-ships are hard and that's what I talk to our young people about.[75]

McDonald clearly articulates a set of criteria for Haudenosaunee mate selection based on maturity and wisdom, not simply romantic affections. These criteria have survived despite the many social, cultural, economic, and faith-based changes in the Akwesasne community. This does not mean that romance doesn't exist. As Dearborn reminds us, "she lives with him from love." Rather, we can recognize a tradition, still operating, where partners look for mates who can "carry the weight of a relation-ship." Clearly, prioritizing responsibility over romance has not hampered Haudenosaunee women's sense of personal fulfillment nor diminished their ability to participate in their communities' spiritual, social, and political structures. In the end, Arabella's disgust that Haudenosaunee couples do not share her culture's prioritization of marital "choice" does not prove Haudenosaunee women's "slave" status, but rather her own bigotry; hers is not an accurate measure of Haudenosaunee women's agency.

Reevaluating the Marriage Plot, Rethinking Choice(s)

With a fuller sense of the contexts of eighteenth-century Mohawk and British marriage practices, it becomes clear that contrary to Arabella's claims, neither Mohawk nor British couples in the period were entirely independent when making marital decisions. For instance, Brooke's Arabella Fermor and Emily Montague are not as free from parental influence as they might like to believe. Robert Merrett notes that both heroines eventually marry the partners their fathers choose for them.[76] Moreover, Julie Ellison insists that "there and back again" plots—where characters travel to the colonies to acquire a fortune, only to return home and uphold the status quo—are often initiated by financial instability and frequently circulate around courtship narratives.[77] Despite their best efforts to live on love, Emily and Edward express a continual concern for an insufficient income. In the end, they marry despite financial concerns. But they are happy to discover after they are already married that Emily's father, whom she has never met, has decided to marry her to Edward (an old family friend's son) and to give them his vast income acquired in the East Indies. The surprise ending allows the couple to claim true love as the motivating force for their marriage, while underwriting their continued happiness through colonial wealth. Ingrid Tague argues that this pitting of "mercenary" marriage motives against the ideal of companionate marriage was altogether common in conduct books and imaginative literature of the early eighteenth century.[78] Although Brooke presents fortune and love as necessarily separate, the marriage plot reveals these issues to be complementary.

However, Arabella's insistence that choosing a spouse is a form of personal freedom both more satisfying and valuable than Native women's political rights proves a more insidious and persistent myth about the value of Western-style romantic love. As Elizabeth Povinelli surveys it, the "intimate event" (normative romantic love) is formed by the intersection of two starkly opposed sets of discourses: the "autological subject"— expressed in Enlightenment notions of self-making, self-sovereignty, and individual freedom—and the "genealogical society"—expressed in notions of familial constraints and the historical debts of empire that supposedly limit the autological subject.[79] What we see in action in Arabella's disgust with Haudenosaunee arranged marriages is the way that liberal discourses of love "measure the worth of a life, and a society, relative to its capacity to constitute and vest sovereignty in the individual" or, as Arabella defines it, in her freedom to choose a husband.[80] As Foucault and others have theorized, Enlightenment freedom begins by claiming the power of self-management and self-discipline. Emerging in conjunction with the Enlightenment demand for freedom and self-management, social theorists such as Jürgen Habermas and Niklas Luhmann trace the achievement of the subject-in-love as a foundational source for democratic revolutions and representative democracy. Taken together, what we have here are a series of discourses and practices of the autological subject (a male subject, we might note) that are discursively opposed to the constraints on the individual imposed by kinship, sociological inheritances, and other forms of genealogical collectivity.

In my reading of Arabella's binary split between English liberty and savage slavery, the significance of pitting the autological subject against genealogical collective becomes clear: English romantic love, in the specific historical form of the companionate-marriage ideal, is more civilized because it invests the individual with sovereignty. As I noted earlier, with the significant influence of parents in our female protagonists' marriage choices, the illusion of independence is just that, an illusion. In reality, the autological subject and normative love are not free from or opposed to genealogical dependencies. Ultimately, "the intimate event and genealogical society function not as isolated discourses and practices, but as co-constitutive fields, riveted together in such a way that they secure and distribute power and wealth in the liberal diaspora."[81]

Despite Brooke's imperialist invocation of the constraints of the genealogical collective in Haudenosaunee practices of arranged marriage, her comparative framework provides the necessary structure through which readers such as Abigail Adams could recognize competing systems of intimacy and demand alternatives to existing patriarchal practices. Reading against the grain of Brooke's Enlightenment marriage comparisons, one finds the reflective space required to ask, as Edward Rivers does, why *are* eighteenth-century British women, as a class, excluded from participating in the governance of their nation? Why are British and Anglophone family structures *this* way rather than *that* way? Does women's status *really* improve with the adoption of companionate marriage? Ultimately, Brooke dismisses Native women's greater capacity for expressing agency when she endorses the marriage plot and its telos of progress through marital companionship.

Instead of a happy ending, the novel's conclusion proves compulsively colonizing as it closes off such questions in order to show the happily married couples living in close proximity in the rural English country-side. In order for the marriage plot to be successful, all traces of indig-enous Canadian romantic (and political) alternatives to companionate marriage must be conveniently left behind. The novel's conclusion takes place in a mythic pastoral space, Georgic in its peace and prosperity. It is free of the taint of imperialism and cultural otherness. Indeed, all traces of non-English identity are erased in the novel's concluding volume; the "circle of friends" continually reiterates their shared, even singular, per-spective on love, friendship, and the pleasures of rural life. This is an idyllic England that never really existed; it is a fantasy world, pure and simple. By relocating the major characters back to England, the novel frees these erstwhile immigrants of the taint of New World courtship. In the end, Canada functions as a time delay on the inevitable resolution of the British marriage plot.

Nevertheless, Brooke *has* revised the traditional marriage plot by jux-taposing it with representations of indigenous peoples' marital diversity. For readers such as Abigail Adams, dissatisfaction lingers long after the characters' transatlantic voyage back home. Listening to Mitchell's, Mc-Donald's, and Herne's accounts of Mohawk marriage, we realize how much we have missed in trying to explain what marriage (in a singular form) meant in the past and, concomitantly, how much we miss when we insist on doing so today.

[3]

MAKING ROOM FOR COQUETTES
AND FALLEN WOMEN

THIS CHAPTER COMPARES GEOGRAPHICALLY distinct discourses of seduction in two novels, *Secret History; or, The Horrors of St. Domingo* (1808) and *Laura* (1809), by American author Leonora Sansay. I argue that Sansay's critiques of two dominant US fictional paradigms of her moment, stories of coquettes and fallen women, are conditioned by the geographically specific gender norms and sexual practices of each novel's setting. Where Sansay's Haitian Revolution novel compares Caribbean and early national US domesticities as a means of rejecting the meaning and morality of the US seduction plot, Sansay's Philadelphia-based novel more discreetly revises that plot. Across both novels, Sansay observes the ill effects of women's economic dependence, offering women's friendships as a salve to romantic disillusionment.

Relocating Victims of Seduction

The 2007 reprinting of Leonora Sansay's *Secret History* testifies to an increasing critical interest in early prose fiction's generic complexities; it also marks a wider scope for the study of early American literature. Welcoming Sansay into the canon means extending our discussions of difference beyond the geographical borders of the US and contextualizing her work within a larger revolutionary Atlantic world. While recent criticism has debated the appropriate generic label for Sansay's extraordinarily slippery text as well as its place within the archive of materials on the Haitian Revolution, there has been relatively little work contextualizing Sansay's comparative assessments of women's sociality in Saint-Domingue.[1] Based on her firsthand experience of what will come to be known as the Haitian Revolution, Sansay's epistolary novel catalogues the numerous types of inhabitants living in what was the most profitable New World colony precisely as it was falling to pieces.[2] In the midst of this contentious geopolitical crisis, Sansay's two US narrators, sisters Mary and Clara, rather unaccountably document the flirtations, petty jealousies, and sexual relationships experienced by a wide swath of women in Saint-Domingue.

While this attention to romance may strike some readers as a distraction from the real business of describing "the horrors" of economic, political, and racial turmoil in early nineteenth-century Saint-Domingue, Mary's and Clara's focus on women's sexual lives is, I would argue, precisely what makes this text worth studying. Mary's and Clara's seemingly out-of-place observations on the complexities of sexual exchange in revolutionary-era Saint-Domingue provide the context for a larger comparative critique of marriage customs and the real limitations women faced both inside and outside of wedlock. As the sisters query the differences between Caribbean and US women's romantic expectations and their lived realities, they deploy this new understanding of gender's geographies to revise their own nontraditional, transnational stories. Capitalizing on her Caribbean setting, Sansay revolutionizes US readers' expectations about the shapes of women's stories and how those stories, in turn, shape women's lives.

Critics frequently comment on the bifurcation of Sansay's semiautobiographical account of her travels in Saint-Domingue across two narrators —the romantic, coquettish Clara (whose story more closely follows Sansay's own biographical experiences) and her more practical and cautious single sister, Mary. Distributing her critique of marriage across these two narrative perspectives enables Sansay to achieve the maximum effect on her readers as she moves between a microcosmic study of Clara's abusive marriage and a macrocosmic protoethnographic perspective of Caribbean women's sociality in Mary's letters. These dual narrative perspectives effectively combine to demonstrate the restrictions and dangers nineteenth-century married women face; the existing and alternative possibilities to marriage such as mulatto women's *ménagère* relationships, described later; and, finally, the utopian vision of homosocial domestic arrangements enabled by these alternatives and the social upheaval of the revolution. More broadly, the novel's comparisons of women's differences usefully disrupt simplistic narratives of nineteenth-century gender roles (i.e., the republican mother, the cult of true womanhood) by demonstrating various women's complex negotiations with multiple, competing, and geographically specific romantic ideologies. It is little wonder that such insights produce an excitingly new and difficult-to-label piece of fiction.

Published in 1808 after Leonora Sansay abandoned her French husband in Saint-Domingue to return to the United States, after the formerly enslaved peoples of Saint-Domingue won their freedom and renamed their country Haiti, and after Aaron Burr—to whom Sansay dedicates her book—had been tried and acquitted for treason, Sansay's text capitalizes on sensational descriptions of racial violence and on Burr's scandalous character.[3] Written as a series of letters from Mary to Aaron Burr, with a brief interlude as Mary's sister Clara explains how and why she leaves her husband, *Secret History* documents an important transition period in the revolution. Napoleon—eager to secure "the pearl of the Antilles" for the French Empire—sends Madame and General Leclerc (his sister and brother-in-law) to stamp out the slave revolt and restore order to the colony. With the arrest of the insurgent leader, Toussaint-Louverture, it seems likely that the French will succeed. However, the insurgents execute several stunning political and tactical moves, ultimately winning their freedom and declaring the newly renamed "Haiti" an independent nation. It remains the world's only successful slave revolt. In a brilliant juxtaposition of macro- and microrevolutions, *Secret History* parallels "the horrors" of political upheaval and racial warfare with the horrors of domestic abuse. In Saint-Domingue, Mary and Clara witness a remarkable number of revolutionary acts—formerly enslaved peoples of both sexes struggling to maintain their newly won freedom; women of color boycotting unreasonable sumptuary restrictions; and even former plantation mistresses working to support themselves—before Clara undertakes her own revolution against her abusive husband.

Attention to Clara's disastrous marriage holds together the rather rambling plot of *Secret History*. Mary writes to Burr: "My sister . . . repents every day having so precipitately chosen a husband: it is impossible for two creatures to be more different, and I foresee that she will be wretched." A few pages later, Mary confirms that Clara's "aversion to her husband is unqualified and unconquerable. He is vain, illiterate, talkative. A silent fool may be borne, but from a loquacious one there is no relief. . . . She finds no sympathy in the bosom of her husband. She is alone and she is wretched."[4] Here Mary employs the rhetoric of companionate marriage—the most prominent romantic ideology circulating in the early national United States—to assess Clara's situation. Unlike arranged marriage, where upper-class parents match their children in order to consolidate wealth or establish alliances across families, companionate marriage is a union of the heart where partners choose one another on the basis of mutual affection. In revolutionary and early national US discourse, women's sexual fidelity and happiness become a "barometer," in John Adams's phrase, of the virtue of the nation and of women's overall progress.[5] As in the British marriage-rites genre discussed in chapter 1, early national US marriage-rites texts frequently ask women to compare their own happy marriage customs with the misery of women in the seraglio, the Indian hut, or the African wilds.[6] In contrast to the supposed drudgery expected of "savage" wives, the sensual usage of polygamous brides, or prearranged marriages where women have little or no say, the US woman's ability to choose her own spouse supposedly ensures her a loving and emotionally bonded marriage. This freely chosen union of hearts was thought to result in women's more progressive treatment and, by extension, an increase in the nation's overall civility. Companionate marriage was, in the rhetoric of the period, a boon for women and the nation. As demonstrated in chapter 1, such comparisons attempt to prove that companionate marriage is the best domestic arrangement for women.

But this is not the case in *Secret History*. To return to the novel, in Mary's estimation, the problem with Clara's husband, St. Louis, is not simply that he is foolish and vain, but that he is unsympathetic. Again and again Mary describes him as unequal to his wife; St. Louis cannot appreciate her. Mary notes that he is "jealous as a Turk" and describes the marriage as unwisely recommended by Clara's guardian in order to secure her an income: "the fortune of her husband was his only advantage." Without regard for compatibility, Clara's marriage is based on money. Mary continues, "Though to me he has been invariably kind yet my heart is torn with regret at the torments which his irascible temper inflict on his wife. They force her to seek relief in the paths of pleasure, whilst destined . . . [for] domestic felicity."[7] Faced with the impossibility of a companionate marriage, Clara turns to another popular US romantic narrative to script her life's story: she styles herself a coquette.

In the popular didactic literature of the early nineteenth century, the coquette is usually a single young woman, a female rebel who fails to subscribe to the protocols of monogamous heterosexual marriage. The coquette is invariably punished for her rebellion, often falling prey to a libertine seducer and dying in shame, scorned by society at the end of the tale. Sansay's use of the coquette/seduction plot is, structurally, a strange turn in an already strange text. Traditionally, the unmarried coquette must either tame her flirtatious behavior in preparation for a happy marriage or die for her refusal to submit; in *Secret History*, an incompatible marriage leads an otherwise good wife to become a coquette. Like many coquettes, Clara's mistake is that she imagines she is autonomous; that is, she assumes that she is an independent agent with the power to act for herself (as most men could do). As a married woman, though, Clara has no right to circulate herself. Her body is taken off the market, so to speak, when she marries the French planter, St. Louis. Given the fact that the French were stereotypically known for pragmatic marriages and extramarital relationships, Clara's mistake is especially ironic: "The French appear to understand less than any other people the delights arising from an union of the hearts. They seek only the gratification of their sensual appetites. They gather the flowers but taste not the fruits of love."[8] Clara might coquettishly imagine that with a French husband she could also maintain a lover, but St. Louis is that unfortunate breed, a jealous French husband. He tenaciously maintains his right to control Clara's body.

The most famous early American literary example of the coquette is Hannah Foster's *The Coquette* (1797), inspired by the true story of Elizabeth Whitman, a Connecticut woman who fails to secure a suitable marriage proposal only to be seduced and eventually die in childbirth. Previous scholarship on *The Coquette* typically reads the dilemma of the heroine, Eliza Wharton, as an allegory for the dangers of democracy; more recently, in *The Gender of Freedom,* Elizabeth Dillon has argued against such allegorical readings, claiming that the novel explores competing US views on sociality. Eliza maintains a position of "open sociality" —where social contact works as a *generative force* for shaping feminine subjectivity—but her friends and community understand women's sociality as "closed"—a means for displaying a *preexisting* feminine subjectivity with the end goal of organizing private individuals into proper heterosexual couples.[9] Dillon's models of open and closed sociality help to explain why the trope of the coquette (a position of open sociality) might appeal to a woman such as Clara, invested as she is in expanding the possibilities for circulating in public, even in a violent, war-torn public. Already married, Clara's traditional window for autonomy—courtship— is now closed. The only way she can imagine to reopen it is to inhabit the coquette's narrative. But this role seems a poor choice for an intelligent and ambitious woman; everyone knows that the coquette inevitably dies as a result of her refusal to follow the norm.

Clara, however, is not in Connecticut, where Elizabeth Whitman/Eliza Wharton was seduced, or in Philadelphia, where Sansay was the mistress of Aaron Burr prior to her marriage. Caribbean sexual mores have the ability to transform the coquette's narrative function and meaning via the seduction plot. For instance, Clara's sister observes, "In this country that unfortunate class of beings, so numerous in my own—victims of

seduction, devoted to public contempt and universal scorn, is unknown."
Indeed, free mulatto women are "destined from their birth to a life of
pleasure" and to that destiny "no infamy is attached." Of French Creole
women, Mary notes, "Here a false step is rarely made by an unmarried
lady, and a married lady, who does not make one, is as rare." French
Creole women generally find pleasure outside of marriage: "Every girl
sighs to be married to escape the restraint with which she is held whilst
single, and to enjoy the unbounded liberty she so often sees abused by
her mother." Taking a lover is, according to Mary, standard procedure
here. With no choice over her spouse, a woman is likely to find affection
any way she may: "A husband is necessary to give [a wife] a place in
society; but is considered of so little importance to her happiness, that
in the choice of one her inclination is very seldom consulted."[10] One can
imagine that in the context of Saint-Domingue, the coquette's typical
ending—infamy and death—might seem less likely. Clara's decision to
become a coquette appears less disastrous in a French Caribbean setting,
where the morality of the seduction plot would seem completely alien.
However, it is not only the logic of the seduction narrative that Mary
finds inoperable here; she also notes that the adultery plot seems quite
distinct here. Unlike the insistence on US women's strict adherence to
marital monogamy, upper-class French Creole women practice a form
of discreet adultery that was widely known and socially sanctioned as
long as it remained covert. While it might seem obvious, Mary effectively
demonstrates via comparison that experiences of and discourses about
seduction vary by geography. As her characters observe and analyze Caribbean customs and manners, Sansay uses this enlarged scope of acceptable
sexual practices to rewrite popular US romantic narratives such as that of
the coquette's inevitable "fall." In short, in the narrative formula of the typical US seduction plot, Clara's coquettish behavior demands punishment;
however, in colonial Saint-Domingue, it is far from extraordinary.

Although Clara flirts with the newly appointed General Rochambeau
out of boredom (Rochambeau replaces General Leclerc after his sudden
death), she loves him no more than she loves her husband. Hoping for
distraction, she finds only more trouble. Rochambeau's attentions prove
more dangerous than her initial situation. Clara realizes the seriousness
of her mistake when the general sends St. Louis to fight on the front,
denying him much-needed reinforcements. Thinking Clara has used this
time to conduct an affair, St. Louis returns home without permission and
imprisons Clara. Mary writes, "St. Louis is unworthy of her: he thinks it
would be possible to force her to love him:—how much more would a

generous confidence influence a heart like hers! . . . But I believe Clara is not the first wife that has been locked up at St. Domingo."[11] If Clara's body is a valuable commodity legally owned by St. Louis and highly desired by Rochambeau, St. Louis decisively takes her out of circulation. As his legal property, Clara has no right to challenge him, no recourse from his claims to control her.

Of course, in Saint-Domingue Clara is not the first person to lose her liberty without cause. Sansay's brilliant juxtaposition of "the horrors" of a tyrannical husband alongside "the horrors" of slave revolt brings to light two separate but related forms of domination. Both wives and enslaved peoples are property, equally subject to the whims and suspicions of domineering white males. As the violence of the revolution increases and formerly enslaved peoples gain strength, St. Louis desperately strives to maintain control over his property. *Secret History* quietly suggests that when men abuse their power—over enslaved peoples and over wives—revolution is the inevitable result.

The political situation in Saint-Domingue produces opposite effects on St. Louis and Clara. As a property owner and slaveholder, the slave insurgency makes St. Louis more tyrannical, while it inspires Clara to escape and start a new life. Clara hears many examples of women resisting exploitative power structures; all around her, emboldened enslaved and mixed-race persons, including many women, bravely risk their lives for their own freedom and the freedom of others. For instance, Mary relates the story of an unnamed insurgent chief and his wife who, after being captured, were about to be executed: "As they walked to the place of execution the chief seemed deeply impressed with the horror of his approaching fate: but his wife went cheerfully along, endeavoured to console him and reproached his want of courage. When they arrived on the field in which their grave was already dug, she refused to have her eyes bound; and turning to the soldiers who were to execute their sentence, said 'Be expeditious, and don't make me linger.' She received their fire without shrinking, and expired without uttering a groan."[12] Loosely based on the true story of Sanite Belair's death, this account illustrates how some women not only participated in the events of the revolution, but even outranked men in their performance of bravery as well.[13] As in Aphra Behn's well-known depictions of the fictional Oroonoko, Belair "expired without uttering a groan," the most recognizable of stoic, masculine behaviors. Mary notably describes this couple as "black" and refuses them specific names. Mary's story of Zuline, another example of female bravery, offers a more traditional model of sympathetic femininity in a light-skinned mulatto woman living with an American man.[14] Attuned to the needs of white men, the beautiful Zuline begs a mulatto soldier to spare the life of a Frenchman (probably a planter): "She sunk at his feet, and pressed his hands which were reeking with blood. Dear brother, she said, spare for my sake this unfortunate man. He never injured you. . . . She was beautiful; she wept, and beauty in tears has seldom been resisted. Yet this unrelenting savage did resist. . . . The mulatto, enraged, asked if the Frenchman was anything to her? Nothing, she replied; I never saw him before; but to save the life of an innocent person how trifling would appear the sacrifice I offer."[15] These two examples show brave women acting to secure freedom for themselves and others. Color difference and gender performance obviously shape Mary's perception of these women. She freely admits her "admiration" for the recognizably feminine and light-skinned Zuline, while calling the bold black insurgent a "fury in female form."[16] This difference is consistent with contemporary stereotypes representing mixed-race individuals as more civilized because they are more white.[17] The nameless chief's wife and Zuline actively participate in the affairs of the revolution; they draw upon tremendous inner resources, resisting others' attempts to define or limit their involvement in the fight for freedom. While she values their efforts differently, Mary clearly admires the mental and emotional fortitude these women exert in the face of danger.

In addition to heroic stories of black and mixed-race women's participation in the revolution, Clara's decision to end her unhappy marriage might also be influenced by the surprising examples of strength she finds in French Creole women who flee Saint-Domingue after Rochambeau surrenders the island to Dessalines. Unattended by male relatives, who remain behind to fight for their property, French Creole women quickly discover their previously untapped survival skills. Mary observes how mass dislocation makes French Creole women stronger:

> The cheerfulness with which they bear misfortune, and the industry they employ to procure themselves a subsistence, cannot be sufficiently admired. I know ladies who from their infancy were surrounded by slaves, anticipating their slightest wishes, now working from the dawn of day till midnight to support themselves and their families. . . .
>
> Though I liked not entirely their manner, whilst surrounded by the festivity and splendor of the Cape, I now confess that they excite my warmest admiration.[18]

Struggling to survive, French Creole women have less time for splendor and excess; like good domestic women, they must now *cheerfully* bear misfortune. Although Mary and Clara are also caught up in this mass exodus of women, they continue to see themselves as outsiders, us citizens who may yet return home. Mary adds, "In the same circumstances I fear I should be inferior to them both [in cheerfulness and fortitude]."[19] Clara, however, responds differently. All around her women are surviving on their own. When her marriage becomes unbearable, she follows the example of the many brave women, black and white, remaking their lives right beside her.

In a moment of crisis Clara flees her husband. We read her story retrospectively from her own pen. Significantly, this change in narration transforms Clara from an object of male desire and sisterly curiosity to a writer with the power to relate her own story. Unlike the distant, ethnographic tone of Mary's letters, Clara writes with an intensity and intimacy that surprises readers accustomed to Mary's travelogue style. In explaining how and why she left St. Louis, Clara testifies to her experience as a victim of abuse, yet she assertively writes her way out of that role. "The night before I left him," Clara writes to her sister,

> he came home in a transport of fury, dragged me from my bed, said it was his intention to destroy me, and swore that he would render me horrible by rubbing aqua-fortis [nitric acid] in my face. This last menace deprived me of the power of utterance. . . . The only thought I dwelt on was, how to escape from this monster, and, at break of day, I was still sitting, as if rendered motionless by his threats. From this stupor I was roused by his caresses, or rather by his brutal approaches, for he always finds my person provoking, and often, whilst pouring on my head abuse which would seem dictated by the most violent hatred, he has sought in my arms gratification which should be solicited with affection and granted to love alone.[20]

Clara vividly describes the shock and stupor she felt as a victim of physical and sexual assault. She was speechless and motionless. She could not fight; her only thought was to run away.

When Clara leaves St. Louis, she takes the road to Cobre, the site of a large slave revolt in Cuba.[21] The cobreros, a maroon colony that formed after the revolt, lived in the surrounding mountains and welcomed runaway enslaved peoples from throughout the Caribbean. Clara's description of her flight is reinforced by her choice to relocate via Cobre, a site of black resistance and struggle. Like the maroons who surely found the way to Cobre through a dense network of social relations, Clara draws upon her social connections to secure herself an asylum: "I knew that, as soon as I was missed, the town would be diligently searched for me, but of the retreat I had chosen St. Louis could have no idea, for he was totally unacquainted with the residence of Madame V——. To this lady I had rendered some essential services [in Saint-Domingue], which gave me a claim on her friendship. She . . . lives in the greatest retirement. I had heard of her by accident, and thought it the surest retreat I could find."[22] Clara's choice illustrates a community of French Creole women, US and Caribbean, banding together after the disruptions of the revolution. For Clara's flight is just one more dislocation, one more close escape, in the many stories gathered here of resourceful women reorganizing their lives. Though she freely chooses it, Clara's single status is not unusual in the chaos of the revolution. Intense bonds of sympathy forged through mutual loss and suffering unite French Creole women across the American hemisphere.

Clara relates her close friendships with other women as part of the various traumas they all have survived. Subsequent to leaving her husband, she makes two new women friends: Madame V—— and Madame St. Clair. Madame V—— is a friend from Saint-Domingue who also relocates to Cuba. She accepts Clara without any explanation of her sudden appearance:

> Seizing my hand, she led me to her chamber, where, pressed in her arms, I felt that I had found a friend, and the tears that flowed on her bosom were proofs of my gratefulness.
>
> I began to explain my situation. "I know it all!" she cried, "you have escaped your husband. My predictions are verified, though a little later than I expected." There was no necessity for giving her a reason for having left my husband. She had always been at a loss to find one for my staying with him so long.[23]

Where Mary suspects Clara's motives and unsympathetically accuses her of behaving with want of propriety, Clara's friend understands the situation without words. There is a caring tenderness expressed as Madame V—— provides Clara with new clothes, a place to rest, and food. Clara describes a new kind of Caribbean domesticity, a single women's sympathetic collective.

This reciprocal care and responsibility harkens a new status for Clara and the Creole women remaking their lives outside of Saint-Domingue; they can be dependent on one another while remaining independent, thinking beings. This domestic sphere does not require gender subordination, but rather mutual sympathy and respect. After a few days with Madame V——, Clara finds that a popular festival will make her hideout less secluded. The women then decide to visit Madame St. Clair in another remote part of Cuba. These women immediately become so intimate that "Madame St. Clair, seduced by the description I have made of our peaceful country . . . intends going with me to Philadelphia."[24] Here, America figures as a space for forging hemispheric Creole alliances that transcend national borders. It holds the promise of a quasi-feminist utopia, free from the legal claims men hold over women's bodies. Moreover, Clara "seduces" another women with her utopian vision; this seduction does not end in ruin, however. Instead, both women find hope in relocating together; their alternative domesticity is not divorced from politics, but bred in and of it.

This ending surprises readers with its reversal of the traditional courtship plot structure. Where such texts typically begin with a homosocial community of single women pursuing acceptable marriage partners and end with several happily married heterosexual couples, *Secret History* revises this structure by beginning with an unhappily married heterosexual couple, transforming the wife into a coquette, and ending with an international homosocial community of single women. To return to Elizabeth Dillon's models of sociality, by the end of the novel, Clara successfully engages in a form of open sociality. Circulating in a new international community of sympathetic Creole women, Clara finds the opportunity for self-development that Foster's Eliza Wharton desires, but cannot obtain. Clara also escapes the narrative conclusion of the seduction plot that seemed to loom over her coquettish behavior. In fact, the seduction plot is entirely rejected. There is no death, no social isolation, no punishment by painful, fatal childbirth here. Instead, Clara authors a remarkable new story for herself.

Oddly, the geopolitics of colonial and racial violence make this utopian hemispheric alliance possible. Nearly every woman has survived the loss of a male loved one or the disruption of a marriage. Clara's own Creole identity connects her with other Caribbean Creole women, even as she plans to return to the United States.[25] Her story is a "revolution" from the dominant US narrative conventions of her time, radically revising the narrative formulas of both early national US courtship and seduction plots. Clara does not find another husband, take a lover, or die from a broken heart or shame. Rather, she uses her network of international women friends to rebuild her life and create a new international family. This Creole rejection of the seduction narrative provides a powerful counterdiscourse to the hegemony of domestic morality in British and American fiction of the same period.

Caribbean Domesticities

Thus far I have argued that Clara draws on the strong examples of black and white Caribbean women fighting and surviving the horrific social conditions of the revolution as she decisively breaks free from her abusive marriage and forms her own utopian community of transnational women friends. However, these are only a few instances of the geographically distinct sexual and social relations that inspire Sansay to break with the narrative conventions that might trap Clara in a seduction plot. I now turn from the microcosmic framing of Clara's individual romantic revolution to consider how Mary's travelogue-style comparative analyses of Caribbean social and sexual mores provide a macrocosmic frame for the novel's revolutionary rejection of the seduction plot.

A number of scholars have demonstrated how the Caribbean served as a foil for more wholesome forms of British and US morality.[26] In myriad period depictions, black, white, and biracial women in the Caribbean colonies are described as oversexed, irrationally violent, and morally depraved. To speak, then, of Caribbean domesticity would seem oxymoronic. However, Sansay identifies a surprising source for Caribbean domesticity: the class of free mixed-race mulatto women living in Saint-Domingue. Described as the most "fervent priestesses of the American Venus," as well as the most constant and tender companions, renowned for their expert household management, free mulatto women were the preferred sexual and domestic partners of white men in Saint-Domingue.[27] In a letter to Aaron Burr, Mary champions mulatto women "housekeepers" (also known as *ménagères*) for their sexual fidelity and economic acumen, observing, "The mulatto women are the hated but successful rivals of the Creole ladies. Many of them are extremely beautiful; and, being destined from their birth to a life of pleasure, they are taught to heighten the power of their charms by all the aids of art. . . . To the destiny of the women of colour no infamy is attached."[28] In this brief description, Mary reveals a wealth of contemporary assumptions about the differences between mixed-race mulatto women and their rivals, French Creole women born in the Caribbean. Although neither of these groups of women is enslaved, neither is truly free. Both compete for powerful white men's affections as well as the prestige, wealth, and consumer goods that such relationships bring.

What Mary describes here and throughout her letters is that even as mulatto and French Creole women compete with one another, the romantic relationships that they form with white men are quite distinct.

Whereas French Creole women marry for long-term legal and economic security, transmitting property through their legitimately produced heirs, Mary notes that mulatto women pursue a different "destiny." Rather remarkably, Mary's comparisons establish nonmarital sexual relations and alternative domesticities as acceptable social realities for at least some women living in colonial Saint-Domingue. Of course, as one credits Mary's comparative observations for their perceptive analyses of local gender norms, one must also acknowledge that Mary's unsympathetic observations on her sister's abusive marriage and her overt racism render her a less than objective narrator. Still, by championing mulatto women's sexual fidelity and economic resourcefulness, Mary identifies an overlooked source of domesticity in the turbulent social reality of the Haitian Revolution. From Mary's admittedly questionable perspective, mulatto women's domestic partnerships offer some unique advantages over the system of coverture governing US married women's lives.[29]

In this section I focus on Mary's extended observations on the differences between French Creole and free mulatto women's sexual relationships with white men, as well as the island's system of *plaçage,* another alternative to legal marriage, as additional sources of inspiration for the novel's pathbreaking conclusion: the utopian women's community Clara envisions. I juxtapose Mary's representations of local Caribbean women with similar commentary by contemporary male writers such as Michel-René Hilliard d'Auberteuil and M. L. E. Moreau de Saint-Méry to make visible how Mary's comparisons of local heterosexual practices lead toward a quasi-feminist social imaginary at the novel's end. Compared to French metropolitan male observers who, by and large, demonize mulatto women, Mary marvels at mixed-race women's wider range of social, sexual, and economic freedoms.

Not French, but influenced by French manners; not Afro-Caribbean, but marked by the local dialect; not Oriental, but managing to be imperious and voluptuous at the same time, Mary describes French Creoles as a blend of various national characteristics: "The Creole ladies have an air of voluptuous languor which renders them extremely interesting . . . they have acquired from the habit of commanding their slaves, an air of dignity which adds to their charms. Almost too indolent to pronounce their words they speak with a drawling accent that is very agreeable. . . . Those who, having been educated in France, unite the French vivacity to the Creole sweetness, are the most irresistible creatures that the imagination can conceive."[30] In addition to an ambiguously identified "Creole sweetness," an abiding feature of contemporary descriptions of French

Creole women is their idle and pampered lifestyle. Speaking somewhat ironically of the heyday of slavery Mary writes:

> I wish [the negroes] were reduced to order that I might see the so much vaunted habitations where I should repose beneath the shade of orange groves; walk on carpets of rose leaves and frenchipone; be fanned to sleep by silent slaves, or have my feet tickled into extacy [sic] by the soft hand of the female attendant.
>
> Such were the pleasures of the Creole ladies whose time was divided between the bath, the table, the toilette and the lover. . . .
>
> But the moment of enjoying these pleasures is, I fear, far distant. The negroes have felt during ten years the blessing of liberty, for a blessing it certainly is, however acquired, and they will not be easily deprived of it.[31]

Although Mary acknowledges enslaved peoples' legitimate desire for liberty, neither she nor her sister actively supports emancipation. They are part of the planter class, even if by marriage. In this passage, Mary explicitly imagines herself as a Creole lady, "tickled into extacy," *not* an enslaved female obliged to fulfill the mistress's every demand. As a US woman from Pennsylvania,[32] Mary is both attracted to and appalled by slave-owning Creole women's indulgence. She may fantasize about the former luxuries of plantation mistresses, but Mary is neither the mistress nor the servant. Her remarks register the distance between her and these two ranks of Caribbean women. Still, Mary does recognize that such pleasures are only possible through slavery. Once enslaved peoples rebel, "the moment of enjoying these pleasures is . . . far distant."

In contrast to idle and pampered French Creole ladies, mulatto women —"the hated but successful rivals of the Creole ladies"—are "destined from their birth to a life of pleasure."[33] Mary uses the categories "mulatto" and "women of colour" interchangeably, but she is primarily interested in a group of women who frequently act as mistresses and housekeepers, or *ménagères,* to single and married white men. Many mulatto women traded their sexual capital (their beauty, allure, and reputation for sexual prowess) for the material goods, monetary payments, and increase in status associated with such employment. C. L. R. James notes, "In 1789, of 7,000 mulatto women, 5,000 were either prostitutes or the 'kept mistresses' of white men."[34] However, contemporary travel writers and historians insist that free women of color were not prostitutes; these relationships are more stable and more sentimentally domestic than one might expect.[35] Although white men might also hire enslaved women to be *ménagères,* preference was often given to free mixed-race women who sometimes possessed considerable personal wealth or property, becoming genuine economic assets to their employers. Uncovering the complex rhetorical strategies that French Creole planters used to describe these relationships, Doris Garraway observes that "as early as 1734, official correspondence noted the frequency with which newly arrived French settlers sought their fortunes not on the sugar plantation but in marriage with free women of color possessing considerable savings."[36] Later in the eighteenth century, these marriages were stigmatized as "*mésalliances*" and punished through social exclusion and acts of discrimination. Thus, extralegal marriages known as *plaçage* (discussed more fully later) and other contract arrangements for sexual and domestic unions became increasingly popular and were often still referred to as "marriage" without facing the legal punishments for breaking *mésalliance* laws. For instance, eighteenth-century travel writer, politician, and scientist Girod de Chantrans explains, "Not only do domiciled whites consider it necessary to their pleasures and advantageous for their interests to have a woman of this species at the head of their household, it is even a common practice of etiquette and good taste among them."[37] Not only did *ménagères* usually receive salaries for their domestic work, but, more important, they also helped their employers establish necessary social and business contacts, recommended merchants or service providers, and directed household spending. As Garraway notes, the free mulatto was both the sign and symbol of white male sexual hegemony, and also one of the colony's most controversial figures: she "stands as a privileged icon of colonial libertinage, embodying the very nexus of concupiscence, luxury, and consumption that came to signify the Antilles in the French colonial imagination."[38]

Male authors such as Girod de Chantrans and Hilliard d'Auberteuil justify crossing the legally established racial barrier by describing white women, Creole, French, or otherwise, as rapidly losing their attractiveness in the damaging tropical climate and lacking in the supposed sexual prowess that made mulatto women desirable sexual partners.[39] Period accounts of free mulatto women grant them a kind of corrupting agency, actively displacing the responsibility for white men's miscegenation onto supposedly calculating, voluptuous mixed-race women.

Although French marriage laws ensured lawfully wedded wives long-term economic maintenance—a security *ménagères* lacked—in practice, *ménagères* had considerable authority in the supervision of the household and in personal relationships with their employers. As Mary notes, in Saint-Domingue, "no infamy is attached" to such women. In Mary's representations, *ménagères* use their relationships with white men to increase their social and economic power in the larger community, thereby revising standard assumptions about domesticity and women's separate sphere.[40] While Mary's perspective does not attend to the lack of options free mulatto women had for exercising agency, nor does it critique the ways that this supposed form of agency reduces mulatto women to sexualized bodies, it does recognize that free mulatto women's particular relationships with white men afford them a different status than white US, Creole, or even metropolitan French women could claim. While mulatto women might be "fallen women," they are clearly not "victims of seduction." Far from being "universally scorned," as Mary notes that fallen women in the United States were, here, free mulatto women are powerful social and sexual actors, the "hated but successful rivals of the Creole ladies."[41]

If, in the Caribbean, it was especially obvious that women's bodies were fundamentally commodities purchased for their physical and reproductive capabilities, then mulatto women, in Mary's account, capitalize on the commodity potential of their bodies in ways that white US and Creole women could not. From Mary's historically limited point of view, mulatto women maintain a surprising level of social and economic power and personal autonomy. As contracted labor, unmarried *ménagères* may leave or find other employment if the situation proves unsatisfactory. Unlike Clara and other married women who find themselves divested of control over their desirable bodies, *ménagères* maintain limited control over their bodies by retaining the right to exchange those bodies on the free market. Moreover, *ménagères* turn their pay into increased opportunities for social and economic power in the larger community by lending money at interest or renting properties for additional income.[42]

Obviously there are ethical concerns and serious limitations to arguments that make a woman's "agency" equivalent to her ability to trade her body for payment, especially in a patriarchal and fundamentally racist slave-based economy. I am not making such a claim here. Nor am I defending capitalist systems that render women and their bodies commodities. More simply, I want to draw attention to the relative positions of various groups of women in this specific historic period and geographic locale. Comparatively, free unmarried mulatto women in Saint-Domingue express more control over their lives when acting outside of the legal marriage system. While their power originates in the domestic sphere via sexual relationships with and household management for white men, it is not limited to the domestic sphere. Separated from the function of producing legal heirs and, consequently, from interconnected discourses of domesticity, reproduction, and the nation, *ménagères* forge distinct domesticities in Saint-Domingue. More broadly, Mary's sustained comparisons of mulatto women's domesticities suggest how these alternatives become a powerful force in the novel's revision of US coquettes and fallen women.

Mary is not alone in characterizing mulatto *ménagères* as powerful players in their local communities and economies. As Garraway argues, the mulatto woman was the locus of a contradictory set of rhetorical assertions and representations in prerevolutionary Saint-Domingue: she was "a racially hybrid marker of sexual excess, material extravagance, and domestic virtue."[43] The *ménagère* was typically part of a relatively stable and committed domestic partnership; however, male observers often describe women of color as the most outrageous of libertines. In the heady realm of Caribbean fantasy and desire, mulatto women—themselves the products of interracial sexual union—become symbolically equated with the interracial desire denoted in their biracial origins.[44] Eighteenth-century white male travel writers, former plantation owners, and historians frequently offer up assessments of mulatto women more properly located in fiction. For example, Hilliard d'Auberteuil, the French colonial lawyer and author of *Considérations sur l'état présent de la colonie française de Saint-Domingue*, writes, "The mulâtresses are in general much less docile than mulatto men because they have arrogated to themselves an empire over most of the whites, founded on libertinage. They are well made, their movements are guided by voluptuousness; the affectation of their attire does not sit badly with them."[45] Plantation owner and historian Moreau de Saint-Méry offers a more pointed analysis of mulatto women's sexual power: "The sole occupation of the numerous class of women who are the fruit of the mixture of whites with slave women is to avenge themselves, with weapons of pleasure, for being condemned to abasement."[46] In both of these accounts, mulatto women's sexuality is a form of "empire" over white men. In the seductive hands of the mulatto temptress, sexuality is a weapon for gaining ascendency in the racial hierarchy. On the surface at least, white men grant women of color a limited kind of sovereignty; but as several critics note, these statements shuffle the responsibility for white male sexuality onto the shoulders of free mulatto women.

For Garraway, historical sources that "document" the sexual proclivities and/or the faithful loyalty of mulatto women continue to make available the projections of white male sexual hegemony at work in Saint-

Domingue prior to the revolution. Similarly, Mary's perception of mulatto women's social and sexual power is the product of her narrow ideological preconceptions and interpretations. It is not the goal of this chapter to critique the limitations of Mary's observations—obviously mulatto women had limited power and means for wielding that power—rather, my aim is to trace the way that Mary's position as a white US woman affords her a different perspective on mulatto women's sexual power. To be clear, I do not claim that Mary (or Sansay) accurately represents mulatto women in revolutionary Saint-Domingue. Instead, I argue that the differences in her attitude toward mulatto women's sexual, social, and economic power—as she perceives it—are worth further reflection.

While Hilliard d'Auberteuil and Moreau de Saint-Méry charge mulatto women with a sexual empire over white men, Julien Raimond, an educated mulatto man from Saint-Domingue, describes a distinct free and wealthy class of mixed-race "people of color," which developed from affectionate interracial sexual relations. In "Observations on the Origin and Progression of the White Colonists' Prejudice against Men of Color" (1791), written to persuade the French National Assembly to grant political rights to free colored people, Raimond observes: "Though they [white men] called them [mulatto mistresses] housekeepers, they made them into wives. As soon as these women had children with their masters, they became free, as did their children, who were always raised like free children. . . . There was no dishonor in knowing them, spending time with them, living with them, forming relationships with their daughters." Racial prejudice begins, according to Raimond, when white women arrive and find themselves in competition with *ménagères* and wealthy women of color: "Many Europeans crossed the sea, including large numbers of poor women who came to seek their fortunes. Mothers brought their daughters to marry them to rich colonists. They were frequently disappointed. Since these immigrant women brought no resources, many of the young men who came to the colony to get rich preferred to marry girls of color, whose dowries included land and slaves they could use profitably. Such preferences began to inspire jealousy in white women."[47] In sharp contrast to white male travel writers' demonizing accounts of mulatto women's sexuality, Raimond historicizes white colonial men's participation in the creation of a free mulatto class and those planters' preferences for economically advantageous matches over racial solidarity through marriage with white women.

Like Raimond, Mary notes that French Creole women were a prime source of racial hostilities, frequently complaining of their husbands' bankrolling mulatto women's luxurious consumption habits. White Creole women witnessed mulatto women's power most visibly in the expensive material goods such as lace, linen, silk, gold, and even real estate that they acquired from white lovers. In exchange for their valuable domestic and sexual services, women of color gained coveted trade goods and the social éclat that accompanied them. In her vivid account of mulatto women's sexual, social, and economic power, Mary describes how Creole women became so jealous of women of color and "their influence over the men . . . that they complained to the council" about family fortunes lavished on mixed-race mistresses. Mary observes that Creole women rallied to pass sumptuary laws to shame their rivals: "No woman of colour was to wear silk . . . nor to appear in public without a handkerchief on her head." But women of color understood their power; in the face of new sumptuary laws, they boycotted by "shut[ting] themselves up in their houses, and appear[ing] no more in public." Refusing to be victims of economic exchange, women of color withdrew themselves and their considerable wealth from public circulation. The results were immediate: "The merchants soon felt the bad effects of this determination, and represented so forcibly the injury the decree did to commerce, that it was reversed, and the olive beauties triumphed."[48] Of course, mulatto women's boycotting tactics were not particularly new. European women frequently organized riots when the cost of bread exceeded peasant families' ability to purchase this staple. But whereas European women rioted when basic staples were inaccessible, the sumptuary-law boycotts in Saint-Domingue were not about being out-priced. Rather, these boycotts demonstrate mulatto women's social and economic powers over and against supposedly elite white Creole women. These boycotts proved that mulatto women could exercise limited independence from race-based economic constraints by withdrawing their bodies (and their extensive capital) from circulating in the market. In this case, a retreat to the domestic sphere serves to increase mulatto women's social power—a power remarked by white men and imitated by white women.

The madras headscarf, which was meant to be a symbol of mulatto women's humiliation and second-class status, becomes instead a sign of regional pride and female sensuality. Interestingly, madras cloth was manufactured in the East Indies and used to trade for slaves on the West African coast, where it functioned as a highly symbolic material sign of wealth and became a kind of currency in and of itself.[49] That mulatto women chose madras as the cloth used to cover their heads in obedience to sumptuary laws should, then, be interpreted as the highest form of irony, even an outright statement of rebellion. These women are no one's slaves; instead, they swathe themselves in the wealth-generating materials of the slave trade. As Elizabeth Dillon argues, the madras scarf becomes synonymous with the generative force of Creole culture itself.[50] It demonstrates that the colonies were far from passive consumers of metropolitan culture, but that they could and did generate their own distinct cultures and fashions. Indeed, white women as high-ranking as Napoleon's sister imitated sultry Caribbean women of color as they donned the stylish madras headscarf. Baron de Wimpffen writes that mulatto women "are the envy and despair of the white ladies, who aspire to imitate them, and who do not see that it is impossible for strong and glaring colours, calculated to animate the monotonous and livid hue of the mulatto, to harmonize with the alabaster and the rose of Europe!"[51] While I agree with Dillon's reading that the scene demonstrates the generative possibilities of Creole culture, I argue that white women's appropriation of the madras headscarf also serves to illustrate another less documented fantasy: a desire for the kind of sexual dominance and power reportedly possessed by local free mulatto women. Although jealous French Creole women initially sought to prevent their rivals from displaying their luxury consumer goods, they—and their metropolitan French counterparts—finally came to imitate their successful rivals' style and demeanor. French Creole women's imitation of mulatto fashion further illustrates the power that Mary perceives mixed-race women had, not just over their white male partners, but over white women as well.

While Dillon reads the madras headscarf as "the first signal of a counter-discourse of creolism in the novel," this chapter argues that Mary's persistent comparisons of the Caribbean's competing domestic and romantic ideologies denaturalizes all such belief systems as cultural constructions. Mary's macrocosmic perspective on the differing levels of romantic and social agency across the various classes of women in Saint-Domingue combats essentialized notions of gender and sexuality that were increasingly popular in the nineteenth-century United States. In this way, Mary's attentive comparisons of the differentiated romantic and social customs in Saint-Domingue make visible the local Creole culture Dillon identifies. As I have tried to show, those comparisons are grounded in her own difference as a US outsider. Mary's expectations for love are trained to a different romantic script; as a US woman, she maintains the companionate-marriage ideal. Rather than reacting to mulatto women with jealousy or imitation, Mary contrasts mixed-race women's quite public sexual and economic power to the distinctly private emotional fulfillment touted in US discourses of companionate marriage. Mixed-race women's domestic partnerships model an alternative to the limitations of the companionate-marriage ideal, where women are encouraged to find their sole satisfaction in wedlock. Mary's analysis of mulatto women demonstrates that these women could contract for their own exchange value *and* be emotional companions and successful household managers; indeed, women of color did all this without the legal restrictions placed on married US women and their property.

Sansay's novel of the Haitian Revolution exceeds the traditional confines of US women's stories by reworking the courtship and seduction plots and refiguring their coquettes and fallen woman. Yet, her narrator, Mary, maintains bourgeois values such as romantic faithfulness and domestic loyalty even as she criticizes the legal and social restrictions of institutionalized marriage. For instance, in contrast to her critique of coquettish French Creole women who cannot wait to find extramarital lovers, Mary finds much to praise about women of color: "There is a friendliness and simplicity in their manners. . . . [They] breathe nothing but affection and love."[52] One can imagine many Creole women disagreeing with Mary's assessment; she does seem to be projecting her own domestic expectations onto mulatto women. Indeed, she makes her domestic ideals explicit when she argues that suitably matched partners produce satisfying long-term attachments: "In such a situation [where partners are suitably matched] the heart is always occupied, and always full. For those who live [this way] their home is the world; their feelings, their powers, their talents are employed. They go into society as a ramble; it affords transient amusement, but becomes not a habit. Their thoughts, their wishes dwell at home, and they are good because they are happy."[53] Unlike Clara's attempt at open sociality, where her community helps to generate her subjectivity, Mary's ideal companionate couple finds fulfillment through a form of closed sociality—they are already complete and need nothing outside of this partnership. Mary's concern, though, is with attachments, affections, and domestic yearnings; she speaks of equally matched men and women, *not* husbands and wives. From Mary's point of view, *marriage* makes US women legal dependents, subject to the tyrannical whims of their husbands. She witnesses this firsthand in her sister's unhappy marriage. However, in her view, mulatto women suffer no such legal or social restrictions in their committed domestic partnerships.

As Tess Chakkalakal argues, the "fiction" of slave marriages in the United States—marriages that have no legal standing, but that carry all the weight of marriage in terms of commitment and affection—may actually have helped early feminists and social reformers to imagine an alternative to legal marriage. According to Chakkalakal, "as a marital relation that had little to do with either property or power, the slave-marriage came to embody the principles of an ideal marriage, a union of souls that transcended the earthly concerns upon which legal marriage was based."[54] Although obviously the position of the *ménagère*, a (usually) paid employee of a white planter, is not the same as a bond of affection between two enslaved persons, we might usefully think about the way that alternative models such as *ménagères* or US slave marriages helped women writers and social reformers to imagine and to tell stories about other forms of domesticity.

In contrast to the *ménagère*, who works for a white male employer, there are numerous other traditions of consensual domestic arrangements between black men and women in Saint-Domingue. One such arrangement is *plaçage*: a consensual, committed relationship without the official forms of church and state. The term comes from the colonial word *place* (domain), where to place oneself means to establish both a household and agricultural cultivation. There is a sense of rootedness in these relationships, of claiming a place with another. The anthropologist Serge-Henri Vieux describes *plaçage* as the predominant form of conjugal union in Haiti; it is not a common-law marriage, nor is it concubinage.[55] Rather, it demands elaborate rituals. Also, a man might have more than one *placée*. Because of historical and economic factors such as the expense of a marriage license and the historical legacies of colonization and slavery, most of the rural peasant population in Haiti still chooses *plaçage* over marriage.[56] According to Joan Dayan, many peasant women living in Haiti today prefer *plaçage* to marriage "since they believe *plasaj* preserves women's independence" as marriage does not.[57] Although the male partner owns the land, the female *placée* maintains her own small agricultural fields, sells her agricultural and domestic goods at the local market, and keeps the profits. In sharp contrast to Western familial structures that render women's bodies men's property and legally divest women of their economic contributions (where their earnings accrue to a male head of household), economist Sidney Mintz notes that a Haitian peasant woman's earnings accrue "to the woman herself, rather than to some other member of her group, as an individual or as an executor of group wealth."[58] Mintz argues that Haitian peasant society "acknowledges an equal economic status for women in local, culturally-prescribed terms."[59] Practiced both before and after the revolution, *plaçage* is one of many forms of domestic union offering women a more expansive sense of individual agency than has heretofore been recognized. Peasant couples practicing *plaçage* and plantation owners hiring *ménagères* are far from the domestic world envisioned in nineteenth-century British and US fiction, yet clearly these alternative domestic models have the potential to denaturalize familiar Anglo-American romantic scripts. Although *Secret History* clearly overlooks the coercion and lack of opportunities that pushed women of color into long-term sexual relationships with white men, Mary and Clara envision positive change for women through the alternative domestic relationships they encounter in Saint-Domingue.

Such partnerships would undoubtedly have interested Sansay, whose sexual relationship with Aaron Burr continued even after her marriage.[60] Although Sansay provides no direct statement comparing her own status (or those of her two protagonists) to that of *ménagères* or of "placed" women, her narrator's relatively positive assessments of unmarried mulatto women's domestic loyalty and economic successes invite readers to make biographical comparisons. In his *Memoirs,* Aaron Burr sidesteps Sansay's marginal position in society, suggesting that she "is too well known by the name of 'Leonora.'"[61] Michael Drexler interprets this comment more directly: "Sansay was a public woman, a coquette."[62] Would Sansay recognize herself in popular fictional depictions of the "fallen woman" of the time? Mary writes, in Saint-Domingue, "that unfortunate class of beings, so numerous in my own,—victims of seduction, devoted to public contempt and universal scorn, is unknown."[63] While early national US fiction is littered with the corpses of women who transgress sexual mores, Sansay must have marveled at the stories she heard of Caribbean women's lives. Here are no whimpering Charlotte Temples or remorseful Eliza Whartons, but Sanite Belairs, Zulines, Madame V——s, and Madame St. Clairs. At a moment when biology was on the horizon of becoming destiny, when racial and sexual categories were ossifying, when one's body signaled one's full or limited human status, Sansay's novel demands that readers notice how supposedly essentialized identity categories vary across geographic locales and even within defined geopolitical borders.[64] Mary argues that there are no victims of seduction in Saint-Domingue; consequently, we might ask, could a seduction plot be staged in Saint-Domingue? Where else could Sansay set a story that challenged the United States' most basic standards for acceptable feminine behavior? How else could US readers of sentimental and didactic fiction accept such a story?

If labels such as "fallen woman" are geographically local, their effects on women's lives and women's stories are very real. Revolutionary-era

Saint-Domingue allows Sansay to make room for alternative domesticities and alternative women's plots in US fiction. She concludes *Secret History* with a homosocial female utopia, a "New World" for white women from across the Americas. While not without its limitations—for instance, there is no room for minority women in Clara's utopian vision—Sansay's revolutionary text shatters nineteenth-century fictional norms and, in the process, revises what it was possible to say about women's lives and women's relationships. Witnessing alternative romantic ideologies and competing domestic arrangements firsthand, Sansay imagined new possibilities, new stories, and new words and worlds for women.

A Philadelphia Seduction Story

I have argued that Sansay rejects the seduction plot in her Caribbean-based novel, but what are the implications of this rejection for her Philadelphia-based novel, *Laura* (1809)? Could the nonmarital domestic alternatives Sansay conjures in Saint-Domingue hold in Philadelphia? Sansay's second novel, *Laura,* seems worlds away from the racial violence and colonial excesses reported in *Secret History,* but it, too, revises the seduction plot in surprising ways.

The story begins by tracing how Laura's mother, Rosina, runs away from a convent in Lisbon to secretly marry her brother's friend. Rosina and her new husband, William, move to Philadelphia to avoid public scandal; however, before he informs his family of their marriage, William dies in a transatlantic voyage, leaving Rosina and her unborn child penniless and friendless. Rosina gives birth to a daughter, Laura, and after struggling through years of poverty, she reluctantly remarries. Laura matures under her mother's loving guidance. Then, at the age of fifteen, Rosina dies, leaving Laura under the supervision of her less tender stepfather. Rather than marry the man her stepfather chooses for her, Laura elopes with her sympathetic and beloved beau, Belfield, an impoverished medical student. Like her mother, Laura chooses love as an escape route. However, Rosina's experiences school readers to carefully weigh the slim differences between the mother's marginally "respectable" elopement and the daughter's similar yet scandalous actions. Comparing the mother's and daughter's stories, readers learn that married or unmarried, women are vulnerable when their sexual relationships are not publicly recognized and sanctioned by family or community.

Although Belfield is a worthy and respectable young man, his financial situation renders him dependent on an older brother while he continues as a student. He finds that he is not in a position to marry, even as he encourages Laura to reject her father's proposed match and run away with him. In short, Belfield is rash. By deferring their marriage, Belfield sacrifices Laura's reputation and mars their future happiness together. Young and in love, the couple engages in premarital sex and Laura becomes pregnant. However, unlike more popular fallen heroines such as Charlotte Temple or Eliza Wharton, Laura retains a dignity, even an innocence, despite her premarital sexual activity. This innocence—perhaps we might better call it a deep trust in Belfield's good intentions—is threatened when Laura finds herself placed in a brothel by Belfield. Hurrying to get Laura out of the house before his family visits, Belfield does not investigate the true nature of the lodgings. As an occupant at a brothel, Laura is subjected to the sexual advances of anyone who might pay the right price and, not surprisingly, this is exactly what happens. Laura flees the house, rejecting the terms of her status as a "fallen woman." However, she is without resources. An orphan with no living family, Laura turns to the aid of her mother's former friends. Now she must see herself as she is viewed in the eyes of her community. Her mother's onetime friend rails: "We know very well where you have been. So instead of marrying the honest husband your father had chosen, you went off with George Belfield; and after all the expense, that was foolishly thrown away on you, turned out no better than you should be. And now Belfield's tired of you and casts you off and you come to me, as if you thought I should have any thing to do with you! No, no, I shall not injure my character by harbouring such creatures." After this tirade, Laura silently prepares to leave; she passes the unnamed hostile woman with a "calm look of indignation, and left the inhospitable roof."[65] Laura's withering silent reproach is almost unimaginable from the desperate Charlotte Temple or the humiliated Eliza Wharton. However, Laura tries another of her mother's friends, the more sympathetic Sophia, and here she finds respite. Laura's turn toward her mother's friends for shelter and sympathy echoes Clara's newly formed community of displaced women in *Secret History*. However, here it is not the ravages of war that disrupt families and render women dependent. The everyday experiences of the death of a spouse, a husband abandoning his wife, or any other number of reasons that women faced poverty suggest that for dependent women, Philadelphia, too, could be a precarious place. Sansay's previous solution, a close-knit community of women sharing resources and caring for one another, works in Philadelphia as well. Although it might seem less utopian than the female community she envisions in *Secret History*, on her own return from the Caribbean, Sansay established for herself and others a form of women's community in Philadelphia, a factory for manufacturing artificial flowers where she employed young girls. As Michael Drexler notes, this venture is "another example of Sansay's willingness to try out alternative social arrangements."[66] Laura does not end her days bonding (or commiserating) with her sympathetic friend Sophia, though. Instead, she reconciles with Belfield, who finally realizes the significant sacrifice of reputation Laura endures for his sake and makes arrangements for their marriage.

Before Belfield can make good on his promise of marriage, however, he is fatally wounded in a duel to defend Laura's honor. He dies on their wedding day, before marrying Laura and legitimating their unborn child. By accepting the challenge to duel (from the same man who threatened Laura in the brothel), Belfield aims to prove in the symbolic logic of dueling that Laura is pure, that she is no "fallen woman." Belfield believes himself in the right. His intentions to Laura are true; moreover, she has been true to him. In the honor logic of the duel, however, Belfield's death suggests that private intentions and personal feelings are irrelevant. A publicly recognized marriage is the only way to save Laura's reputation, and now she will be deprived of this narrow chance for "redemption."

Dressed for her wedding, Laura arrives at her lover's deathbed. Although she desperately crawls into Belfield's funeral bier hoping to die, she survives his loss. Sansay concludes the novel with this stringent, but curious, moral: "To trace Laura through the many vicissitudes that awaited her, would be a task too painful. She became a mother,—She found protection from the gentleman [to] whom Belfield had recommended her. . . . thro' every stage of her varying existence, happiness remained a stranger to her bosom; and her life was an exemplification of this truth:—'that perpetual uneasiness, disquietude, and irreversible misery, are the certain consequences of fatal misconduct in a woman; however gifted, or however reclaimed.'"[67] While "perpetual uneasiness, disquietude, and irreversible misery" are certainly not happy endings, this is, nevertheless, a notable divergence from the seduction plot's inevitable conclusion in death (usually in or after painful childbirth). Most obviously, Laura does not die, and that alone makes her story stand out from previous seduction novels. More than this, though, Belfield takes the full brunt of punishment—death—typically reserved for the fallen woman. In the end, Belfield atones for his "crime" by claiming her as his wife on his deathbed.

Though not without its didactic moralizing, the novel's conclusion is remarkable for the way that it inverts the seduction plot's traditional sexual double standard, killing Belfield and giving Laura the typically male part of grieving, repentant survivor. Not only does Laura live, though, she learns; and her learning is not restricted to remorsefully reviewing her previous sexual misconduct. As the narrator observes, despite the "many vicissitudes that awaited her," "her beauty continued unimpaired; her mind acquired new brilliancy."[68] In those short lines, Sansay offers her most interesting commentary on the significance of the geographies of seduction. In Philadelphia, Sansay cannot eradicate the seduction plot; the story is too central to US conceptions of gender and sexuality. Yet, by reversing the terms of punishment, Sansay's novel questions the fairness of unequally punishing women for a sexual misstep that both partners make. Sansay's conclusion raises the question, *why* should Laura and others like her die? Although she does not provide her heroine with a happy ending, Sansay significantly revises the terms of the seduction plot in the United States by allowing Laura to survive.

Comparing geographically specific discourses of seduction in two novels by Leonora Sansay demonstrates how the logic and narrative demands of seduction differ across two unique settings in a single author's fiction. In *Secret History*, Sansay rejects the morality of the seduction plot, transforming readers' expectations for the typical coquette and fallen woman stories by providing alternative Caribbean domesticities as counterpoints to familiar US figures. Although Sansay does not jettison the seduction plot in her Philadelphia story, she radically revises the dominant and conventional conclusion, the death of the fallen woman. By killing Belfield, Sansay places the guilt of premarital sex on the male partner, reversing the sexual double standard that demands women pay the price for non-marital sexual activity. Although Sansay's Philadelphia-based seduction story is more circumspect in its challenges to the narrative conventions of sex and gender, like *Secret History* it, too, envisions female-centered community as a necessary support structure for women betrayed by the romantic scripts they are taught to inhabit. Sansay's comparative Caribbean novel launches the critique of seduction she continues, if more moderately, in the City of Brotherly Love.

[4]

A POSTCOLONIAL HEROINE "WRITES BACK"

WRITTEN FROM THE POINT of view of an upper-class Jamaican mulatto woman, the anonymously published *The Woman of Colour: A Tale* (1808) begins in Jamaica when Olivia Fairfield, the daughter of a black slave and an English master, discovers that she must travel to England and marry her unknown white cousin, Augustus Merton, in order to retain her father's fortune. For the sensitive and sprightly Olivia, marriage to an unknown man who may be repulsed by her biracial heritage is a cruel legacy from a beloved father. Although the stipulation in Mr. Fairfield's will is meant to protect his daughter from the racial and sexual oppression that most black and biracial Caribbean women experienced, by linking Olivia's inheritance to her sexual relationship with a white man, Mr. Fairfield forcefully reiterates the very racial and sexual oppression he seeks to prevent. As an epistolary novel, the narrative is relayed through Olivia's first-person letters to her white governess, Mrs. Milbanke, in Jamaica. From Olivia's biracial and colonial point of view, what might be a typical English courtship plot becomes instantly comparative. For in the relative privacy of her letters, Olivia reveals how she patiently suffers insensitive British racism, discovers a deep love for Augustus, and realizes he returns her affections.

Unlike the heroines of Jane Austen whose stories inevitably end with marriage, this is not the conclusion to Olivia's story. Olivia suffers a surprising and deep loss after Augustus's first wife reappears and, with no malicious intention, renders Olivia's seemingly perfect marriage null. If readers are initially led to believe that the worthy Olivia achieves her ideal, attains the status of successful domestic heroine, and triumphs over racism through her happy marriage, they are forced to question the value of the marriage plot when Olivia's happy ending is torn from her. In her correspondence with Mrs. Milbanke after Augustus's first wife returns, Olivia expresses her determination to live a single life and, in doing so, rejects the two powerful narrative conclusions available for fictional women: marriage or death. By the novel's end, Olivia's rejection of both the marriage and seduction plots becomes a critical commentary on the significance of race and colonial oppression in metropolitan social reproduction. Continuing to insist on her respectability and domesticity despite the loss of her marriage and the shocking reality that she has been made to reenact her slave mother's past concubinage, Olivia simultaneously claims and alters the typical role of the domestic heroine, making it less exclusively metropolitan and more racially diverse. In effect, Olivia's pathbreaking conclusion creates a new pattern of domesticity accessible to Caribbean tropicopolitans, Srinivas Aravamudan's term for colonized persons subjected to colonial discourse. She makes a place for herself and for the Caribbean within the dominant ideology of domesticity.

A Tropicopolitan Heroine

It must have been difficult for many nineteenth-century British readers to contemplate a virtuous mixed-race woman as the primary heroine of a domestic novel. Two of the three extant reviews of the novel cannot resist a bit of cutting commentary on the protagonist's race. For instance, the reviewer for the *British Critic* notes that "this Woman of Colour is by no means illiterate or without ingenuity of contrivance," as he or she presumably expects. Although the reviewer for the *Critical Review* notes that Olivia "displays much good sense and feeling," the review also notes that "the character of her black servant Dido, is the most natural of any."[1] Such commentary suggests that reviewers read with racist expectations and are most gratified when those expectations are met (as in the more stereotyped depictions of the less educated Dido). In contrast to popular stereotypes of lascivious mixed-race Caribbean women, Olivia is an altogether successful nineteenth-century domestic woman.[2] She shares several features—such as her virtue, independent spirit, and confidence—in common with other heroines of British Romantic fiction. She is clearly a domestic woman in Nancy Armstrong's terms; she has learned to "turn behavior into psychological events" and, in the act of claiming her superior moral value, she regulates her own desire.[3] In the past thirty years, literary scholars such as Nancy Armstrong, Joseph Allen Boone, Christopher Flint, and others have demonstrated how the British domestic novel naturalized a changing set of historically specific family relations and gender roles; namely, companionate marriage and the rise of the domestic woman.[4] While historians are now revising previous notions about the pervasiveness of companionate marriage in actual historic couples' lives and literary critics are rethinking the function of the domestic woman in fiction, the companionate-marriage *ideal* certainly structured the plots of many nineteenth-century domestic novels.

Revising Nancy Armstrong's classic account of the domestic novel as an ideological tool for shaping bourgeois women's gender roles, Eve Tavor Bannet argues that eighteenth-century British women novelists played an active role in creating the domestic woman ideal and in claiming the domestic sphere for feminist purposes.[5] Eighteenth-century feminist fiction writers, Bannet observes, politicized the domestic realm by making it a space where women could critique unjust practices and even claim power for themselves. For instance, in response to the 1753 Marriage Act, British women novelists as diverse as Mary Wollstonecraft, Mary Hays, Hannah More, and Jane West made marriage, sexuality, and the legality of those relationships central to the fiction of the period. Many women recognized that the law, which claimed to reform marriage and protect family relations, needlessly complicated common-law marriages as well as local customs and practices. In restructuring the rules and procedures required to marry, eighteenth-century British law actually voided many marriages and rendered some children illegitimate. In Bannet's account, women novelists recognized such injustices and vigorously portrayed the ill effects on women and families in their own fictional representations of domestic life.

If Bannet notes the ways that eighteenth-century women both participated in the construction of domesticity and questioned its results, Helen Thompson argues that feminist theorizations of agency have limited our ability to see representations of women's compliance to patriarchal power in eighteenth-century domestic novels as a form of political agency.[6] To comply, in Thompson's reading, is a conscious act of will that points out, rather than supports, the Lockean fantasy of a "universal" (male) individual imbued with natural rights. The domestic heroine's compliance shows that gender hierarchies are not natural or inherent in the body. Thompson's theory of compliance is particularly useful for thinking about the ways that Olivia Fairfield participates in a problematic liberal, bourgeois domestic ideology. For Olivia's compliance to the dictates of domestic fiction radically ensures that she is recognized as a domestic heroine, a role she would not ordinarily be eligible to fill as a biracial Caribbean woman.

A valuable instance of Olivia's qualification for domestic heroine status, her capacity to "turn behavior into psychological event" (and thereby regulate her desire) can be seen in a conversation in which Olivia begs Augustus to clarify his feelings for her.[7] Exceeding the "limits usually prescribed to my sex," Olivia requests a private conversation with her cousin. However, this breach of conduct is easily forgiven when Olivia explains that, although she is already engaged, she fears he intends to marry her for her fortune. In "a beseeching attitude," Olivia begs her fiancé to reconsider the engagement "if it is to unite you to an object, for whom you feel no regard." Olivia's actions reveal an uncommon depth and sensitivity. She cannot be satisfied with an ordinary marriage; her love must be returned before she can be happy. This plea, couched in the language and demeanor of a "trembling abashed woman," finally forces Augustus to confess "that I am warmly, sincerely interested for your happiness!"[8]

In a final clarification of feelings, Olivia inadvertently reveals the depth of her love for Augustus, but not before regulating that desire with a modest concealment: "'I resolve to *refuse* your hand?' cried [Olivia], scarcely knowing what I said, 'Oh, Mr. Merton how can you—If, indeed'—Alas! I found out that I was betraying myself, by the eager gaze of Augustus."[9] In a quick turn, Olivia modulates her behavior in order to regulate her desire. She worries, in recalling these events, that she has "been too forward," but the reader is satisfied that her motivation—a desire for mutual respect and true affection—proves Olivia's worth and Augustus's satisfactory appreciation of her.

Even in this encounter, though, Olivia's status as woman of color means that she must not only comply with the standards of domesticity, but she must constantly prove that a biracial woman can be a domestic woman as well. Olivia's complexion renders her body, rather than her virtue, the primary object of interest among her English acquaintances. In Armstrong's account, the new morally superior female subject must shed the aristocratic display of the body in favor of her psychological depth. But Olivia must constantly remind others—even Augustus—that "the good qualities, which I may possess, are not to be discerned in my countenance."[10] She is more than her "olive" outside. These reminders seek not just to redress Augustus's potential racism, but also lingering doubts held by nineteenth-century British readers. As gently as Olivia reproves her family's racism, the novel, too, expands its readers' sympathies through an imagined intimacy with a thoroughly respectable colonized domestic woman.

In the familiar conventions of the domestic novel, Olivia's reward for complying with the standards of domesticity should be a happy marriage to a loving husband. Indeed, contemporary reviews of the novel expressed their disappointment with the story's surprise bigamy in no uncertain terms.

A writer for the *British Critic* [March 1810] succinctly notes: "It is very hard after all, that the poor heroine does not get a husband, for she is made very much to deserve one." Another reviewer observes, "We do not see what good is to accrue from reading a story, in which an amiable female is despoiled of her name and station in society . . . and three worthy characters [Augustus, Olivia, and the first wife] made wretched for no reason in the world."[11] What is the reader to learn from Olivia's experiences, this critic demands. To what purpose is such a story written? Our heroine's decision to describe herself a "widow" may be the first clue to understanding "what good is to accrue" from this novel. In Rachel Blau DuPlessis's terms, Olivia writes "beyond" the narrative demands of marriage or death in the usual heroine's ending: "Writing beyond the ending means the transgressive invention of narrative strategies, strategies that express critical dissent from the dominant narrative." Indeed, it "produces a narrative that denies or reconstructs seductive patterns of feeling that are culturally mandated, internally policed, hegemonically poised."[12] If, then, Olivia amply qualifies for the role of domestic heroine, she rejects this role (and its reverse, the fallen woman) for a new life story and a new pattern of domesticity.

A Brave New Domestic World

The Woman of Colour clearly shares many of the features Bannet outlines for eighteenth-century British feminist fiction's critique of the institution of marriage. Augustus Merton's secret first marriage is duly punished. His clandestine arrangements produce misery when he and his first wife are separated by the evil machinations of a jealous lover who incorrectly leads him to believe the first wife has died, and, again, when his happiness with Olivia is overturned by the untimely reappearance of his first wife. Still, *The Woman of Color* achieves more than a critique of clandestine marriage or even the unjust influences of greedy and/or overprotective parents. With her mixed-race Caribbean heritage and respectable femininity, Olivia challenges nineteenth-century British claims that the mother country is the sacrosanct domestic space, while the colonies are degenerate corruptions. Although some readers might question whether Olivia's narrative with its story of a good marriage lost simply reinforces the companionate-marriage ideal, as I note in more detail later, Olivia's outsider position enables her to constantly compare and critique the supposedly more civilized British marriage system with the social norms of Jamaica. Though set primarily in England, *The Woman of Colour* nonetheless offers a strong comparative-marriage plot.

Olivia calmly claims her right to the title of domestic woman with each instance of racism she patiently endures and corrects. However, her biracial heritage complicates her antiracist position. She is neither black nor white, neither English nor Afro-Caribbean; we might call her *Creole* —that hybrid blend of racial and cultural inheritances that comprises the legacy of colonial domination in the Caribbean—but in 1808 that term was used to define *white* West Indians.[13] Explaining her biracial social status to her racist white relations, Olivia makes a distinction between her own position and that of the slave populations in Jamaica. At the same time, she surprises readers by claiming her affiliation with her African heritage. In response to her hostile, racist cousin Mrs. Merton's claim that "I thought that Miss Fairfield—I understood that people of your—I thought that you almost *lived* on rice . . . and so I ordered some to be got." Olivia notes, "This was evidently meant to mortify your Olivia; it was blending *her* with the poor negro slaves of the West Indies! It was meant to show her, that, in Mrs. Merton's idea, there was no distinction between us—you will believe that I *could not* be wounded at being classified with my brethren!"[14] The dizzying use of exclamation points and the constant reference to "our poor slaves" belies Olivia's claim to remain unwounded by the comparison. Yet this educated and immensely respectable heiress does not flatly reject her slave heritage; rather, this "not them, but of them" logic forcefully highlights her "mixed" position.

Olivia continually rises above such race-baiting, turning the sting of racism into learning opportunities for her family (and, no doubt, for some readers). Just after the rice incident mentioned previously, Olivia teaches a young relative that her black maid's skin is not dirty and will not rub off. Quite patiently she explains, "The same God that made *you* made me . . . the poor black woman—the whole world—and every creature in it! A great part of this world is peopled by creatures with skins as black as Dido's, and as yellow as mine. God chose it should be so, and we cannot make our skins white, any more than you can make yours black."[15] And in reply to her young cousin's question about whether the color would rub off, Olivia gives the child her handkerchief to try it on her own skin. Successfully winning over little George, Olivia patiently battles the prejudices of others. In the process, she successfully defines her virtue and worth as a long-suffering domestic woman in the face of—perhaps even because of—her family's obvious racism. Olivia's outsider perspective challenges the supposed superiority of Britons and British culture with her frequent and uniquely positioned cultural comparisons.

Yet even as Olivia proves her domestic virtue in the face of British racism, she radically questions some British women's claims to the same status. For instance, Olivia compares the fashionable Mrs. Merton, her would-be sister-in-law, to a "languid" West Indian woman; indeed, Mrs. Merton beats any of the "supine" West Indians she has observed in Jamaica: "Nothing more frequently excited my surprise, and I may add, disgust, than the languid affectation and supine manners of some of our West Indians; but I never saw any one of them who could in the least compare with Mrs. Merton, who seems to have attained the very height of inaction." Describing her relation as "pretty by anyone who looks for feature only," Olivia characterizes Mrs. Merton as an unpleasant combination of self-importance, spleen, and racial prejudice. More telling, though, is the way Olivia connects her unpleasant personality to her mimicry of fashionable colonial mannerisms. For instance, Mrs. Merton speaks with "the languid drawl of a fine lady" and "preceded us down the stairs with a languid careless step, which could not have been exceeded by the most die-away lady in the whole island of Jamaica."[16] While Mrs. Merton dislikes Olivia and works to embarrass her at every turn, she performs what is, to Olivia, clearly a familiar (and disgusting) form of Caribbean sensuality—a sensuality that Olivia understands as connected via white Creoles back to fashionable women of color. Olivia confirms her understanding that Mrs. Merton's fashionable sensuality originates in the Caribbean through her careful distribution of the word *languid* over the course of several pages as she first describes her cousin's wife. Mrs. Merton's manners are certainly consciously performed; the question is whether and how she understands them to be colonial imports, directly mimicked from the Caribbean women of color she is so intent to belittle.[17]

Sharon Harrow has argued that in eighteenth-century British literature, colonial otherness is "a force that would underwrite financial stability [even] as it undermined social hierarchy and infected or adulterated a feminized English virtue."[18] Olivia's relationship to Mrs. Merton (and others whom she finds contaminated by colonial customs) is a fascinating instance of such an infected feminine virtue, for Olivia is a colonized other commenting on the transmission of "languid" Jamaican manners into English society. While Olivia's disdain for Mrs. Merton's "die-away" inactivity seems to fit Harrow's description, Olivia's position as colonized woman of color changes the dynamics of her commentary. Olivia's performance of domesticity and her critique of Mrs. Merton's lack of domesticity fit within Homi Bhabha's theory of colonial "mimicry": a mode of behavior inculcated by British colonizers that aims to produce colonized subjects who are "almost . . . but not quite" British.[19] Bhabha notes the ways that this "not quite" status affords colonized peoples the space in which to creatively adapt to colonization. Olivia's mimicry of, or her "compliance" to, British domesticity oddly opens the way for Olivia to inhabit an alternative domestic scene, a Caribbean domesticity.

If Olivia's mimicry confirms Harrow's claim that "bourgeois domesticity [was seen] as the means by which England should dispossess itself of the vices of empire," she also highlights that domesticity is not a "native" English attribute. Olivia avers that domesticity—as an ideological set of values—is not moored to particular environments such as the "pure" English countryside, or to particular (white) bodies. She performs her domesticity as well as—indeed, better than—Mrs. Merton. And if Mrs. Merton continually insists on Olivia's difference, her inability to ever truly be English (or white), Olivia counters Mrs. Merton by confirming their difference. She turns the tables by being more English than the English. Unlike the languid Mrs. Merton, Olivia is active in both body and mind; she frequently walks for exercise and performs mental gymnastics around her dull-witted acquaintances.[20] In an exemplary sardonic quip, Olivia observes that Mrs. Merton "considers me as but one remove from the brute creation," but "I seem hardly to consider her as a rational being," "so here, perhaps, we meet on equal terms." Similarly, Olivia reverses the colonizing gaze when she bluntly assesses her colonizers: "I am disappointed in England: I expected to meet with sensible, liberal, well informed and rational people, and I have not found them; I see a compound of folly and dissimulation."[21] Olivia's canny reversals do not simply satirize British foibles as do previous "exotic" narrators such as Oliver Goldsmith's *The Citizen of the World*; in her letters to Mrs. Milbanke, Olivia authors herself as a full-fledged domestic heroine, a role she intently revises by insisting on her own place within it.[22]

In Olivia's next encounter with Britons who have been tainted by colonial experiences, Olivia's moral character is confirmed through comparisons with the outlandish behavior of three English "nabobs," a married couple and their son who have just returned from India. The encounter shows that it is not the geography, climate, or extent of one's experience in the colonies that corrupt "native" English morals, but rather the conscious adherence to domestic values, especially the appropriate performance of gender that ensures one's continued moral integrity. Lady Ingot, "a masculine woman; very hard-favoured, and of a forbidding countenance," hopes Olivia, another immigrant from the empire, will prove an ally against the "narrow minded, prejudiced beings" who have never "set a foot out of England."[23] While Lady Ingot is willing to overlook racial dif-

ference in the hopes of finding cosmopolitan similarities with her potential new friend, Olivia will have none of it. She counters the admittedly
ridiculous Lady Ingot with a most peculiar set of claims:

> "I rather lean towards old customs, and old notions, and can trace one
> of *my ideas* as far back as the *Old* Testament, where a lady of some note,
> being asked, whether she would be spoken of to the king or the captain
> of the boat, answered, with true feminine modesty—'I dwell amongst my
> own people!' It has always struck me as a most beautiful reply. Retirement
> seems the peculiar and appropriate station of our sex; and, the enlargement
> of the mind, and the conquest of prejudice, is not always achieved, perhaps,
> by visiting foreign climes!"
>
> "You speak like a *perfect* English woman," said Lady Ingot; "I see you
> have already imbibed our air."
>
> "I thank your ladyship for the compliment," said I: "I do consider my-
> self as more than *half* an English woman, and, it has always been my ardent
> wish to prove myself worthy of the *title!*"[24]

This passage leaves one with an abundance of questions: How can the
dislocated Olivia ever "dwell amongst my own people"? Who are her
people, exactly? Furthermore, how is Olivia "*more* than half" English?
Olivia's efforts to prove herself worthy of the title of domestic woman
serve only to reinforce her outsider position. She will, of course, never
be more than half-English even if she perfects the sensible, liberal per-
sona she expects to have met in England. In her conservative defense of
"old customs, and old notions," Olivia attempts to prove that learned
behaviors, one's manners and moral integrity, can outweigh race and/
or colonial geography (that is, that a mulatto West Indian woman could
be a legitimate domestic woman). By complying with the hegemonic expectations of domesticity, including performing an appropriately demure
femininity, Olivia actually does prove that domesticity is not the result of
"imbib[ing] the air," but learned and vigilantly performed behavior.

More pointedly, Olivia understands her performance of retiring feminine modesty to trump Lady Ingot's performance of masculine/racist
assertiveness. Indeed, in Olivia's view, Lady Ingot belittles others and
assumes an unjustified, pompous authority because she is used to seeing herself as better than the indigenous Indian populations whom she
has always dominated. If Lady Ingot believes her travels have made her
more open-minded, Olivia critiques this understanding with her retort
that "the enlargement of the mind, and the conquest of prejudice, is not
always achieved, perhaps, by visiting foreign climes!"[25] Of course, from

Olivia's colonized perspective, Britons' travels to "foreign climes" in the service of the empire could hardly be said to enlarge the mind or alleviate prejudice. More narrowly, one concludes that Lady Ingot's regular exertion of her authority renders her masculine, the ultimate colonial degeneracy. Although Lady Ingot might naturally seek an ally in a colonial heiress, Olivia puts pressure on the assumption that they share an equivalent position. Olivia is the daughter of a plantation owner; she is even served by a black maid. But she does not preside over others as does Lady Ingot. If her current performance of British domesticity makes her *more* than half-English, Olivia still claims her slave mother and that history of oppression.

How should we account for Olivia's comparative critiques of Britons' "reverse" mimicry? Prior to the strictly essentialist, biological understanding of inherent racial characteristics that develops in the late nineteenth century, in the eighteenth and early nineteenth century, the "taint" of the colonies is described as a disease contracted through exposure to unhealthy or foreign contaminants. We can see this in reverse in Lady Ingot's statement that Olivia has "imbibed our air." Examples from literature include *The Secret Garden* in which the sickly orphan Mary returns to England after her family dies in India and subsequently recovers by gardening in the rural English countryside. This colonial taint is usually "cured," as in Mary's case, with a restorative connection to a more congenial British climate and simplistic, ruddy nature. A more serious form of colonial contamination is "going native"—which frequently carries the suggestion of trading in one's culture for another. Going native implies a radical reprioritizing of assumptions, beliefs, values, and practices. It is not a hybrid blending of identities, but a wholesale exchange of one set of values for another. The danger of colonial travel is that one might "pick up" colonial habits or modes of being against one's will. Neither of these contamination models adequately accounts for the transformation of British manners Olivia notes in the cases of Mrs. Merton and Lady Ingot.

Colonialism from the Inside: Critiquing Cultural Tourism by "Writing Back"

The Woman of Colour posits British mimicry of colonial otherness as a form of consumerism. Otherness becomes a commodity available for use by white Britons, with or without actual colonial contact. In *Black Looks,* bell hooks calls this complex phenomenon the "commodification of otherness"—whereby mainstream consumers try on otherness without "relinquish[ing] forever one's mainstream positionality."[26] This "cultural tourism" is a temporary fad, much like this year's excitement over stripes will quickly be superseded by some new fashion trend. "Currently," hooks argues, "the commodification of difference promotes paradigms of consumption wherein whatever difference the Other inhabits is eradicated, via exchange, by a consumer cannibalism that not only displaces the Other but denies the significance of that Other's history through a process of decontextualization."[27] In her concern about the displacement of the other and the decontextualization of the other's history, hooks names the problem I outlined earlier about whether and how Mrs. Merton understood that her "languid drawl" and mannerisms were inherited from Caribbean "women of colour." For Mrs. Merton, this mode of sensuality is most likely generically exotic, though Olivia is careful to connect it to Jamaica. It is Olivia's role as "recontextualizer"—the way that she insists we see Mrs. Merton as enacting a form of "die-away" Jamaican femininity or the way that she subtly corrects Lady Ingot's assertion that travel enlarges the mind—that I find not just satiric, but potentially postcolonial.

Although we do not know who wrote *The Woman of Colour,* I suggest viewing the anonymous author as, at the very least, sympathetic to a tropicopolitan position.[28] The question becomes, how does a tropicopolitan like Olivia understand cultural tourism? What do we gain from her colonized perspective that we do not find in more mainstream notions of colonial contact as contamination documented by Sharon Harrow? Tropicopolitan narrators such as Olivia demonstrate a nuanced understanding of the choices that colonized and colonizing subjects make in fashioning identities. British cultural tourism, as Olivia observes it, is dangerous because this mode of commodifying otherness eradicates difference and homogenizes culture, thereby removing the threat implicit in Bhabha's theory. There is no danger or potential loss in this mode of mimicry—rather, it is a lifestyle choice, easily exchanged for the next exotic fashion. Still, Olivia's account of British mimicry makes whiteness recognizable as a set of discrete cultural practices subject to change, rather than a biologically inherent set of traits. In its temporary "trying on" of otherness, cultural tourism allows the British mimic to use "the backdrop of otherness" to connote the mimic's own status as sensual, worldly, or cool by association, if you will. Scholars have more work ahead to differentiate between the cultural tourism that Olivia witnesses in nineteenth-century Britain and the twentieth-century cultural tourism that hooks and others observe in postmodern late capitalist America. Of value here is how *The Woman of Colour* insists that we recognize the commodification of otherness as a reciprocal form of mimesis intimately linked to colonial power structures.

As a colonial mimic herself, Olivia is in a unique position to comment on the mimicry of others. Olivia obviously patterns herself after a domestic woman, but her performance is more than mimetic; I argue it is also an early instance of a colonized character "writing back to the center."[29] In making such a claim, I proceed with caution. Olivia does not express a postcolonial identity—there is no "post" to her colonial experiences; no Jamaican nation yet exists. Neither does she identify with or champion the black Jamaican population. As a tropicopolitan, Olivia both participates in and resists colonizing discourses; however, even as she asserts British domestic values, Olivia occupies a position of difference from the colonizing culture. She begins the process of "writing back to the center" by imagining a place for herself within British domesticity; by the novel's conclusion she will go even further, writing, in Rachel Blau DuPlessis's terms, "beyond" Britain and British narrative conventions for women's stories, as she imagines a new mode of domesticity and a new ending for herself in the Caribbean.

Just as events seem poised to ensure Olivia's future happiness, Augustus's first wife returns; Olivia and Augustus discover that they are accidental bigamists. One way to understand this sudden turn toward bigamy is, like Bannet, to place *The Woman of Colour* in the context of other women writers such as Mary Wollstonecraft and Mary Hays who actively critiqued British marriage laws and the sexual restrictions placed on women. Olivia has every right to complain; by the sexual standards of the time, she has just been reduced to a concubine. Her relationship with Augustus has at once been rendered outside the law and outside the bounds of morality. Recognizing the impossibility of continuing their marriage, Olivia relinquishes Augustus to his first wife. In doing so, she gives up on marriage completely: "I scruple not to own to you, that, as my husband, I loved you with the warmest affection; that tie no longer exists, it is now become my duty to force you from my heart,—painful, difficult I acknowledge this to be, for your virtues had enthroned you there! But this world is not our abiding place. I look forward with faith and hope to that eternally happy state where there is neither 'marrying nor giving in marriage,' where there shall be no more sorrow, and where 'all tears shall be wiped away from all eyes!'"[30] Seeking a future state where there is "neither marrying nor giving in marriage," Olivia hopes to find peace; significantly, it is the state of marriage, not just Augustus's earlier and secret marriage, that seems to be the problem. When a Mr. Honeycomb later proposes to Olivia, she makes the most direct refusal possible: "I *now,* and to the *last* moment of my existence, *shall* consider myself the widowed wife of Augustus Merton."[31] As a "widow," Olivia assumes authority over the devastating situation by controlling the terms of her unbelievable status reversal from legal wife to fallen woman; with this new label, she rejects the seduction plot entirely. Like Lydia Maria Child's Hobomok, a character addressed in this book's introduction, Olivia is a victim of circumstance when a previous claimant to her husband's heart returns. But unlike Hobomok, whose romantic sacrifice also becomes emblematic of a tidy resolution to the United States' so-called Indian problem, Olivia refuses to "forever pass away,"[32] to vanish out of existence for the convenience of white folks. In fact, she symbolically kills her beloved as she obstinately authorizes the terms of her experience.[33]

By declaring herself a "widow," Olivia frees herself from the position of mistress, but she also frees herself from the unequal partnership of marriage and the dictates of the marriage plot. Olivia elaborates on her situation later when she explains that there is no room in her heart for another "lord:" "I feel consolation—a romantic satisfaction, in imagining myself as the widow of my love! Had death taken from me the object of my affections, *this bosom never could have known another lord.* Think then . . . how much more acute was my misfortune, when, by a single stroke, an instance almost unparalleled—duty—religion—even honour, bade me instantly to resign my living husband."[34] The term *lord* is pointed. It is, of course, a formal phrase for a husband, but this usage is old-fashioned by the early nineteenth century—replaced, in the companionate-marriage tradition, with the husband's first name.[35] That Olivia uses the word *lord* to describe her husband suggests to the reader something important about the depth of her love. Augustus was her superior, more than a friend or companion. She describes him as "a model of manly beauty and grace" and "a singularly prepossessing young man."[36] When they are married, she notes: "I am thankful to Heaven, for my happy, thrice happy lot; and humbly pray, that my Augustus's happiness may be as perfect as my own." Noting his occasional sadness, but unable to find any reason for it, Olivia adds, "I will not quarrel with my husband, because *his* cup of felicity does not overflow."[37] When his source of sadness is finally revealed, Olivia turns to religion and the Lord God to find peace.

In turning to religion, Olivia expresses a fairly typical response to her extraordinary circumstances. However, unlike other heroines who re-treat or die in shame and frustration, Olivia understands that her ex-perience is not an individual or isolated event. Instead, she turns to her Afro-Caribbean heritage to make sense of her loss. Connecting her own situation with the experiences of her slave mother, Olivia observes to her pastor: "My mother, though an *African slave,* when once she had felt the power of that holy religion which *you* preach, from *that* hour she relin-quished him, who had been dearer to her than existence! And shall I then shrink from a conflict she sustained?"[38] Although Olivia's mother freed herself from what she felt was a sinful sexual relationship with her literal master, Olivia must learn to free herself from the "lord" of her heart. The invisible hand of fate—or, in our terms, systematic racial and sexual oppression—dooms the daughter to repeat her mother's renunciation of a white man to whom she has no legal tie. In the context of the novel, this repetition does *not* reflect on Olivia and her mother, but rather on the failings of men who abuse their partners' trust and on the failings of the supposedly superior British marriage system that ultimately fails to protect women. Mr. Fairfield wouldn't consider marrying his slave, but he did dictate his daughter's marital choice and subject her to white male control. By hiding his first marriage, Augustus risks Olivia's happiness and fails to be a true partner. Both men act wrongly, but it is the virtuous black/biracial women who are made to suffer.

In the terms of this novel, Olivia's choice to pronounce herself a widow is equivalent to declaring her independence; her failed marriage teaches her that no human should be lord over another. As Jane West said, the liberty that women sought was "not the power of doing what you please, for that is licentiousness, but the security that others shall not do what they please to you."[39] This critique is especially poignant for the daughter of a black slave. Olivia, a cultural and racial hybrid afloat in an Atlantic world, can and must set the terms for her own value. Though the ending is not happy in the traditional sense of a happily-ever-after marriage—the usual reward for a proper domestic woman—Olivia has created a new kind of happy ending, one in which she determines her own future. In this sense, *The Woman of Colour* enables Olivia to move "beyond" the con-fines of the traditional conclusions of a woman's story, marriage or death. In her new life as a "widow," Olivia will make her own decisions without the permission of her white relations. She will not return to Jamaica to become a white man's mistress; her father's inheritance, which she even-tually regains, makes her financially as well as physically and mentally independent. Instead, she plans to rejoin her governess and devote herself to charitable racial-uplift projects. Olivia proves through her sacrificing love that she deserves the title of domestic woman, but she does not die from the loss of traditional respectability that her bigamy might entail. Rather, she returns to Jamaica ready to share her unique brand of domesticity in her modestly feminine capacity. She remakes Jamaica into a domestic retreat from the psychic damage of the metropole—a move that expressly reverses the typical domestic fiction plot in which virtuous British women return to rural England to restore health and morality after exposure to the vices of the West Indies. In contrast, Olivia's Jamaica is not a seat of libertinage, nor is it a hermitage where she will isolate herself to mourn Augustus. Rather, Olivia makes herself a bountiful patroness for those most in need. While we might question her class privilege and the relation she assumes to other enslaved and colonized persons, she is, remarkably, a self-determined woman.

Like most British heroines, Olivia Fairfield longs for a companionate marriage, but when that life is made impossible by circumstances out of her control, Olivia has a unique perspective on being single. She returns to the Caribbean, where she must have seen many examples of successful unmarried women of color living life on their own terms. I do not want to suggest that black or mixed-race women in the Caribbean did not face their own intense battles with race, gender, and class oppression or, on the opposite spectrum, that they served as early feminist icons. More modestly, I claim that as a Caribbean woman of color, Olivia has many models of successful single black and mixed-race women surviving and thriving.

Recent historical work demonstrates that late eighteenth-century free women of color played significant social and economic roles in the Caribbean: they traded and sold commercial goods and produce, owned shops, bought and sold real estate, rented property, lent money, and profited in the slave trade.[40] Affluent women of color sent their children to be educated in Europe. In Barbados, women of color owned inns; in Jamaica, free women of color organized their own social clubs, put on dances, and maintained prominent positions in society. Although it is unclear how much of the capital traded in these transactions was the result of sex work, inheritance from white slave-owning fathers, and so on, women of color were successful, even shrewd, financial managers.

Inserting the newly "widowed" Olivia Fairfield into this picture, one sees her as a potentially powerful social leader in the free colored community; she also has the necessary wealth to shape opinions and generate substantive changes in the lives of others. As Susan Socolow observes,

"The majority of free women of color certainly led precarious economic lives, but [public records] suggest that many played important roles in the local economy, acting independently, unlike white women, who were rarely visible acting on their own."[41] In this context it is possible that Olivia, an independently wealthy woman of color, could be freer than many of her white counterparts in England or Jamaica. Olivia makes Jamaica her home and, in doing so, she challenges stereotyped representations of Caribbean sensuality and significantly "writes back" and "beyond" the restrictions of the domestic novel and its marriage plot. However, it is important to qualify this moment by noting that the price Olivia pays for this oppositional stance is to accept and to mimic, even in a now-altered form, the ideology of domesticity with fairly standard definitions of femininity.

Olivia Fairfield is certainly an unusual Atlantic world heroine. As a domestic woman she shares many values and assumptions about gender, marriage, and the family with other heroines of British domestic fiction. However, Olivia's biracial tropicopolitan position sets her apart in ways that challenge her to define her worth in nonracist, postcolonial terms. Much like the gesture of Haitian mulatto women wrapping their heads in madras cloth in "obedience" to sumptuary laws, Olivia's narrative embraces the values of the domestic novel, even as it defiantly relocates the domestic and its cultural and moral authority to the Caribbean. Written in the same year as Sansay's *Secret History*, *The Woman of Colour* powerfully reclaims the Caribbean as a domestic space, a genuine home; as scholars continue to uncover more information about free women of color in the Caribbean, readers may more readily imagine Olivia returning to Jamaica finally able to "dwell among her people."

[5]

BUNGLING BUNDLING

IN "THE AMERICAN ORIGINS of 'Yankee Doodle,'" J. A. Leo Lemay locates a surprising instance of bundling in a lesser-known version of "Yankee Doodle." The lines read: "Two and two may go to bed / Two and two together / And if there is not room enough / Lie one atop the other."[1] Alongside the song's cheeky refrain to "keep it up" and "with the girls be handy," these lines reveal that colonial Americans were none too shy about the outright sexual nature of courtship. Bundling was an early American courtship practice popular in seventeenth- and eighteenth-century New England and mid-Atlantic colonies that presented a young unmarried couple with the opportunity to spend the night together in the female partner's family home for the purposes of getting to know one another. Although couples were customarily expected to retain at least some undergarments and had nominal parental supervision during the process, demographic studies show that, in this period, as many as 30 percent of all first births were conceived prior to marriage. The historian Richard Godbeer has argued that bundling was a pragmatic solution to colonial couples' demands for independence and privacy, as parents with knowledge of their daughter's sexual partners could intervene to force a marriage if necessary.[2]

Lemay's identification of bundling in "Yankee Doodle" is significant because he dates the song to the 1740s, much earlier than previous critics, demonstrating how the song was an early site of colonial identity or, as Lemay argues, "American self-characterization." Until Lemay's pathbreaking article, most scholars believed that "Yankee Doodle" was a satiric British production created to mock colonials, especially New Englanders, and their provincialism. However, Lemay claims that the song was actually a colonial production ridiculing British snobbery. Posing as backward "bumpkins," colonial Americans turned the tables on British stereotypes of ignorant Yankees by highlighting English credulity: "If [the English] were taken in, the Americans had reversed the snobbery and proven that the English were credulous and foolish."[3] Lines that had previously been read as British criticisms of colonial provinciality are, Lemay argues, a colonial rejection of metropolitan disdain. The same can be said about bundling. In "Yankee Doodle," bundling jokes are not just another British jab at colonials and their crude lovemaking, but evidence of a self-mocking Yankee humor tradition that points to the emergence of a distinctly colonial culture. If Lemay's dating is correct, then postrevolutionary-era bundling references by Royall Tyler and Washington Irving discussed later in this chapter continue a well-established rhetorical tradition of deploying Yankee bundlers as evidence of a distinct colonial-turned-national romantic heritage available for comparison.

In contrast to the comparative marriage plots previously discussed, this chapter traces a variety of eighteenth- and early nineteenth-century discursive traditions that position bundling as a courtship practice representative of the US nation and its values. However, the value of bundling's representativeness largely depends on who is speaking and to whom they are speaking. In works as diverse as European travel writing; popular ballads such as "Yankee Doodle" and "Jonathan's Courting"; Royall Tyler's *The Contrast* (1787); Washington Irving's *A History of New York* (1809); and the pseudonymous picaresque novels, *The Adventures of Jonathan Corncob* (1787) and *The Life and Adventures of Obadiah Benjamin Franklin Bloomfield, M.D.* (1818), bundling scenes provide Americans with a lively romantic tradition.[4] However, there are few straightforward celebrations of bundling in this archive, and for good reasons: bundling is only one of the many competing courtship traditions to choose from in the ethnically and religiously diverse United States; it is frequently associated with rustic "bumpkin" characters and many Americans are understandably concerned to espouse such a provincial national identity; and, finally, this provincialism is not in line with the popular cosmopolitan sensibilities that many US writers and readers want to adopt. Instead of provincialism, many early American novelists choose rather to adapt familiar and seemingly more sophisticated British literary conventions of sensibility.

In the final section of this chapter I argue that *The Life and Adventures of Obadiah Benjamin Franklin Bloomfield, M.D.*, rejects the hierarchical evaluative tendencies of Enlightenment comparison and instead embraces the cacophony of competing romantic discourses present in early national print culture. The novel humorously capitalizes on the almost overwhelming diversity of US romantic practices and belief systems, satirizing a consistent strain in contemporary print culture to single out romantic traditions as accurately representative of the nation. With its dizzying play of forms, conventions, and voices, this novel's exciting heteroglossia of romantic discourses celebrates the messy tangle of romantic doings and sayings that comprise the early US romantic imaginary.

Comparing Courtships: The Marriage-Rites Genre in the United States

In chapter 1 I traced the ways that comparative anthologies of "ceremonies used in marriage, by every nation in the known world" cull proto-ethnographic descriptions of courtship and marriage from various travel accounts and assemble them into attractive compendiums of exotic marriage customs.[5] During the course of the eighteenth century, these collections evolve from the titillating to the didactic and are popular with a wide variety of readers. Such books claim to provide a systemized approach to understanding and classifying the diversity of marriage rites around the globe by applying Enlightenment principles for organizing knowledge to materials aimed at a popular audience. Lisa O'Connell argues that the marriage-rites genre, coinciding as it did with British legal reformations such as Hardwicke's Marriage Act of 1753, becomes a tool for proclaiming nationalist sentiments about British women's supposedly more civilized treatment. In O'Connell's account, by the mid-eighteenth century, comparative representations of courtship and marriage practices are recognized tools for distinguishing national cultures and evaluating the differences in women's status across national borderlines. However, nationalizing projects obviously pose problems for the recently postcolonial United States.[6] Did the United States possess any of its own distinct romantic traditions, and would they be worthy of international comparison? The problem might more accurately be deciding *which* of the many traditions—indigenous, imported, or blended—to cast as *the* romantic practice representative of the new nation.

Almost as soon as the United States existed, American authors began inserting US marriage rites into their comparative texts. However, US versions of the marriage-rites genre are generally more anxious about the nationalist claims they make. For instance, in a lengthy 1787 letter "To the Editor of the Columbian Magazine" by "A Friend to the Fair Sex," the author compares American Quaker traditions to other global marital practices in order to prove that American customs are among the best: "With a wish to reconcile [single women] to what is absolutely necessary [marriage] . . . I would beg leave to offer the following facts and ideas on the subject—and have thought it most eligible to collect a short account of the foreign marriage ceremonies, the barbarities and absurdities of which, will have a tendency to reconcile us to the moderation and delicacy of our own." After detailing customs among the Laplanders, Russian peasants, Germans, Italians, Turks, Chinese, East Indians, Norwegians, Hottentots, and French, the author describes the customs of local American Quakers. While many marriageable individuals in Philadelphia apparently complained about the Quaker church's requirement to proclaim the banns, necessitating a wait of several weeks between engagement and marriage, the author explains that this minor delay pales in comparison to the "absurd institutions of other countries, and even of some of the sects in our own state." So, far from being a deterrent to marriage, the author argues that public professions of commitment and the "privilege of selecting the man she loves for a companion in her journey through life" ought to encourage matrimony. Whereas financial interests and "fortune-hunting" govern marriage considerations in "the old crowded cities" of Europe, "contracts, settlements of fortunes, etc. are scarcely understood by the inhabitants of America." In this depiction of a youthful, innocent America, love reigns supreme: "After all, the best criterion of what is right in courtship or wedlock, is the portion of happiness enjoyed by the aggregate of married inhabitants in any given country: and whoever attempts to make a scale of this kind for the whole world, must place America in a very elevated situation."[7] Here, the text's cross-cultural comparisons use a metric of personal happiness imported from the Scottish Enlightenment to prove that *America* possesses some of the best marriage arrangements. According to "A Friend," women are happiest and most esteemed in this new and flourishing country where domestic virtues and individual choice are highly prized and money matters are relatively unimportant. As this example demonstrates, the marriage-rites genre becomes one site in which discreet accounts of particular US marriage practices prove not only the nation's civility, but, on a more fundamental level, the very existence of culture in the United States. Comparison becomes a vehicle for positioning the United States and its romantic practices as the equivalent of other nations' long-standing cultural traditions; however, as "To the Editor" underscores, even in the state of Pennsylvania there are many religious "sects" with their own "absurd institutions." Making strong claims about the nation's supposedly progressive social mores and customs proves difficult in the face of the overwhelming diversity of us peoples, belief systems, and cultural practices. Which customs are progressive and which are absurd?

Before a national culture could be determined, then, a specific courtship ritual or marriage custom must be nominated above others as representative of the nation's values and character. Lacking a majority, it seems that the Quaker romantic tradition promoted by "A Friend" did not establish itself as the representative romantic practice in the larger field of the marriage-rites genre. However, the problem of locating representative traditions among a diverse and divided us population was further complicated by early nineteenth-century Romantic-era beliefs that national culture emerges from long-standing "indigenous" customs; most often this meant local, rural folk practice. Many early nationals argued that former colonies, lacking a unique language and deep historical connections to their geography, could not yet muster the necessary requirements for a unique national culture. For instance, in his well-known 1815 "Essay on American Language and Literature," William Ellery Channing claims that given the colonial origins of the United States, there could be no "native" language and, thus, no basis for a us national literary tradition.[8] From this point of view, the United States might well remain a mere clone of British traditions with no "native" literature of which to speak. Channing continues his explanation for the disappointing lack of American literature in the early national period with his additional charge that the new nation had yet to develop a market for us authors, in large part because American readers continue to import their reading materials from abroad. Clearly, whatever us culture, romantic or otherwise, would be, it would be a blend of existing British traditions with those of more recent us construction; but, in this sense, it was not so far removed from the Romantic-era efforts of Celtic nationalists such as Sir Walter Scott, whose well-documented invention of "traditional" Scottish culture took the literary world by storm with his landmark novel *Waverly* (1814).[9]

What might appear to be the seeming limitations of bundling as a national romantic practice—its regional association with New England Yankees and its reputation as a lower-class practice—could be seen, according to Romantic-period values, as assets for bundling's authenticity as folk tradition. This Romantic-era turn to bundling is rather surprisingly initiated by the complicated maneuver Lemay tracks in "Yankee

Doodle": a colonial investment in and reclaiming of seeming provincial-isms as authentic "heritage."

"A little peaceable bundling": Yankee Romance as Heritage

Before a romantic practice can become a tradition, it must be widely recognized as social protocol. To be a meaningful marker of "heritage," the same romantic practice must be invested with historical meaning as a source of local identity and pride. For bundling to be a heritage tradition, it must not only be a romantic practice from the past, but it must also carry with it a useful set of values and meanings for contemporary people about how their collective, regional, and, in this case, romantic identity has come to be. For New Englanders, bundling's heritage standing stems from what Edward Said calls a *contrapuntal reading strategy* in which colonials value a practice in direct opposition to European criticisms of that same practice.[10]

European travelers frequently comment on the widespread practice of bundling across the northern and middle North American colonies, recognizing in it a form of colonial alterity. For instance, according to British lieutenant Thomas Anburey's *Travels through the Interior Parts of America* (1789), bundling is an "unaccountable" colonial oddity.[11] In a scene that might have come directly from a British sentimental novel, Anburey describes the temptations he faces when his colonial hosts offer their daughter, the "very pretty black-eyed" Jemima, as his bedmate. Because beds were scarce, Jemima's parents view sharing a bed as an obvious and completely innocent solution. Anburey, however, finds the sexual temptation exceedingly great and finally rejects this "test of virtue," exclaiming "how cold the American constitution" must be to withstand Jemima's allure.

As this example shows, bundling could include nonsexual bed-sharing activities (think, for example, of Melville's Queequeg and Ishmael snugly sharing a bed at an overcrowded inn). However, most European travelers comment on bundling as a specific courtship ritual, also known as "girling of it," and "staying with."[12] Andrew Burnaby notes during his 1759–60 tour of Massachusetts that after the parents retire, "leaving the young ones to settle matters as they can," the lovers "get into bed together also, but without pulling off their undergarments, in order to prevent scandal."[13] Johann Schoepf, a German botanist and chief surgeon for a group of Hessian forces during the revolution, observes reassuringly that "the young woman's good name [is] no ways impaired" by the liaison. Far from stealthy nocturnal visits, "parents are advised" of these meetings and engagement is not a prerequisite; rather, "these meetings happen when the pair is enamored and merely wish to know each other better."[14] Taken together, though, these repeated European expressions of surprise, shock, and suspicion underscore the ways that metropolitan writers see bundling as an expression of colonial alterity.

For their parts, many colonists responded to Europeans' scandalized reports with righteous indignation. For instance, in 1781, the Reverend Samuel Peters rebutted such reports by insisting that bundling was an innocent practice: "Why it should be thought incredible for a young man and young woman innocently and virtuously to lie down together in a bed with a great part of their clothes on, I cannot conceive." Speaking from a position of church authority, Peters's support for bundling is one of the strongest contrapuntal interpretations. More broadly, though, he speaks to a revolutionary-era sensitivity to European condescension by turning the tables to question European morals: "It may seem very strange to find this custom of bundling in bed attended with so much innocence in New England, while in Europe it is thought not safe or scarcely decent to permit a young man and maid to be together in private anywhere. . . . Europe will discover that there is more Christian philosophy in American bundling than can be found in the customs of nations more polite."[15] In Peters's defensive comparison, bundling easily fits within preexisting comparative marriage-rites frameworks for evaluating national "politeness," and in his account, American bundling trumps Europe's false modesty. From this perspective, bundling is primarily an opportunity for carefully regulated privacy, where couples might forge an emotional bond. It is a testing ground for the likelihood of long-term emotional and physical compatibility, and, as such, neatly fits young couples' increasing demands for companionate marriage.[16]

The historian Richard Godbeer argues that by the mid-eighteenth century, bundling accommodated both young colonial couples' increasing insistence on sexual and marital independence as well as a pragmatic parental desire for sexual surveillance. Thus, in the event that premarital sexual intimacy ended in conception, parents with knowledge of their child's sexual partners could intervene to promote a timely marriage. As mentioned previously, as many as 30 percent of all first births in the revolutionary era were conceived prior to marriage.[17] These numbers indicate that, contrary to Anburey's claim, colonials were anything but "cold" in bed.

Published in London, the pseudonymous picaresque novel *The Adventures of Jonathan Corncob, Loyal American Refugee* (1787) loads its protagonist with stereotypical Yankee features, including a predilection for bundling. Because little is known about the publication history of *Corncob*, it is difficult to ascertain the novel's origins. As R. W. G. Vail suggests, it is highly probable that it was written by an English author satirizing the stings of recent revolutionary losses.[18] Jonathan describes himself as a Loyalist, but at the start of the novel he explains that he has been exiled from England for unpaid debts, and continues in his habits of exceeding his income in his present location, a garret apartment in Flanders. Writing from necessity, but also for amusement, Corncob relives his previous adventures on the page. Although he never disavows his Massachusetts Bay roots, neither does he embrace a metropolitan English identity. As Henri Petter notes, Jonathan's loyalty is "to himself rather than any country or institution."[19] He is adrift in the world, hilariously pursuing pleasures and experiencing many amusing setbacks along the way.

Yet Jonathan never learns from his mistakes, never tempers his desire. Indeed, he never acknowledges any genuine impropriety on his part, whether sexual, political, or commercial. This overconfidence leads the reader to question Jonathan's morality, for any time Jonathan faces punishment, he runs away or switches sides. Cathy Davidson observes that Jonathan's penchant for moving to a new setting, which she calls *global episodism*, is quite common in picaresque novels of this period. Looking back, Jonathan traces his rambling lifestyle to "the first little mistake I ever made in bundling."[20] Since he also tells his reader that he has "already bundled with half the girls in the neighborhood," the reader presumes that Jonathan only regrets that in this particular instance, bundling led to his fathering an illegitimate child. Jonathan marks his bundling "American beauty," Miss Desire Slawbunk, with highly racial descriptors: she is a "little dusky" and has a "certain languor in her look that was not displeasing." Desire also has a sweet tooth, leading to the overconsumption of "melasses" and the loss of six upper and six lower teeth.[21] Tying the "dusky" Desire to sugar consumption gives readers a new vantage on Desire's oversexed behavior. Like many profit-hungry New Englanders, Desire is tied to the triangle trade of slaves, sugar, and manufactured goods.

When Jonathan arrives at the Slawbunk house, he announces his intention to "tarry" with Desire and is accepted by her. After some unremarkable conversation on the cold, Desire observes that the fire is "by no means brilliant." She begins to fan the flames with her petticoats, giving Jonathan a view "that vied with all the snow and forests of the continent. Without improving the fire, she had produced an equal effect . . . I could not help proposing to bundle." Quickly stepping to the bed, the couple undresses "according to the rules of bundling, scrupulously reserving the breeches and underpetticoat," but this last reserve of modesty is no match for this clever couple. After a little tickling match, Corncob observes "we exceeded all the bounds of bundling. Heaven only can tell what become of the petticoat during the night, but in the morning we found it kicked out of the foot of the bed."[22] After a few months, it is clear that Desire is pregnant and a committee forms to resolve the situation. Jonathan is faced with the choice of marrying Miss Slawbunk or paying a fine of fifty pounds. Jonathan chooses instead to abscond to New York, a Loyalist stronghold. What is remarkable about this passage is how explicit Jonathan is about the bundling—no other scene I have found offers so much detail—and how assertively Desire plays her part in the action. She is no victim of deceit, no naïve or misguided waif, no passionless nineteenth-century angel in the house. She literally and purposely fans the flames in this encounter.

Rather surprisingly, Desire returns several times during the course of the novel to aid Jonathan in times of need. She seems to have something of a soft spot for him, despite his abandoning her. Indeed, Desire roguishly makes the best of her situation. After an unfortunate miscarriage, resulting in her losing Corncob's child, Desire beds with another young man and this time she lands herself a husband. Speaking in the first person, Desire informs Jonathan: "The committee of safety was consequently assembled, and it was determined, that for the security of the township, the captain should be put in gaol, and forfeit all right to his exchange, unless he married me: in this dilemma, Seeclear Sedley chose rather to become a sober husband, and I am now the captain's lady at your service."[23] Later, Desire unaccountably shows up in the jail cell next to Jonathan and digs a passageway between their cells. She relays news of Seeclear's murder while defending her from sexual threats by an Irish soldier; how she was forced to live with the Irishman until he was hanged as a deserter; and how she was then taken captive by a Hessian mercenary from whom she eventually escapes. Finally, Desire locates a relation of her former husband's in a Boston jail, but when the cousin escapes, Desire is accused of assisting him. Consequently, she suffers tarring and feathering and is put in prison for her supposed offense. While in jail, Desire restores Jonathan to her embraces and adds the jailor to her increasing list of lovers. Although she is only a minor character and clearly operates outside the bounds of socially prescribed feminine modesty, Desire Slawbunk, like Defoe's Moll Flanders before her, is a survivor and an adventuress.

She always seems to land on her feet. I cannot help admiring Desire's pluck, but she is certainly not a model of appropriate behavior or a satisfactory stand-in for the nation. US readers in 1787 would be understandably reluctant to valorize a racially marked, passionate, roguish woman such as Desire. *Corncob* is anti-American satire, then, not a genuine endorsement of colonial sexuality. After the sting of military defeat, it seems that a little brazen bundling humor may have provided a balm for at least some London readers.

In contrast to these condescending British portraits of Yankee bundling, Cameron Nickels claims that the rustic Yankee stock character, "Jonathan," "had become . . . the archetypal American, the embodiment of the common man"; moreover, Jonathan's predilection for bundling and his bumpkinish courting style are central to his characterization.[24] Although Nickels does not frame Jonathan's representativeness as a contrapuntal revaluing of colonial provinciality, his study usefully identifies bundling as a key feature of his representativeness. For a look at how Americans attempt to claim Yankee provincial lovemaking as heritage, Thomas Fessenden's popular 1795 broadside "Jonathan's Courting, or, The Country Lovers" provides an arch example: "And now the people went to bed: / They guessed for what he'd come, sir; / But Jonathan was much afraid, / and wish'd himself at home, sir / . . . / Sal cast a sheep's eye at the dunce, / Then turn'd towards the fire, / He muster'd courage, all at once, / And hitch'd a little nigher."[25] Far bolder than her "sparking" partner, Sally teases Jonathan until he begins to twitch with nervous energy, leading Sally to respond by dousing Jonathan with a bucket of water. In short, Fessenden depicts Jonathan as an incompetent lover. This popular broadside was frequently anthologized in later nineteenth-century collections of American literature. Fusing this protracted moment of bungled bundling to the tune of "Yankee Doodle," Fessenden's celebration of colonial provinciality resonated with the historical weight of revolutionary patriotism and victory against the British.

The dilemma posed by using provincial folk culture to establish a colonial identity is that it risks presenting all Americans as naïve and rustic.[26] Royall Tyler's *The Contrast* (1787) registers this problem by comparing the courtship styles of stock characters such as Jonathan, the typical rustic Yankee, with the respectable Captain Manly and the foppish Billy Dimple. Tyler's Jonathan speaks in crude dialect and his uncouth manners are humorously out of fashion; he finds urban customs and manners altogether incomprehensible. After unsuccessfully wooing a city housemaid, Jonathan declares: "Gor! she's gone off in a swinging passion, before I had time to think of consequences. If this is the way with your city ladies, give me the twenty acres of rock, the Bible, the cow, and Tabitha, and a little peaceable bundling."[27] Of course, while Jonathan's bundling might serve as an "indigenous" source of American identity and cultural traditions, Jonathan is not the hero of Tyler's play. Instead, Captain Manly embodies the best of American masculinity in his sentiment, virtue, and class standing. As Cameron Nickels comments, "The more identifiable and thus indigenous those qualities were made . . . the more clearly they represented social, cultural, and even political distinctions that were undesirable."[28] Claiming bundling proves a double-edged sword in that it promotes US distinctiveness by admitting its own provinciality—even Tyler could not avoid a postcolonial anxiety that "Jonathan" and his bundling would be criticized as outré in Europe.

Tyler walks a middle path by maintaining the tensions between "bumkinish" bundling and the fashionable cosmopolitan culture of sensibility circulating in the Atlantic world. With Manly as the hero, Tyler essentially has it both ways by including a stock Jonathan—a nod to colonial heritage—while clearly endorsing the more sophisticated masculinity of Manly. But the sharp class divisions Tyler depicts between bundlers and nonbundlers may not be entirely accurate. For although many accounts represent bundling as a primarily lower-class, folk practice, even the future president John Adams recommended that when practiced with discretion, couples could benefit from the test of compatibility it provided. And, during the same year that Adams and his future fiancée, Abigail Smith, went on a seemingly unchaperoned weekend trip together, he wrote that he could "not wholly disapprove of bundling."[29] With no proof that the future first couple actually bundled, we must instead be satisfied with the fact that even an ambitious man like Adams found some charm in the idea of bundling.

In *A History of New York* (1809), Washington Irving continues the satiric treatment of bundling, although he manages this satire in such a clever contrapuntal twist as to reverse many condescending British attitudes about the supposed cultural inferiority of the former colonies. Writing as Diedrich Knickerbocker, Irving humorously ascribes both the population growth and peculiar characteristics of the "Yankee race" to New England bundling: "This amazing increase may, indeed, be partly ascribed to a singular custom prevalent among them, commonly known by the name of bundling—a superstitious rite observed by the young people of both sexes, with which they usually terminated their festivities, and which was kept up with religious strictness by the more bigoted part of the community."[30] Irving's obviously biased Knickerbocker describes bundling in titillating, yet oblique terms. This "singular custom" is not only "superstitious" and "primitive," but it also serves more generally as a representative species of regional culture—that is, Yankee "shrewdness" in bargaining: "Thus early did this cunning and ingenious people display a shrewdness of making a bargain which has ever since distinguished them, and a strict adherence to the good old vulgar maxim about 'buying a pig in a poke.'" Knickerbocker polarizes upstart invading Yankees against previous generations of Dutch populations of New York by giving each group distinctive, if unflattering, features. In Knickerbocker's assessment, Yankee courtship perversely begins where "ours" ends; that is, in bed. As an "indispensable preliminary," bundling prioritizes sexual intimacy and physical compatibility; yet, in Knickerbocker's humorously biased account, Yankee bundling is morally suspect. The latent irony, here, is that despite its morally suspect nature, bundling is particularly generative. Knickerbocker claims:

> To this sagacious custom, therefore, do I chiefly attribute the unparalleled increase of the Yanokie or Yankee race: for it is a certain fact, well authenticated by court records and parish registers, that wherever the practice of bundling prevailed, there was an amazing number of sturdy brats annually born unto the state, without the license of the law or the benefit of clergy. Neither did the irregularity of their birth operate in the least to their disparagement. On the contrary, they grew up a long-sided, raw-boned, hardy race of whalers, wood-cutters, fishermen, and pedlars, and strapping corn-fed wenches, who, by their united efforts, tended marvelously toward peopling those notable tracts of country called Nantucket, Piscataway, and Cape Cod.[31]

With a good deal of tongue in his cheek, Irving via Knickerbocker shows how bundling not only produces "sturdy brats," it also produces a distinct, local culture with its own sexual codes and customs.

In contrast to charges of New World degeneracy posed by the French natural historian Count Buffon, for instance, who hypothesized that the cold North American climate decreased sexual libido, shrinking both the stature and the population size of all North American life, Irving insists that colonial courtship practices produce an abundant population.[32] Far from something to shrink at, Irving jokes, colonial America's supposed sexual and moral degeneracy *generates* a distinctly Yankee race with its own "singular" customs. Despite the custom's negative reception by European travel writers, Irving recognizes that bundling is an authentic source of US difference—even if that difference is valued negatively in Europe. Echoing Buffon, British lieutenant Thomas Anburey's assessment of Americans' "cold" sexual constitution could not be further from the truth, Knickerbocker retorts, as he describes Yankees as a passionate "race of brisk, likely, pleasant-tongued varlets," who "soon seduced the light affections of the simple damsels from their ponderous Dutch gallants."[33] Indeed, Knickerbocker's "brisk" Yankees make quick work of courting in order to get on to the more serious business of squatting on Dutch New Yorkers' lands. Through ingenious satire, Irving transforms Anburey's report on the "unaccountable" custom into the site of a distinctive local romantic tradition, "brats" and all.

Where *Jonathan Corncob* gives us salacious detail, Irving couples quasi-ethnographic accounts of bundling with Yankee stereotypes to "authenticate" America's unique romantic heritage. Irving ups the ante on Knickerbocker's credulous historical account when he humorously reverses bundling's actual origins from the Old World to the New. In open defiance of common knowledge that bundling was adapted from the Dutch practice of *queesting*, Knickerbocker argues that, in fact, obnoxious Yankees teach the Dutch to bundle rather than the other way around. When it comes to bundling, Knickerbocker explains, American colonials are the innovators: "Among other hideous customs . . . [Yankees] attempted to introduce . . . [was] bundling, which the Dutch lasses of the [New] Nederlandts, with that eager passion for novelty and foreign fashions natural to their sex, seemed very well inclined to follow, but that their mothers, being more experienced in the world, and better acquainted with men and things, strenuously discountenanced all such outlandish innovations."[34] Colonizing logic dictates that Europe is the source of "civilized" culture. By denying that colonial peoples possess their own civilized culture, the metropole benefits by selling consumer luxuries to eager colonials anxious about their own supposed lack of culture.[35] In his humorous reversal of the origins of bundling, Irving unseats Europe as the generative site of culture by pointing to the "innovation" of Yankee bundling. When it comes to love, Yankees have creativity and a growing population on their side. Of course, in Knickerbocker's representation Yankee bundling is not civilized; nevertheless, it is an export commodity, taken up by the Dutch. In Irving's savvy hands, distinctive Yankee heritage becomes a complex vehicle for debating the sources and meanings of culture.

Atlantic Currents of Seduction: Connecting the
Local and the Global

If bundling receives ambiguous support from John Adams, Royall Tyler, and others, we might characterize it as an early and unwieldy form of local color writing, rather dangerously advertising its own provinciality. As such it offers only a limited regionalism, rather than the patriotic nationalism demanded by Channing and others. As authors recognize the problems of promoting their own provinciality, bundling does not make its way into the larger repertoire of American literature and seems to fade away in actual practice as well. The historian Richard Godbeer has a different explanation for bundling's disappearance at the turn of the nineteenth century. He argues for a linear progression from previously permissive attitudes toward bundling that gradually give way to a "widespread anxiety about the vulnerability of women," manifest in the prevalence of seduction literature in the 1790s. However, Alan Taylor suggests yet another explanation: "A more satisfactory explanation for the apparent coexistence of pragmatic courtship [embodied in bundling] and literary hysteria [seduction fiction] is that they derived from, and spoke to, two different generations in two distinct social orbits: one mid-eighteenth-century, rural, and traditional; the other late-eighteenth-century, cosmopolitan, and upwardly mobile. . . . The print media spoke first and foremost to the middle-class Americans who longed to perfect the manners and the morality that comprised 'gentility'—a standard that derived from an idealized image of the British gentry as found in Jane Austen's novels."[36] I tend to agree with Taylor, although on this last point, I would suggest that the fictional models are a slightly older set of sentimental novelists still popular in the United States: Richardson and Sterne. American readers infatuated with *Charlotte Temple* prefer the more direct confrontation with seduction initiated by Richardson over the more subtle seduction subplots found in Austen.

Seduction fiction in the vein of Samuel Richardson favors the machinations of a powerful male who victimizes a virtuous female, undeserving of such treatment. As Cathy Davidson notes, "women are seduced in the novel[s] not by their own uncontrollable desire but by the verbal chicanery of men."[37] While this might suggest that women were powerless dupes to rakish men, many authors of seduction fiction encouraged women readers to see through a seducer's duplicitous words, to be cautious, and even to educate themselves against such seductive arts. As many literary critics have argued, the theme of vulnerable women was especially appealing to US readers who saw their new political situation in such seduction scenarios; as John Adams observed, "Democracy is Lovelace, and the people are Clarissa."[38]

More recently, though, scholars of seduction fiction have pushed back at these nation-centered and US-centric interpretations. For instance, Toni Bowers recovers a long history of British seduction stories stretching back to the seventeenth century, a timely reminder that seduction themes have a long provenance before the emergence of the United States or US reading publics.[39] In his deft account of Richardson's popularity in the colonial and early national United States, Leonard Tennenhouse argues that American fiction is deeply indebted to British literary traditions; so much so that Tennenhouse argues it fostered diasporic ties well into the nineteenth century.[40] Rather than a specifically homegrown plot or readerly priority, seduction fiction registers a cosmopolitan sensibility that exceeds the borders of the United States. As Bowers and Chico argue, seduction and sentiment belong instead to "synergistically" connected eighteenth-century Atlantic readers and their worlds.[41]

Tracing the development of the early American novel in an Atlantic world-system, Steven Shapiro similarly claims that national frameworks are inadequate to the task of meaningfully accounting for the changes in the early American novel. Shapiro identifies the difficult ruptures in colonial structures of feeling caused by the revolution and explores how traditional forms of communication were no longer adequate to convey new postrevolutionary patterns of thought. At the same time, new forms and conventions of expression had not yet emerged to describe postrevolutionary social relations. Shapiro convincingly locates this problematic transition period in the United States alongside a larger Atlantic world geoculture organized around sensibility, sensational consumption, slavery, and sentimental cultural productions, such as novels. In brief, Shapiro notes how a merchant class largely outside of the revolutionary politics of the 1770s and 1780s eschewed nationalist discourses that alienated potential trade relations, instead adapting "older forms of expression, like those caught within the slightly obsolete British and French sentimental novel, to represent their anxieties and experiences."[42] US readers' embrace of seduction fiction and its cosmopolitan morality appears to be not only a salient metaphor for US political anxieties, but also an avenue for displaying one's knowledge and performance of already established currents of European taste. Oddly, seduction fiction was a safely approved vehicle for the demonstration of cosmopolitan sensibility, whereas bundling still invited European smirks. For Americans who hoped to participate in Atlantic world mercantile exchange, adapting cosmopolitan forms and conventions of sentiment proved more advantageous than provincial or national forms of expression.

This perspective helps to explain how Susanna Rowson's most famous novel, *Charlotte Temple* (1791), a relative flop upon its original publication in London, became a US best seller reprinted 161 times.[43] In the ample extant commentary on *Charlotte Temple,* critics have largely overlooked the novel's surprising lack of attention to its transatlantic settings.[44] For instance, Rowson does not capitalize on her firsthand experiences of Atlantic crossings; instead, the Atlantic is more of an allegorical divide between Charlotte's innocent past and troubled future. In every respect, the spaces of England and America are culturally and geographically indistinct. My point is that unlike the provincially located activity of bundling, seduction is not associated with a specific place or time. This lack of specificity proves an asset as the novel's solicitation of a cosmopolitan sensibility allowed US readers to feel themselves part of a larger network of social relations across disputed borders.[45] Political differences do not prevent sentimental readers from sharing emotional bonds forged through sympathy with Charlotte, but most important, those emotional bonds are not dependent on geography. Instead of a regionally limiting and provincially marked romantic practice such as bundling, many US writers and readers preferred to tread familiar novelistic ground by reframing seduction stories for American readers.

Compared to Rowson's indistinct transatlantic settings, Martha Meredith Read's lesser-known *Margaretta; or, The Intricacies of the Heart* (1807) expands the arena of seduction to encompass a larger circuit of the Atlantic world. Read's eponymous heroine faces sexual coercion and assault first in rural Maryland, and then again in Philadelphia, Baltimore, Saint-Domingue, and England, before finally marrying and moving to the idyllic Susquehanna Valley. Although these various settings are far from fully developed chronotopes, Read gives each setting a level of detail that infuses her endless cycle of seductions with some variety. Because *Margaretta* is an epistolary novel, each setting gains a distinctness through Margaretta's first-person observations. Much like Samuel Richardson's *Pamela, Margaretta*'s heroine is a strikingly attractive country girl whose manners and beauty draw the attention of a socially superior set. Without getting too mired in the plot, Margaretta, like Richardson's Pamela, relies on her own ingenuity and the kindness of strangers to escape repeated assaults on her virtue; and, like Pamela, she is rewarded by a loving marriage to a man who has learned to properly prize that virtue. If in every part of the Atlantic world Margaretta faces sexual assault, it is also true, as Richard Pressman observes, that as a symbol of the vulnerable nation, Margaretta is never penetrated.[46] Read adapts Richardson's slightly out-moded epistolary style, recasting his claustrophobic fantasy of English bourgeois ascendancy in a wider Atlantic world. Read rejects the provin-cialism of Tyler or Washington, but she does not reject the idyllic fantasy of a safe and conservative US elite. As it turns out, Margaretta is an aris-tocrat by birth, lost to her English family by their own snobbish pride and misfortune. At the novel's end, she finds her true family, her true love, and her true place ensconced among the (Federalist) US elite. In contrast to *Margaretta*'s impenetrable vision of a consolidated United States, in the final section of this chapter, I explore how and why Obadiah Benjamin Franklin Bloomfield instead ventriloquizes the many cosmopolitan and local varieties of romantic discourse proliferating in early national print culture.

Courting Heteroglossia: Representing Romantic
Discourses in the Early United States

Published in Philadelphia and attributed to copyright holder Edward Franklin, *The Life and Adventures of Obadiah Benjamin Franklin Bloom-field, M.D.: A Native of the United States of America, Now on the Tour of Europe. Interspersed with Episodes, and Remarks, Religious, Moral, Pub-lic Spirited, and Humorous* (1818) is a text keenly aware of the ways that romantic practices are seen as evidence of national customs and shared national identity.[47] More than this, though, *Obadiah* demonstrates how a cacophony of romantic discourses from the protoethnographic reports of marriage-rites anthologies to the melodrama of seduction fiction seek to locate an individual (male) subject within a nascent national romantic tradition. A key feature of Obadiah's quirky self-fashioning narrative is his engagement with and literary imitations of Benjamin Franklin, his name-sake, and British sentimentalist Laurence Sterne; I do not address these features of the text here as this chapter attempts a more narrow consider-ation of *Obadiah*'s prolific romantic discourses, including its fascinating scene of bungled bundling.[48]

Like *Jonathan Corncob*, *Obadiah* is a picaresque novel with little in the way of an organized plot.[49] The novel follows the professional as well as the romantic ups and downs of its title character from his early manhood, as he strives to fulfill his father's desire to hear him preach a sermon, to choosing a career as a medical doctor, and, finally, to obtaining the wealth and status that enables his family to tour Europe (at which point the text concludes). Unlike the unreliable Corncob, Obadiah is a generally likeable fellow who unfortunately experiences many romantic difficulties, including a few premarital scrapes and three marriages. Even this brief summary suggests how, like Fielding's *Tom Jones* (1749), Obadiah gradually matures from his early picaresque ramblings toward a kind of respectability, and how this respectability depends on the erotic, sentimental, and legitimating discourses of sex and marriage for achieving status in the Atlantic imperial world.

What makes Obadiah stand out from obvious male precursors such as Tom Jones or Tristram Shandy is the novel's obvious yoking of its protagonist's individual maturation with that of the new nation. Somewhat awkwardly combining the features of a picaresque ramble with the masculine novel of development—sometimes also called an apprentice novel—*Obadiah* strives for a cosmopolitan sensibility that connects its protagonist's waggish romantic adventures to the book's not altogether settled conclusion: for in taking his family on a tour of Europe, Obadiah proves himself still a rambler, though now a slightly tamer, cosmopolitan family man.

Hyperaware of the competing conventions of romance in this period, *Obadiah* humorously moves between the expected objectivity of the marriage-rites anthologies and the sentimental and melodramatic expressions of courtship and seduction fiction with maximum ironic effect. For example, in the novel's first chapter, Obadiah interrupts the story of his birth (à la *Tristram Shandy*) for a long diatribe on "Hottentot" courtship rituals. This ethnic group from South Africa known today as the Khoikhoi was frequently depicted in the racist language of the period as subhuman. Saartjie "Sarah" Baartman, the so-called Venus of Hottentot, was exhibited in freak shows across Great Britain and France; her body was the subject of prurient curiosity among European intellectuals and laypeople alike.[50] Although the story of Baartman's humiliating exploitation is well documented in contemporary scholarship, racist stereotypes about the "crude" customs of "Hottentots" were widely circulated well before Baartman's exhibition, in part due to marriage-rites anthologies such as *Hymen: An Accurate Description of the Ceremonies Used in Marriage, by Every Nation in the Known World* (1760), discussed in chapter 1.[51] In imitation of this genre and of the dialogues of *Tristram Shandy*, Obadiah describes "Hottentot" courtship in a dialogue with a curious female interlocutor. Much of the humor in this scene, racist as it is, relies on Obadiah's use of the protoethnographic conventions of the marriage-rites genre and its naïve Shandian female interlocutor for come-dic effect. The dialogue begins with the unnamed female asking, "Hot-tentot! Pray what description of people are they? I don't recollect ever to have heard of them before?" To which Obadiah replies: "Your curiosity is a very laudable one, my dear, and I will cheerfully gratify it. You must know, then, that the Hottentots are a sort of uncivilized copper-colored folk, more remarkable for their personal cleanliness than the most true of all true musselman, or the French, or the Italians; insomuch as they make it an invariable rule—to bathe a dozen times a day—comb their heads a dozen times a day—perfume themselves a dozen times a day—and, in brief, to do *every thing else which is done by human beings in the same ratio.*" Initially focused on customs and habits, Obadiah describes Khoi-khoi peoples as excessive, even exaggerated, but in this respect they are not much different than similarly stereotyped representations of Muslim or French peoples. The last italicized phrase in the preceding quotation works as a bit of a wink, wink, nudge, nudge, verging on the borders of politeness acceptable in mixed company. Obadiah moves from customs to observations on Khoikhoi bodies, but his commentary works less to racialize Khoikhoi bodies than to satirize the inappropriate curiosity of the female interlocutor: "Moreover, they are made pretty much as we are, having heads, and legs, and arms, &c. procreate in the same manner, and worship gods of their own manufacture." Not receiving the infor-mation she desires, Obadiah's female friend asks more directly, "But you have not explained to us how they manage their love matters, which is a primary consideration to most ladies." Obadiah proceeds to lampoon "Hottentot" lovemaking and his readers' curiosity about "every thing else which is done by human beings" in his fictional protoethnographic account: "You are not to suppose, their extraordinary ablutions to the contrary notwithstanding, that they conduct in that all important and *ticklish* affair as we do." In contrast to the "nonsense" of Western court-ship, "a Hottentot gallant" needs merely to "obtain his own consent and go a wooing, and he is certain of taking a wife to his bosom the self-same night." In ever more ludicrous detail, Obadiah claims: a "[Hottentot] youth resolved to lie alone no longer, rigs himself out in his best attire, borrows the youngest infant which is *come-at-able*, repairs to the residence of the object of his choice, presents it with a grin, after making one of his very best bows, left foot foremost; and awaits in silence. If his addresses are agreeable, his flame takes the child, eagerly kisses [it] . . . smiles, nods her head, and then squats, body and all, as gracefully as does a hare when he is disposed to put the hounds at fault. The *ceremony* is now over."[52] With invented phrases such as "come-at-able" and niggling details such as "left foot foremost," Obadiah capitalizes on the exotic reports contained in the marriage-rites genre to satirize not just the "Hottentots," but readers' insatiable curiosity about other peoples' sexual lives. Generalizing from a specific and obviously absurd instance, Obadiah's report imitates the supposedly neutral protoethnographic language that, in fact, animalizes non-European others. However, the humor lies in recognizing these conventions as *conventions* particular to describing cultural others; and, of course, in the literalizing of a baby positioned between the nubile couples' coupling.

Obadiah's send-up of the marriage-rites anthology has particular purchase for a fledgling nation such as the United States, bent on articulating its own distinct national traditions. Obadiah's marriage-rites satire questions the way these texts comparatively interpret particular details of courtship rituals as evidence of civility or savagery. Indeed, Obadiah renders the polite conventions of Anglo-American courtship such as attendance at balls and the writing of love letters into a kind of "drudgery," the "nonsense of our own creation."[53] If, in Obadiah's report, "Hottentot" courtship rituals are silly, so, too, are "our" customs. This sleight of hand does more than simply ridicule contemporary "love-making" practices, however. It overtly situates US courtship traditions among an unspecified "we" who are different from those "uncivilized" races of "Hottentots." We, Americans, possess romantic practices; we use those practices as the basis for cultural comparisons; and we assert our civility through those comparisons.

Like the literalness of the "Hottentot" baby in the previous scene—a custom that strips away the "nonsense" of balls and love letters—humorous representations of bundling by Irving, Tyler, and others insist on the no-nonsense way Yankee bundlers try out a relationship before marriage. From this perspective, bundling simplifies sentimental novelistic conventions in favor of the practicalities of compatibility such as living and sleeping with another human being. However, the generic divide between satiric prose by Irving, *Corncob*, and *Obadiah* and sentimental fiction modeled after Richardson was deep. Perhaps another reason that it is difficult to find novels that deal with bundling was because it was so challenging to meld the satiric with the sentimental relations favored in this period. That both *Jonathan Corncob* and *Obadiah* draw on Sternean style suggests the ways these texts tried to meld the often crude sexual jesting of Sterne with the popular sentimentality he achieved. If Obadiah draws on familiar marriage-rites comparisons, he ultimately rejects the evaluative goals of such comparison. Rather, our narrator adds a dizzying array of romantic practices and discourses to his narrative.

In true Shandian fashion, I have left my real target—bundling—standing all this while and it is high time I return to it. In yet another dialogic scene, this time between Obadiah and a curious "Yankey," Obadiah begins a long-promised bundling episode with a teasing tautology: "In imitation of that great transatlantic luminary, George Alexander Stevens, . . . who learnedly observes in his profound dissertation on law—that—"the law is the law"—I—Obadiah, junior, announce without fear of contradiction, to Jew and Gentile, Mahometan and Pagan, that bundling—is bundling!" In a tangle of words, ironically staged to free himself from contradiction, Obadiah explains that bundling "—is bundling." The pause indicated by the dash brilliantly conveys the anticipation Obadiah protracts from his "Yankey" friend. Not surprisingly, the "Yankey" angrily retorts that he will not be "hoax[ed]": "You promised us a chapter on bundling, and I will have my pennyworth—I guess as how I will." Teasing still, Obadiah continues, "I can readily perceive by the contour of your phiz. my dear half Yorkshire—half Yankey friend, that you are dying to know what bundling is, and [are] considerably embarrassed thereat; because the *wholesome* practice is kept up in your Yankey state of Connecticut to this day."[54] Here's a true delight, Obadiah seems to suggest, a Yankee "green" to the arts of bundling.

In lieu of a more direct definition, Obadiah circumvents the Yankee's straightforward demand for information by using a personal anecdote; here, I let Obadiah tell his own story: "In my youthful days I set out on a visit of pleasure to New York, accompanied by a friend, much about my own age. . . . We were determined not to let so fair an opportunity of being eye witnesses of the manner in which the humbler class BUNDLE in that state." Obadiah proceeds to relate how he and his friend journey on foot to a farmer's house, "who was said to have some beautiful daughters";[55] they arrive about sunset and receive an uncertain welcome. Ingratiating themselves by paying a great deal for their dinners and throwing out compliments all around, they are finally invited to stay the night. The Yankee interlocutor's suspense has reached such a pitch that he interrupts with little ribald replies in the story's rising action:

There were but two rooms in the house. (*Yankey. So much the better.*) We were directed to sleep next to the chimney; the three girls next to the chamber, and the two young men, their brothers, in the centre; as a barrier betwixt us, I presume. The dame retired to the chamber with the younger children, and was soon followed by her husband, after he had carefully outed the fire and candles, and apologized to us for the necessity he was under of requiring us to undress in the dark. And that is what is termed bundling!!! (*Yankey. True. And I guess as how you both walked in your sleep, ha, ha, ha. Author. That's tellings!!!*)[56]

In contrast to the Yankee's dialect and vulgar interjections, Obadiah's mostly urbane self-presentation shows him to be more cosmopolitan, but also more calculating. Even if his bundling is bungled, Obadiah presents himself as an adventurer in pursuit of sexual escapades. As such, he is less like the bumbling Jonathan of Thomas Fessenden's "Jonathan's Courting" and more like Fielding's likeable rogue, Tom Jones. However, Obadiah's bundling episode also achieves—precisely through its stock characters, regional dialect, and particular country customs—a limited form of local color, which precisely distinguishes it from competing British novels. Bundling signals our waggish protagonist's connection to a productive, prosperous, and "indigenous" colonial American culture.

Thus far I have argued that bundling functions in early national US writing as one particularly resonant example of a distinctive US romantic practice. Of course, bundling was neither local to New England (as it was adapted from the Dutch practice of *queesting*) nor representative of the entire United States. However, by repeatedly citing bundling as "native," local culture authors such as Tyler and Irving infuse bundling with the mythic national status they sought to establish. Anything but simple, the bundling references traced here resist Old World claims of America's supposed degeneracy by insisting on the (re)productive powers of local customs such as bundling to generate an "authentic" American culture. These references actively reverse the colonial logic that locates civilized romantic culture exclusively in the metropole, demonstrating how colonial courtship practices could emphasize romantic compatibility and intimacy over the supposedly mercenary motives of Old World marriages. In each case, US writers claim bundling as a site of American difference; even satiric bundling scenes could be opportunities for developing a distinct US literary mode.

In bungling nationalist attempts to trope bundling as an "authentic" American custom—this Yankee doesn't even know about bundling— *Obadiah* reveals a more complex consideration of US decolonization as a slow process that requires trial and error and a good sense of humor. The nothingness of this bundling episode suggests how early national authors groped in the dark, imitating, multiplying, adapting, and improvising their way toward what Joseph Roach calls "full-blown myths of legitimacy and origin."[57] What *Obadiah* does instead is slot bundling next to satiric marriage-rites entries, exposés of "dark houses," and Obadiah's three sentimental marriages. The novel revels in what Bakhtin names one of the distinctive features of the genre, its heteroglossia, or "many-voiced" perspective.[58] *Obadiah*'s many narrative intrusions, jokes, and plot disruptions might seem to work against it, but this rowdy celebration of proliferating romantic discourses simultaneously undercuts the ideological structures of gender and sexual normativity implicit in these discourses simply by illustrating their competing conventions and aims. No coherent male subject could emerge from such a cacophony, *Obadiah* seems to argue. The pleasure this novel takes in its ostentatious mocking of all romantic conventions makes *Obadiah* a positively queer text. Ranging from the protoethnographic to the erotic to the sentimental, *Obadiah*'s complicated interweaving of competing romance conventions provides its protagonist with a story of the difficulties in obtaining married respectability.

Historians argue that after the revolution, the founders replace the parent-child metaphor so useful for describing the relation of empire to colony with a marital metaphor to describe its citizen's voluntary union and contractual consent.[59] Courtship and marriage are seen as "a training ground of citizenly virtue"; intimate family bonds and the experiences of governing a family would, it was thought, prepare men for the more abstract allegiances and political duties owed to the nation.[60] Elizabeth Maddock Dillon argues that in this same period, "marriage functions as both an intensely private relation and as a form of public ratification" that consolidates the liberal subject's identity through the community's approval of his or her private decisions. The paradox that Dillon uncovers is how "making the *correct* choice means exercising individual consent in relation to socially constructed norms."[61] If courtship novels in this period inevitably end in marriage and, generally, in marriage founded in mutual affection and consent, the events leading up to marriage track the young person's development from dependence and immaturity to mature, married adult. The courtship plot serves as a kind of education narrated as development, with a telos not only of obtaining a respectable partner, but of having properly performed one's gender so as to acquire a suitable partner.[62] As Dillon argues, early national marriage is a "gendering machine: the discourse of marriage and marital passion produces differently sexed bodies—it masculinizes men and feminizes women in an increasingly significant fashion."[63] The plots and characters of courtship novels serve as romantic scripts in this gendering machine, but as Dillon explains, the results of this discourse operate differently on men and women.

Obadiah suggests that before marriage and social responsibility, a man might be allowed a little romantic adventuring. We have seen Obadiah rather unsuccessfully attempt a bit of bundling; another adventure draws on the conventions of seduction fiction even as it reformulates those conventions. After a round of preaching on the Methodist circuit where Obadiah has been secretly training in order to fulfill his father's desire to hear him preach a sermon, Obadiah stays the night at a simple farmhouse and becomes infatuated with the farmer's daughter, Mary.[64] Like Mary Magdalene, this Mary prepares to wash Obadiah's feet, stirring up inappropriate desire. Obadiah coyly dodges Mary's intentional expressions of desire as "accidental" rather than practiced, and his own excitement at the encounter obviates any serious consideration of Mary as sexual agent: "I retired to my apartment, leaving the door open.—Mary soon glided through, and latched it after her—accidentally, no doubt, for she did it without noise. She is upon her knees before me—I can now look upon her without dread of detection." The odd shifts between verb tenses heighten the sexual tension as Obadiah—presumably in the act of writing —imagines Mary in the present tense "upon her knees before me." In the heat of the moment, he acknowledges his feelings of guilt and attempts to dodge them: "The icy heart of a hermit of ninety would have been thawed, and he would have conceited himself nineteen." No one can blame him for what follows, he suggests. The rest of this scene recalls Sterne's teasing conclusion to *A Sentimental Journey* when Yorick breaks in mid-sentence as he catches hold of the Fille de Chambre's [———] as Obadiah interrupts his description with a series of dashes reminiscent of Sterne's evocative groping conclusion: "—The washing proceeded but slowly.—It was a boisterous night—a sudden blast found its way through the pine logs whereof the house was built—and—the—candle—was—extinguished!!!"[65]

Like Sterne, who is explicitly named in the opening "Advertisement" as a literary influence, our narrator leaves us to imagine the ensuing scenario for ourselves by promptly concluding the chapter. The scene perversely implicates the reader for its erotic content as he or she imaginatively fills in the dark space created by the extinguished candle. The suspense mounts when, on turning the page, the reader discovers an entirely unrelated chapter titled "The Enchanted Hat." Written from an completely separate point of view, the story of the enchanted hat follows a rogue

English sailor who swindles two Jewish brothers by leading them to purchase his "enchanted" hat. As a standalone piece that is not referred to again, the story seems inserted purely to delay the conclusion of the Mary affair. Only reading between the lines can we tie the not-so-enchanted hat to Obadiah's guilty sexual conquest. He tells us, when he resumes the narrative, that far from tarnishing Mary's virtue, he discovers that she has "washed the feet" of several other Methodist preachers. Thus, he absolves himself of the crime of seducing an innocent woman. Obadiah's disillusionment with an "enchanted" object spares him the guilt required for the act of seduction. *Obadiah* teases readers attuned to the usual melodrama of the seduction novel by infusing the narrative with the eroticism of that genre while rejecting its harsh condemnations of premarital sex. Mary does not "fall"; Obadiah does not waste his energy on unnecessary regrets.

While the complicated plot continues to twist, turn, and digress, Obadiah's sexual adventuring with Mary as well as the aforementioned bundling scene suggests the episodic picaresque nature of his romantic ramblings. Obadiah's encounter with Mary is merely a placeholder on the seemingly inevitable path to marriage. However, Obadiah's progress toward maturation occurs in a series of fits and starts as he marries three times: first, the sensual and sentimental Louisa, who unfortunately dies in childbirth; next, the passionate Maria, who turns out to be an adulteress; and finally, Sophia, a worthy partner for the now steady and respectable Obadiah. Tried and tested, first by grief and then by cuckoldry, Obadiah proves himself a worthy partner with unfortunate luck in love. But the plot's digressions tend, in *Tristram Shandy* fashion, to divert us from the seemingly inevitable respectability of marriage toward an acknowledgment of the work that a variety of social conventions, including novels and other discursive traditions, play in this gendering machine, to use Dillon's term.

Over the course of the novel, Obadiah confesses to impetuous sexual desire, attempts to make amends for his early faults, and faithfully and lovingly performs his duties as a son, a husband, and father. Obadiah is not a bad guy, but his frequent ramblings and romantic digressions suggest that he is blown off course as easily as he switches between romantic discourses. Shaped by the gendering machine, Obadiah helps his readers to see its tools, especially in the form of conventional literary language. By the novel's conclusion, Obadiah is a man with an independent fortune, a successful career, and a male heir. He has become a respectable male citizen, but that path has not been straight.

Obadiah walks a fine line in the way that it acknowledges and even pardons women's sexual passions. Whereas it dismisses Mary as unworthy of any real guilt, it sanctions Obadiah's initially adulterous relationship with his soon-to-be first wife, Louisa, because her first husband is an abusive scoundrel who quickly dies through no fault of either Obadiah or Louisa. All loveliness itself, Louisa is not a victim of Obadiah's lust, nor a wicked wife. Rather, the text suggests that Louisa very much deserves love and Obadiah is the answer to her prayers. That she finds herself pregnant a little earlier than the wedding does not prove a cause for concern. Although she does die in childbirth, the novel does not make Louisa's death a form of punishment for sexual sins. From Obadiah's perspective, it is simple human tragedy. If the novel's moral code condones Obadiah's initial adulterous relationship with Louisa, it explicitly condemns Obadiah's adulterous second wife, Maria, to a life of "dark houses" and, finally, death. Lacking the excuse of an abusive husband, Maria's sexual crimes are compounded when she is caught in the act, then denies the entire business and engages her brother to duel for her supposed honor. When the truth comes out, Maria flees to New York, reduced to working in a "dark house" (something like a brothel) before Obadiah finally finds and forgives her on her deathbed. After all this loss, the reader feels that Obadiah deserves a lasting love. Although Sophia's family initially rejects Obadiah because he is a poor tradesman's son, they are soon persuaded of his worth and willingly consent to Obadiah's third marriage. Successful in his career, in his friendships, and now in love, the plot appears, finally, to favor Obadiah—until rumors circulate that Obadiah's second wife Maria has returned to sue him for bigamy. This last attack on Obadiah's respectability actually lands him in prison, but Obadiah successfully proves this woman is an imposter.

With his marriage to Sophia back on firm legal terms, Obadiah prepares to take his whole family and a close friend to Europe, a trip that demonstrates both his wealth and his properly developed cosmopolitan taste.[66] Weaving together popular early national romantic discourses in a queer narrative of personal development, *Obadiah* suggests that early national US romantic traditions are complicated acts of appropriation and reconfiguration, drawing on local, regional, multicultural, and transnational sources and styles. Not limited to the local, not adrift in a vague world of Atlantic seduction, full of cultural comparisons, bridging the ethnographic with the personal, *Obadiah* celebrates the cacophony of conventions past and present that comprise early American romantic sensibilities. At times raucous and at other times sentimental, *Obadiah* is a text alive to the diversity of early American experiences. Studying its meanderings provides a necessarily different and, I hope, welcome perspective on the intersection of local and global romantic geographies in early US print culture.

EPILOGUE: WHY MARRIAGE MATTERS NOW

IN A RECENT POST on her blog, *Love, Inc.,* Laurie Essig argues that in the United States, "romance is the ruling ideology."[1] This wasn't always the case, of course. In the late eighteenth and early nineteenth centuries, when an Anglophone Atlantic world practice of companionate marriage became the ideological ideal, some novelists used what I have called a comparative-marriage plot to compare an emerging ideology of companionate marriage with other Atlantic world practices. As I have argued throughout this book, novels proved effective creative spaces for working out problems, trying out alternatives, and rethinking British marital norms. From matrilineal Haudenosaunee (Iroquois) households and Haitian *plaçage* to New England bundling, modes of marriage in the early Americas have always been more diverse than commonly acknowledged. During the course of the nineteenth century, however, the US government increasingly sought to control, contain, and eradicate this diversity by promoting monogamous companionate marriage among nonconforming American Indians, some postemancipation freedpeople, and polygamous Mormons, to name only a few. In contrast to the exploration of alternatives found in fictional comparative-marriage plots, nineteenth-century marriage reformers attempted to legislate and adjudicate their way toward uniform, state-authorized marriage.

"In our culture, romance is the ruling ideology"

Prior to this, in many backcountry locales, local custom allowed for a much wider range of coupling behaviors because marriage officiates were scarce and even relatively low fees for marriage licenses might be cost prohibitive to many poorer couples. Thus, self-marriage, or informal marriage such as common-law relationships, were permissible and frequent occurrences. Common-law marriage had the added advantage of easy self-divorce. Premarital sex and bigamy were also more frequent and more tolerated, especially in the less densely populated rural south. As Nancy Cott observes, local practices could differ significantly, but there was a sense that coupling depended on mutual consent rather than official state recognition.[2]

This more casual approach to marriage was soon to change as state legislators and courts began to regulate marriage with greater force. These changes included new postrevolutionary divorce laws and a series of legislations revising coverture. After the revolution, many Americans applied the rhetoric of escaping tyranny to their unsatisfactory marriages. For instance, in her 1788 petition for divorce in Connecticut, Abigail Strong argued that her duty to obey her husband was ruptured by his insufferable abuse, as "even Kings may forfeit or discharge the allegiance of their subjects."[3] Many state legislators agreed and proceeded to outline the conditions under which divorce might be granted. Similarly, various states revised the legal assumptions of coverture inherited from British common law so that women could hold their own property as separate estates, make contracts that would enable them to buy and sell that property, and keep their own earnings.[4]

As various states redefined the terms and meanings of legal marriage within their borders, the federal government similarly sought to reform and regulate family structures, sexual relations, and forms of coupling in a wide variety of American Indian nations. Although there are significant differences between American Indian communities in terms of kin structures, clan responsibilities, and communal economic policies, Mark Rifkin observes how, taken collectively, these differences registered to most Americans as nonnormative and threatening.[5] Many policy makers argued that assimilating Native families into American-style monogamous, nuclear family households would best prepare Native peoples to accept US rule.

Among Cherokee peoples, for instance, Thomas Jefferson promoted major changes in traditional gender roles by encouraging Cherokee women to give up their customary agricultural work and adapt white women's roles as domestic regulators by taking up the spinning wheel. This "spinning wheel revolution," as Gregory Dowd terms it, had considerable and intentional ripple effects in this matrilineal community. Many households adapted patriarchal male heads, which shifted matrilineal property inheritances and led to a revaluing of women's roles and work, eventually decreasing women's traditional participation in public assemblies.[6] US policy makers envisioned vast Cherokee hunting territories opened to white settlers once Cherokee families learned subsistence farming on smaller tracts of land. In conjunction with local missionary groups and boarding schools, these policies worked to effect culture change on multiple fronts.

Later policies such as the Dawes Act of 1887 (also known as the Allotment Act) intentionally broke up collective tribal-land ownership and nonnuclear households, forcing a redistribution of reservation properties to private households, typically reorganized with male heads of household and new patronymic surnames. These new domestic arrangements and property regulations introduced monogamous, patriarchal nuclear families as the basic requirement for "civilization."[7]

Decrying the destructive effects of slavery on African American marriage was one of the most effective rhetorical strategies deployed by US abolitionists. In this case, white slaveholders were responsible for enslaved peoples' supposed nonconformity with monogamous state-sanctioned marriage. Because enslaved persons were legally the property of their masters, they were denied the right to consent to marriage. Slave law proclaimed that enslaved people could have no will separate from a master's. When enslaved couples married informally, these marriages were often dismissed as nonbinding or contingent on the wishes of either partner's master. No enslaved couple could be sure that they would not be sold or redistributed as part of the splitting of an estate.[8] Although many enslaved persons were denied the right to marry, the reproduction of an enslaved labor force was crucial to the economic success of slavery, especially after 1808 when the United States banned the further importation of enslaved peoples. Formerly enslaved women spoke of forced "breeding" policies, concubinage, and the capitalist culture that quite literally thrived on their sexual assault. Still, many enslaved couples felt themselves deeply committed to one another. As Frances Smith Foster argues, the so-called legacy of broken African American families resulting from slavery ignores the testimony of runaway, freed, and emancipated enslaved persons who continually attest to deep marital bonds maintained in the face of slavery's traumas.[9] As the constitutional amendment to eliminate slavery moved forward, many legislators praised it precisely on marital grounds. Freedom would guarantee formerly enslaved peoples the legal right to consent to marry. Postemancipation reform efforts included policies to encourage freedpeople to adopt state-recognized forms of monogamous marriage; however, this task was complicated by many disrupted relationships and remarriages, an inevitable result of the vagaries of slavery.[10] These concerns were only exacerbated by attempts to legitimate the children of former slaves with multiple marriages. No standardized solution would easily resolve or erase the diversity of family structures that African Americans had necessarily and resourcefully developed during slavery.

The early Mormon Church's practice of polygamy proves yet another instance of US marital diversity contained by federal and state intervention. While only a small proportion of Latter-day Saints practiced polygamy, many antipolygamy reformers vehemently called for federal interposition to enforce a national standard of monogamy. The Morrill Bill of 1862 made bigamy a federal crime, but it proved difficult to enforce as polygamists could deny additional marriages and Mormon jurists were unlikely to convict fellow believers. In protests against the practice, many reform groups and politicians connected the Mormon system of plural wives with racially marginalized groups: "concubines voluntarily," "bound slaves," or "Indian squaws."[11] Such language polarized the practice of monogamy and polygamy along "civilized" and "barbaric" lines that drew directly from Enlightenment stadial theories linking the status of women to "progress" and "civilization" discussed in chapter 1. During the course of the nineteenth century, this metric of progress was itself racialized so that many white Christians equated civilization with whiteness itself.[12] The view of polygamy as a right guaranteed through religious freedom was officially overruled in 1878 when the United States Supreme Court determined in *Reynolds v. United States* that constitutional guarantees of religious freedom were restricted to beliefs only and did not protect actions in violation of the law. Nine years later, the Church of Jesus Christ of Latter-day Saints overturned its public support of polygamy when legal suits against the Edmunds-Tucker Act, which repealed the church's act of incorporation and threatened to seize the church's property, failed. In September 1890, the church publicly advised its members to avoid marriages "forbidden by the law of the land."[13] The legal showdown over polygamy demonstrates how marriage is far from a private or natural relation; as Nancy Cott argues, marriage is primarily a "political creation" subject to change and interpretation.[14]

The histories of marital diversity contained in this study matter in our own moment because they demonstrate that marriages can be quite flexible arrangements with multiple legal, familial, and economic meanings. Recalling the historical flexibility and multiplicity of styles and meanings that marriage has been able to encompass proves not only a valuable but also a timely project. In November 2013, my home state of Illinois passed the Religious Freedom and Marriage Fairness Bill formally licensing and recognizing same-sex marriages. For many same-sex couples, the marital relation conveys significant, tangible benefits: rights to attend a sick or dying spouse in the hospital, tax benefits, spousal inheritance rights, and so on. Marriage also offers many same-sex couples equal access to the powerful mythology of the marriage plot, with all its promises of personal happiness, relationship stability, and respectability. This mythology is what Rachel Brownstein describes as the opportunity for a "finished identity" or for what Joseph Allen Boone understands as the relationship goal that defines a "fully experienced life."[15] Arguably, access to this shared ideal of marriage, with its rhetoric of stability and completeness, is just as important for many same-sex couples as hospital visitation rights. As one same-sex-marriage activist group argues, "Marriage says 'we are family' in a way that no other word does."[16] Although new legislation and court decisions are quickly changing available data, at the time of this writing, thirty-five states as well as the District of Columbia and some counties in Missouri allow same-sex marriage, although those promarriage rulings are now under appeal. In April 2015, the United States Supreme Court is slated to take up several same-sex marriage cases. A favorable ruling could ensure access to marriage for same-sex couples nationwide. In Illinois, the rapid transformation in public opinion on this matter suggests that in recent years more Illinoisans agree that marriage—a relation that conveys specific legal benefits as well as an archetype of the "finished" self—should be equally available to all.[17]

I support same-sex marriage as a civil right and I believe that anyone who wants to marry should have the right to do so. Still, I wonder if we might also be missing a historic opportunity to rethink marriage and our cultural privileging of the couple, straight or gay. As more Americans take up the work of extending marriage rights to same-sex couples, we should understand that marriage is fundamentally a discriminating category. It offers privileges to those who agree to its terms while denying those same benefits to all those who do not live in a state-sanctioned, ostensibly permanent coupling. As queer and feminist critics of the same-sex marriage movement, such as Michael Warner, Nicola Barker, Nancy Polikoff, and the Beyond Marriage movement, have argued, same-sex marriage continues to exclude many nontraditional households and family structures from the benefits that same-sex married couples seek.[18] One solution, recommended in a report titled *Beyond Conjugality* by the Law Commission of Canada, is to distribute the legal benefits of marriage such as inheritance rights, health insurance, and lower rates for a host of services across a diversity of adult relationships, including nonconjugal house-holds of both relatives and nonrelatives.[19] In practice, all households rais-ing children should receive the same benefits that married couples with children now receive. Moreover, households comprised of nonrelatives such as a collective of senior citizens living together might also benefit by extending certain privileges now conferred only to the married, such as designating other persons in their collective household as responsible and duly able to make health-care decisions for them as necessary. As the Law Commission of Canada's report suggests, the state should "remain neutral with regard to the form or status of relationships and not accord one form of relationship more benefits or legal support than others."[20] As Suzanna Danutta Walters urges, "Let's not imagine that this [same-sex marriage] is all we can imagine."[21]

Rather than insisting that same-sex couples share the "same love," as Grammy award–winning hip-hop rapper Macklemore asserts in his crit-ically acclaimed 2013 hit, we might focus instead on making it easier for all persons, single or married, to live the lives they choose—whether that love looks the "same" or not.[22] In short, we ought not to lose sight of what is gained when we compare structures for coupling and domestic arrangements with the aim of recognizing all families. We are not limited to conferring privilege on the married, gay or straight. Focusing on the rights of households, rather than marriage, accommodates a range of couples, singles, and blood-related and nonfamilial household dynamics and economic structures.

Anglophone novelists in the late eighteenth and early nineteenth cen-turies used a comparative strategy of recognizing and evaluating marital diversity in order to achieve critical insights on the new trend toward companionate marriage. Recognizing the value of assessing cultural dif-ferences, these novelists created fictional worlds that plumbed, rather than effaced, significant alternatives to companionate marriage. We, too, should explore what individuals from all walks of life stand to gain from "New Worlds" of domestic arrangements. I hope this book contributes some historical contexts for long-standing comparative analyses of alter-native forms of courtship, marriage, and family making.

NOTES

Introduction

1. Ian Watt argues that the eighteenth-century English novel underwent a dramatic shift as it moved from previously episodic plots to focus on a single event, courtship. In return, the novel "supplies [love] with its doctrines and rituals." See Watt, *The Rise of the Novel: Studies in Defoe, Richardson, and Fielding* (Berkeley: University of California Press, 1964), 135–36. Other studies of romantic love and the marriage plot include: Leslie Fiedler, *Love and Death in the American Novel* (Champaign, IL: Dalkey Archive Press, 2003); Evelyn J. Hinz, "Hierogamy versus Wedlock: Types of Marriage Plots and Their Relationships to Genres of Prose Fiction," *PMLA* 91 (1976): 900–913; Nina Baym, *Woman's Fiction: A Guide to Novels by and about Women in America, 1820–1870* (Ithaca, NY: Cornell University Press, 1978); Tony Tanner, *Adultery in the Novel: Contract and Transgression* (Baltimore: Johns Hopkins University Press, 1979); Nancy K. Miller, *The Heroine's Text: Readings in the French and English Novel, 1722–1782* (New York: Columbia University Press, 1980); Nancy Armstrong, *Desire and Domestic Fiction: A Political History of the Novel* (New York: Oxford University Press, 1987); Katherine Sobba Green, *The Courtship Novel, 1740–1820* (Lexington: University Press of Kentucky, 1991). More recent studies question the centrality of the canonical Austen-style marriage plot: Ruth Perry, *Novel Relations: The Transformation of Kinship in English Literature and Culture, 1748–1818* (Cambridge: Cambridge University Press, 2004); Jennifer Golightly, *The Family, Marriage, and Radicalism in British Women's Novels of the 1790s* (Lewisburg, PA: Bucknell University Press, 2012).

2. This and the previous quote are taken from Jeffrey Eugenides, Interview for audiobook, *The Marriage Plot* (New York: Macmillan Audio, 2011). For an update of this line of feminist critique, see Susan Ostrov Weisser, *The Glass Slipper: Women and Love Stories* (New Brunswick, NJ: Rutgers University Press, 2013).

3. Although the collection does not focus on comparative marriage plots, Toni Bowers and Tita Chico address related themes in *Atlantic Worlds in the Long Eighteenth Century: Seduction and Sentiment* (New York: Palgrave Macmillan, 2012).

4. Niklas Luhmann, *Love as Passion: The Codification of Intimacy*, trans. Jeremy Gaines and Doris L. Jones (Stanford, CA: Stanford University Press, 1998); Niklas Luhmann, *Love: A Sketch*, ed. Andre Kieserling, trans. Kathleen Cross (Malden, MA: Polity Press, 2010).

5. Edmund Leites, *The Puritan Conscience and Modern Sexuality* (New Haven,

CT: Yale University Press, 1986), 92–100. Amanda Porterfield outlines the debate about whether companionate marriage was beneficial to Puritan women in *Female Piety in Puritan New England: The Emergence of Religious Humanism* (New York: Oxford University Press, 1992). Edmund Sears Morgan describes the Puritan's faith relationship to the church as a marital one in "The Puritan's Marriage with God," *South Atlantic Quarterly* 49 (1949): 107–12. On friendship in American literature, see Ivy Schweitzer, *Perfecting Friendship: Politics and Affiliation in Early American Literature* (Chapel Hill: University of North Carolina Press, 2006).

6. Lawrence Stone, *The Family, Sex and Marriage in England, 1500–1800* (New York: Harper and Row, 1977). Alan Macfarlane dates this freedom to choose one's marriage partner independent of family interference much earlier than Stone; indeed, his argument describes English individualism occurring earlier than the rest of Europe: Alan Macfarlane, *The Origins of English Individualism: The Family, Property, and Social Transition* (London: Blackwell, 1978). For slightly later and specifically US studies of courtship, see Ellen K. Rothman, *Hands and Hearts: A History of Courtship in America* (New York: Basic Books, 1984); Karen Lystra, *Searching the Heart: Women, Men, and Romantic Love in Nineteenth-Century America* (New York: Oxford University Press, 1992). For a general history of marriage, see Stephanie Coontz, *Marriage, a History: How Love Conquered Marriage* (New York: Penguin, 2005); Elizabeth Abbott, *A History of Marriage: From Same Sex Unions to Private Vows and Common Law, the Surprising Diversity of a Tradition* (New York: Penguin, 2010).

7. Lawrence Stone's thesis—that during the eighteenth century companionate marriage replaced older models of familial alliance through marriage—has been challenged by historians and literary critics alike. In literary studies, see esp. Armstrong, *Desire and Domestic Fiction;* Eve Tavor Bannet, *The Domestic Revolution: Enlightenment Feminism and the Novel* (Baltimore: Johns Hopkins University Press, 2000); Joseph Allen Boone, *Tradition Counter Tradition: Love and the Form of Fiction* (Chicago: University of Chicago Press, 1987); Christopher Flint, *Family Fictions: Narrative and Domestic Relations in Britain, 1688–1798* (Stanford, CA: Stanford University Press, 2000); and Perry, *Novel Relations.* Several historians have critiqued Stone's claims: E. P. Thompson, "Happy Families," *Radical History Review* 20 (1979): 42–50; Susan Moller Okin, "Women and the Making of the Sentimental Family," *Philosophy and Public Affairs* 11, no. 1 (1982): 65–88; Alan Macfarlane, *Marriage and Love in England: Modes of Reproduction, 1300–1840* (New York: Blackwell Publishers, 1986); Amanda Vickery, *The Gentleman's Daughter: Women's Lives in Georgian England* (New Haven, CT: Yale University Press, 1998). Other classic histories of the British family include Randolph Trumbach, *The Rise of the Egalitarian Family: Aristocratic Kinship and Domestic Relations in Eighteenth-Century England* (New York: Academic Press, 1978); John R. Gillis, *For Better or Worse: British Marriages, 1600 to the Present* (New York: Oxford University Press, 1985). Beyond Britain, see Abbott, *History of Marriage;* Coontz, *Marriage, a History;* Nancy Cott, *Public Vows: A History of Marriage and the Nation* (Cambridge, MA: Harvard University Press, 2000).

8. Coontz, *Marriage, a History,* 146.

9. Susan Staves, *Players' Scepters: Fictions of Authority in the Restoration* (Lincoln: University of Nebraska Press, 1970).

10. Coontz, *Marriage, a History,* 154–56.

11. Jürgen Habermas, *Structural Transformation of the Public Sphere* (Cambridge, MA: MIT Press, 1989). Although many critics of this position exist, see esp. Elizabeth Maddock Dillon, *The Gender of Freedom: Fictions of Liberalism and the Literary Public Sphere* (Stanford, CA: Stanford University Press, 2004); Cathy N. Davidson and Jessamyn Hatcher, eds., *No More Separate Spheres! A Next Wave American Studies Reader* (Durham, NC: Duke University Press, 2002).

12. Stone, *Family, Sex and Marriage,* 165; Watt, *Rise of the Novel,* 138.

13. Judith Roof, *Come as You Are: Sexuality and Narrative* (New York: Columbia University Press, 1996), 214.

14. See, for instance Winfried Fluck, Donald E. Pease, and John Carlos Rowe, eds., *Re-Framing the Transnational Turn in American Studies* (Lebanon, NH: Dartmouth College Press, 2011); Paul Giles, *The Global Remapping of American Literature* (Princeton, NJ: Princeton University Press, 2011); Donald Pease and Robyn Wiegman, eds., *The Futures of American Studies* (Durham, NC: Duke University Press, 2002); Paul Giles, *Virtual Americas: Transnational Fictions and the Transatlantic Literary Imagination* (Durham, NC: Duke University Press, 2002).

15. Susan Stanford Friedman, *Mappings: Feminism and the Cultural Geographies of Encounter* (Princeton, NJ: Princeton University Press, 1998), 5.

16. Shulamith Firestone, *The Dialectic of Sex: The Case for Feminist Revolution* (New York: Farrar, Straus and Giroux, 2003), 113.

17. Firestone, *Dialectic of Sex,* 119, 131.

18. Anna G. Jónasdóttir, "Feminist Questions, Marx's Method and the Theorisation of 'Love Power,'" in *The Political Interests of Gender Revisited: Redoing Theory and Research with a Feminist Face,* eds. Anna G. Jónasdóttir and Kathleen B. Jones (Tokyo: United Nations University Press, 2009), 62.

19. For instance, see Tania Modleski, *Loving with a Vengeance: Mass-Produced Fantasies for Women* (New York: Routledge, 1990); Janice Radway, *Reading the Romance: Women, Patriarchy, and Popular Literature* (Chapel Hill: University of North Carolina Press, 1984).

20. See Weisser, *Glass Slipper;* Perry, *Novel Relations;* Rachel Brownstein, *Becoming a Heroine: Reading about Women in Novels* (New York: Columbia University Press, 1994); Susan Fraiman, *Unbecoming Women: British Women Writers and the Novel of Development* (New York: Columbia University Press, 1993); Boone, *Tradition Counter Tradition;* Armstrong, *Desire and Domestic Fiction;* Ruth Bernard Yeazell, *Fictions of Modesty: Women and Courtship in the English Novel* (Chicago: University of Chicago Press, 1991); Green, *Courtship Novel;* Miller, *Heroine's Text;* Baym, *Woman's Fiction;* Hinz, "Hierogamy versus Wedlock."

21. Boone, *Tradition Counter Tradition,* 8.

22. Armstrong, *Desire and Domestic Fiction,* 4.

23. Anne DuCille, *The Coupling Convention: Sex, Text, and Tradition in Black Women's Fiction* (New York: Oxford University Press, 1993); see also Belinda Edmondson, "The Black Romance," *Women's Studies Quarterly* 35, no. 1–2 (2007): 191–211.

24. Rachel Blau DuPlessis, *Writing beyond the Ending: Narrative Strategies of Twentieth-Century Women Writers* (Bloomington: Indiana University Press, 1985);

Diana Swanson applies this argument toward women's friendships and possible les-
bian alliances in "Subverting Closure: Compulsory Heterosexuality and Compulsory
Endings in Middle-Class British Women's Novels," in *Sexual Practice, Textual Theory:
Lesbian Cultural Criticism*, ed. Susan J. Wolfe and Julia Penelope (Cambridge, MA:
Blackwell Publishers, 1993), 150–63.

25. Brownstein, *Becoming a Heroine*, xxi, xxiv.

26. Dillon, *Gender of Freedom*; Helen Thompson, *Ingenuous Subjection: Compliance and Power in the Eighteenth-Century Domestic Novel* (Philadelphia: University
of Pennsylvania Press, 2005).

27. For more on enslaved marriages, see Tess Chakkalakal, *Novel Bondage: Slavery, Marriage, and Freedom in Nineteenth-Century America* (Urbana: University of
Illinois Press, 2011); Cott, *Public Vows*; Jennifer L. Morgan, *Laboring Women: Reproduction and Gender in New World Slavery* (Philadelphia: University of Pennsylvania
Press, 2004); Frances Smith Foster, *'Til Death or Distance Do Us Part: Love and Marriage in African America* (New York: Oxford University Press, 2010).

28. See Sharon Harrow, *Adventures in Domesticity: Gender and Colonial Adulteration in Eighteenth-Century British Literature* (New York: AMS Press, 2004).

29. *Hobomok* was not Child's only comparative work; widely read nonfiction such
as *The History of the Condition of Women, in Various Ages and Nations* (1835) and
The Progress of Religious Ideas through Successive Ages (1855) similarly operate in
a comparative frame. Child was a Unitarian and her religious tolerance and liberal
political beliefs led her to publicly advocate for abolitionism, women's suffrage, and
American Indian rights, among other causes. Child's cultural and literary influences
run deep. She published more than fifty books and wrote and edited foundational
children's texts, as well as writing numerous poems, short stories, and newspaper articles. See esp. Carolyn Karcher, "Introduction," in *Hobomok and Other Writings on
Indians* (New Brunswick, NJ: Rutgers University Press, 1986); Carolyn Karcher, *The
First Woman in the Republic: A Cultural Biography of Lydia Maria Child* (Durham,
NC: Duke University Press, 1994).

30. On *Hobomok*, see esp. Harry Brown, "'The Horrid Alternative': Miscegena-
tion and Madness in the Frontier Romance," *Journal of American and Comparative
Cultures* 24, no. 3–4 (2001): 137–51; Karcher, "Introduction"; Lucy Maddox, "Amer-
ican Indians, Civilized Performance, and Civil Rights," *European Contributions to
American Studies* 57 (2004): 53–59; Ezra Tawil, "Domestic Frontier Romance, or,
How the Sentimental Heroine Became White," *Novel: A Forum on Fiction* 32, no. 1
(1998): 99–124. On vanishing Indian rhetoric, see Jonathan Elmer, *On Lingering and
Being Last: Race and Sovereignty in the New World* (New York: Fordham University
Press, 2008); Brian W. Dippie, *The Vanishing American: White Attitudes and U.S.
Indian Policy* (Middletown, CT: Wesleyan University Press, 1982).

31. See Mark Rifkin, *When Did Indians Become Straight? Kinship, the History
of Sexuality, and Native Sovereignty* (New York: Oxford University Press, 2011), 8. I
would not position Child's efforts in the same arena as contemporary Native writers'
work; however, her attempts to locate appropriate ethnographic details demonstrate
how she values a closer approximation of Native traditions over period stereotypes.

32. For instance, Mr. Higginson notes in his sermon that "the threshold of hell is

paved with toleration." Lydia Maria Child, *Hobomok and Other Writings on Indians*, ed. Carolyn L. Karcher (New Brunswick, NJ: Rutgers University Press, 1986), 65. See Karcher's helpful notes identifying historic personages and events throughout, but especially how Child previews the Antinomian controversy and Anne Hutchinson's expulsion: chap. 8, p. 304, n. 2.

33. Baron de Lahontan, Louis Armand de Lom d'Arce, *Mémoires de l'Amérique Septentrionale ou la Suite des Voyages de Mr. Le Baron de Lahontan*, vol. 2, tome second (The Hague: Chez les Frères l'Honoré Marchands Librairies, 1703), image on p. 133. The standard English edition is Baron de Lahontan, *New Voyages to North America*, ed. Reuben Gold Thwaites (Chicago: A. C. McClurg, 1905). Although she does not name her source, Child draws even more obviously from Lahontan in her chapter on American Indian women in *History of the Condition of Women* (1835), which is excerpted in Karcher's edition of *Hobomok*, 171–72.

34. Lahontan's reports of Wendat marriage practices are confirmed by Jesuit missionary reports gathered in Karen Anderson, *Chain Her By One Foot: The Subjugation of Native Women in Seventeenth-Century New France* (New York: Routledge, 1991), esp. chaps. 6–7.

35. This and the preceding quotes appear in Child, *Hobomok*, 124–25.

36. The definitive study is Ann Marie Plane, *Colonial Intimacies: Indian Marriage in Early New England* (Ithaca, NY: Cornell University Press, 2002). Plane includes no archival documents describing traditional Native marriage practices in the New England area. This fact corroborates my own sense that, in the absence of primary documentation on the Wampanoag, Child turned to Lahonton's book, the most richly detailed source available on colonial-era Native wedding ceremonies.

37. Child's revisionist history is most visible in her children's book *The First Settlers of New England: The Conquest of the Pequods and Narragansetts and Pokanokets as Related by a Mother to Her Child* (1829) where she reads primary-source historical documents from New England for their "conquest" story—a move echoing Washington Irving's "Philip of Pokanoket" (1819) and later redeployed by William Apess in *Eulogy on King Philip* (1836).

38. William Wood, *New England's Prospect* (London: Thomas Cotes for John Bellamie, 1634; repr., Boston: John Wilson and Son, 1865), 109.

39. David D. Smits, "The 'Squaw Drudge': A Prime Index of Savagism," *Ethnohistory* 29, no. 4 (1982): 281–306.

40. Baron de Lahontan, "A Conference or Dialogue between the Author and Adario, a Noted Man among the Savages, Containing a Circumstantial View of the Customs and Humors of That People," in *New Voyages to North America*, ed. Reuben Gold Thwaites (Chicago: A. C. McClurg, 1905), 2:605.

41. On the legal status of the feme covert, see Nancy Cott, "Marriage and Women's Citizenship in the United States, 1830–1934," *American Historical Review* 103, no. 5 (1998): 1440–74.

42. According to reports in the *Jesuit Relations*, there was considerable reluctance among the Wendat to convert because of the lack of divorce in Catholic theology. The "indissolubility of marriage," wrote the Jesuit missionary Father Le Jeune in 1633, was one of "the most serious obstacles in the progress of the Gospel," and one finds

the problem of divorce a continuous theme in missionary accounts among the Wendat. Rubin Gold Thwaites, *The Jesuit Relations and Allied Documents* (Cleveland, OH: Burrows Brothers, 1896–1901), 10:63; Anderson, *Chain Her By One Foot*, 76–77 and 115.

43. Child, *Hobomok*, 146.

44. Boone, *Tradition Counter Tradition*, 6.

45. Freedom to Marry, Inc., "Freedom to Marry," accessed January 21, 2014, http://www.freedomtomarry.org/.

46. Freedom to Marry, Inc., "Why Marriage Matters," accessed January 21, 2014, http://www.whymarriagematters.org/.

1. Why Marriage Mattered Then

1. R. Radhakrishnan, "Why Compare?," *New Literary History* 40, no. 3 (Summer 2009): 455.

2. Lisa O'Connell, "'Matrimonial Ceremonies Displayed': Popular Ethnography and Enlightened Imperialism," *Eighteenth-Century Life* 26, no. 3 (Fall 2002): 98–116.

3. Much has been written on the emergence of the nation-state; Anderson remains a useful starting point: Benedict Anderson, *Imagined Communities: Reflections on the Origin and Spread of Nationalism* (New York: Verso, 1991).

4. For more on the relation of the marriage-rites genre to the Marriage Act of 1753, see O'Connell, "'Matrimonial Ceremonies Displayed,'" 98–116.

5. "Uxorious," *Hymen: An Accurate Description of the Ceremonies Used in Marriage, by Every Nation in the Known World. Shewing, the Oddity of Some, the Absurdity of Others, the Drollery of Many, and the Real or Intended Piety of All* (London: I. Pottinger, 1760), accessed July 1, 2014, http://books.google.com/books/reader?id=JIDAAAAQAAJ&printsec=frontcover&output=reader&pg=GBS.PR1.

6. "Uxorious," *Hymen*, 64, 66.

7. Ibid., 179, 223.

8. Ibid., 166, 175.

9. Ibid., vi, viii–ix.

10. William Alexander, *The History of Women* (London: W. Strahan and T. Cadell, 1779; repr. New York: AMS Press, 1976), 111. Although Alexander's singular focus on women's history makes his comparative work noteworthy, his text is largely a compilation of others' theories prepared for a lay audience of women readers; he is especially indebted to the work of John Millar. Jane Rendall questions how many women actually read Alexander's work in "Clio, Mars, and Minerva: The Scottish Enlightenment and the Writing of Women's History," in *Eighteenth-Century Scotland: New Perspectives*, ed. Thomas M. Devine and John R. Young (East Lothian, Scotland: Tuckwell Press, 1999), 134–51. Sylvana Tomaselli asks why women weren't writing conjectural histories even though these texts do enable discussions of women's participation in civilization in "Civilization, Patriotism, and Enlightened Histories of Woman," in *Women, Gender, and Enlightenment*, ed. Sarah Knott and Barbara Taylor (Basingstoke: Palgrave MacMillan, 2005), 117–35.

11. Gayatri Spivack demonstrates how colonizers excused their colonizing actions by claiming that "white men are saving brown women from brown men" in "Can the

Subaltern Speak?" in *Marxism and the Interpretation of Culture*, ed. Cary Nelson and Lawrence Grossberg (Urbana: University of Illinois Press, 1988), 271–313.

12. Versions of this theory appear in Adam Smith's work as well as in the work of William Robertson, Lord Kames, John Millar, and others. However, Smith did not publish his four-stages theory during his lifetime; it was transmitted through students' notes from his University of Glasgow lectures. See Adam Smith, *Lectures on Jurisprudence*, in *The Glasgow Edition of the Works and Correspondence of Adam Smith*, ed. Ronald L. Meek, D. D. Raphael, and Peter Stein, vol. 5 (Oxford: Clarendon Press, 1978). See also Gladys Bryson, *Man and Society: The Scottish Inquiry of the Eighteenth Century* (Princeton, NJ: Princeton University Press, 1945); N. T. Phillipson and Rosalind Mitchison, *Scotland in the Age of Improvement; Essays in Scottish History in the Eighteenth Century* (Edinburgh: Edinburgh University Press, 1970); Ronald Meek, *Social Science and the Ignoble Savage* (Cambridge: Cambridge University Press, 1976); Jane Rendall, ed., *The Origins of the Scottish Enlightenment, 1707–1776* (Basingstoke: Macmillan, 1978); R. H. Campbell and Andrew S. Skinner, eds., *The Origins and Nature of the Scottish Enlightenment* (Edinburgh: John Donald Publishers, 1982); J. G. A. Pocock, *Virtue, Commerce, and History: Essays on Political Thought and History, Chiefly in the Eighteenth Century* (Cambridge: Cambridge University Press, 1985); John Dwyer, *The Age of Passions: An Interpretation of Adam Smith and Scottish Enlightenment Culture* (East Lothian, Scotland: Tuckwell Press, 1998); Stuart Brown, *British Philosophy and the Age of Enlightenment*, vol. 5 of *Routledge History of Philosophy*, ed. G. H. R. Parkinson and S. G. Shanker (London: Routledge, 2003). On progress, see David Spadafora, *The Idea of Progress in Eighteenth-Century Britain* (New Haven, CT: Yale University Press, 1990).

13. Alexander, *History of Women*, 111. For a useful overview of the connection between companionate marriage and the national good, see Mary Catherine Moran, "The Commerce of the Sexes: Gender and the Social Sphere in Scottish Enlightenment Accounts of Civil Society," in *Paradoxes of Civil Society: New Perspectives on Modern German and British History*, ed. Frank Trentmann (New York: Berghahn Books, 2000), 61–85.

14. John Millar, *The Origin of the Distinction of Ranks; or, An Inquiry into the Circumstances Which Give Rise to Influence and Authority, in the Different Members of Society* (Indianapolis: Liberty Fund, 2006).

15. Carol Pateman, *The Sexual Contract* (Stanford, CA: Stanford University Press, 1988).

16. Bowles argues for Millar's genuine curiosity about the status of women in various countries and historical periods, expressly resisting ideological readings of Millar and Scottish Enlightenment history as prescriptive—that is, imposing its normative values on other cultures. The difficulty with this argument, of course, is that it allows Millar's theory to remain scientifically neutral, naïvely glossing over Millar's rhetorical attempts to manage and control the category of women. Bowles's claim for Millar's neutrality proves especially troubling because it erases Millar's attempts to manage the ideological implications of Haudenosaunee (Iroquois) women's authority: see Paul Bowles, "John Millar, the Four-Stages Theory, and Women's Position in Society," *History of Political Economy* 16, no. 4 (1984): 619–38.

17. Rifkin makes an argument for the ways that indigenous kin systems defamiliarize or "queer" Western familial structures in *When Did Indians Become Straight?*

18. Millar, *Origin of the Distinction of Ranks,* 114.

19. Ibid., 95, 98.

20. This argument surprisingly mirrors Niklas Luhmann's more recent theory that mutual recognition is a central process in selecting a romantic partner: Luhmann, *Love as Passion,* 12; Millar, *Origin of the Distinction of Ranks,* 124.

21. Millar, *Origin of the Distinction of Ranks,* 137, 142.

22. Millar's colleague Gilbert Stuart argues, in contrast, that northern Europeans had never treated women the way "savages" supposedly did. Using the poems of Ossian as evidence of the more chivalric and gallant behavior of Highland men toward their women, Stuart plots a different schema for progress in the Germanic and Celtic regions. See Stuart, *A View of Society in Europe, in Its Progress from Rudeness to Refinement* (Edinburgh: Bell, 1778).

23. Millar, *Origin of the Distinction of Ranks,* 124.

24. Ibid., 107.

25. Smits, "The 'Squaw Drudge.'"

26. Millar, *Origin of the Distinction of Ranks,* 110.

27. Some restrictions between the sexes were beneficial, in Millar's view, as too much heterosocial contact could lead to disrespect of women.

28. Millar, *Origin of the Distinction of Ranks,* 144.

29. Ibid., 145.

30. Nancy Armstrong's thesis that conduct books and fiction educated women to find pleasure in the domestic ideal is especially relevant here. See Armstrong, *Desire and Domestic Fiction,* esp. chap. 2.

31. In the late eighteenth century, Mary Wollstonecraft critiqued this species of male gallantry in her *Vindications of the Rights of Woman.* She advocated friendship over romantic love as the true basis of a companionate marriage. According to Barbara Taylor, Wollstonecraft believed that "gallantry was politeness's nastiest manifestation, substituting 'insolent condescension' for true respect and fellow-feeling." See Taylor, "Feminists Versus Gallants: Sexual Manners and Morals in Enlightenment Britain," in *Women, Gender, and Enlightenment,* ed. Sarah Knott and Barbara Taylor (Basingstoke: Palgrave MacMillan, 2005), 43.

32. Millar, *Origin of the Distinction of Ranks,* 144, emphasis added.

33. Anticipating Friedrich Engels's *The Origin of the Family, Private Property, and the State* (1884), Millar argues that patriarchal relations between men and women were the foundation for increasingly complex relations of power—power that he would approve as civilization, but that Engels would critique as oppression. Both wrestled with Haudenosaunee gender traditions as complicating evidence.

34. Millar, *Origin of the Distinction of Ranks,* 117.

35. Ibid., 119, 121.

36. Ibid., 119.

37. Thomas Jefferson makes the circuitous claim that "were we [Europeans and Euro-American colonists] in equal barbarism [with the Indians], our females would be equal drudges." Furthermore, he notes, "It is civilization alone which replaces women

in the enjoyment of their natural equality" in *Notes on the State of Virginia* (Chapel Hill: University of North Carolina Press, 1982), 60.

38. Millar, *Origin of the Distinction of Ranks*, 120.

39. For additional studies of *The Female American*, see Tremaine McDowell, "An American Robinson Crusoe," *American Literature* 3 (1929): 307–9; Betty Joseph, "Re(Playing) Crusoe/Pocahontas: Circum-Atlantic Stagings in *The Female American*," *Criticism* 42, no. 3 (2000): 317–35; Keely Susan Kulman, "Transatlantic Travel and Cultural Exchange in the Early Colonial Era: The Hybrid *American Female* and Her New World Colony" (PhD diss., Washington State University, 2006); Stephen Carl Arch, "The Female American; The Interesting Narrative of the Life of Olaudah Equiano," *Eighteenth-Century Fiction* 14, no. 2 (2002): 240–43; Darlene Everhart, "Accounting and Authorship in Eighteenth-Century Island Narratives" (PhD diss., Carnegie Mellon University, 2009); Matthew Reilly, "'No Eye Has Seen, or Ear Heard': Arabic Sources for Quaker Subjectivity in Unca Eliza Winkfield's *The Female American*," *Eighteenth-Century Studies* 44, no. 2 (2011): 261–83; Laura Stevens, "Reading the Hermit's Manuscript: The Female American and Female Robinsonades," in *Approaches to Teaching Defoe's Robinson Crusoe*, ed. Maximillian Novak and Carl Fisher (New York: MLA, 2005), 140–51; Mary Helen McMurran, "Realism and the Unreal in *The Female American*," *Eighteenth-Century: Theory and Interpretation* 52, no. 3–4 (2011): 323–42; Kristianne Kalata Vaccaro, "'Recollection . . . sets my busy imagination to work': Transatlantic Self-Narration, Performance, and Reception in *The Female American*," *Eighteenth-Century Fiction* 20, no. 2 (2008): 127–50; Adrienne Duvall, "The Ethics of Enterprise: Imagining Colonization in Eighteenth-Century Novels of Colonial Encounter" (PhD diss., University of Oregon, 2008); Janina Nordius, "'Thus Might I Reason with a Heathen . . . ': The Gothic Moment in *The Female American*," *Nordic Journal of English Studies* 7, no. 2 (2008): 1–18; Stephen Wolfe, "Unifying Misnomers: Unca Eliza Winkfield's *The Female American*," *American Studies in Scandinavia* 36, no. 2 (2004): 17–34; Scarlet Bowen, "Via Media: Transatlantic Anglicanism in *The Female American*," *Eighteenth-Century: Theory and Interpretation* 53, no. 2 (2012): 189–207.

40. DuPlessis, *Writing beyond the Ending*.

41. *The Female American; or, The Adventures of Unca Eliza Winkfield* (Petersborough, ON: Broadview, 2001), 35.

42. Ibid., 49.

43. Jonathan Elmer illustrates how rank overrules race in what he calls "the Oroonoko effect": see Elmer, *On Lingering and Being Last*, esp. chap. 1.

44. *Female American*, 50, 51.

45. Quoted in *Female American*, app. A, p. 168. On American nature writing and scientific discovery, see Susan Scott Parrish, *American Curiosity: Cultures of Natural History in the Colonial British Atlantic World* (Chapel Hill: University of North Carolina Press, 2006).

46. Laura Stevens explores the way that missionary groups represented indigenous Americans as in need of rescue spiritually, physically, mentally, and culturally in *The Poor Indians: British Missionaries, Native Americans, and Colonial Sensibility* (Philadelphia: University of Pennsylvania Press, 2004).

47. *Female American*, 110.

48. Ibid., 111–12.

49. On the intersections of Native American and early American oratory, see Sandra M. Gustafson, *Eloquence Is Power: Oratory and Performance in Early America* (Chapel Hill: University of North Carolina Press, 2000).

50. *Female American*, 122, 123.

51. Ibid., 137, 139, 141.

52. I imagine something akin to the theory of Native resistance in the "aiding" of settlement that Anna Brickhouse terms "unsettlement": see Brickhouse, *The Unsettlement of America: Translation, Interpretation, and the Story of Don Luis de Velasco, 1560–1945* (New York: Oxford University Press, 2014).

53. "Uxorious," *Hymen*, viii–ix.

54. *Female American*, 35.

2. *Comparing Rights, Comparing Stories*

1. Sally Roesch Wagner, *Sisters in Spirit: The Haudenosaunee (Iroquois) Influence on Early American Feminists* (Summertown, TN: Book, 2001), 32.

2. Ibid., 28.

3. Abigail Adams, "Letter from Abigail Adams to John Adams, March 31, 1776," in *The Letters of John and Abigail Adams*, ed. Frank Shuffleton (New York: Penguin Classics, 2004), 147–49.

4. Matilda Joslyn Gage, *Women, Church, and State* (Watertown, MA: Persephone Press, 1980), 246. Quoted in Sally Roesch Wagner, "The Root of Oppression Is the Loss of Memory: The Iroquois and the Early Feminist Vision," in *Iroquois Women: An Anthology*, ed. W. G. Spittal (Ohsweken, ON: Iroqrafts, 1990), 224.

5. Lorraine McMullen, *An Odd Attempt in a Woman: The Literary Life of Frances Brooke* (Vancouver: University of British Columbia Press, 1983).

6. Rifkin, *When Did Indians Become Straight?*, 7.

7. Frances Brooke, *The History of Emily Montague* (Toronto: McClelland and Stewart, 1995), 37, 38–39.

8. Thwaites, ed., *Jesuit Relations*. Karen Anderson notes that the Jesuits' only mention of Wendat women's role in political life was to remark that the clans were matrilineal. She makes the claim that Wendat clan mothers could choose chiefs based on the similarity of social organization between the Wendat and Haudenosaunee, backing this claim with reference to Lafitau. Overall, there is more historical evidence for claims of a "gynocracy" among the Haudenosaunee than the Wendat, although the systems may have been fairly similar. See Anderson, *Chain Her By One Foot*. I did not receive a reply to queries made at the Wendake reserve to confirm Wendat clan mothers' roles in the selection of chiefs.

9. Father Joseph-François Lafitau, *Customs of the American Indians Compared with the Customs of Primitive Times*, ed. William Fenton and Elizabeth Moore (Toronto: Champlain Society, 1977), esp. vol. 1, pp. 84–85.

10. Brooke, *Emily Montague*, 38.

11. Ibid., 59.

12. See Coontz, *Marriage, a History*; Nancy Cott, *The Bonds of Womanhood:*

"Woman's Sphere" in New England, 1780–1835 (New Haven, CT: Yale University Press, 1977). See also Cott, *Public Vows*.

13. It was not until 1993 that marital rape was finally recognized as a crime in all fifty United States.

14. Cathy Davidson, *Revolution and the Word: The Rise of the Novel in America* (New York: Oxford University Press, 1986), 123.

15. Following Lawrence Stone's claims that the rise of companionate marriage improved popular conceptions of and attitudes toward women, many historians have qualified and critiqued his claims. See note 7 in this book's introduction.

16. David Lemmings, "Marriage and the Law in the Eighteenth Century: Hardwicke's Marriage Act of 1753," *Historical Journal* 39 (1996): 339–60; Paul Langford, *Public Life and the Propertied Englishman, 1689–1798* (New York: Oxford University Press, 1991), 6–7; Paul Langford, *A Polite and Commercial People: England, 1727–1783* (New York: Oxford University Press, 1983), chap. 1.

17. The groups comprising the Wendat confederacy include the Attignawantan, Attigneenongnahac, Arendaronon, Tahontaenrat, and Ataronchronon. See Daniel K. Richter, *The Ordeal of the Longhouse: The People of the Iroquois League in the Era of European Colonization* (Chapel Hill: University of North Carolina Press, 1991); Jon Parmentar, *The Edge of the Woods: Iroquoia, 1534–1701* (East Lansing: Michigan State University Press, 2010).

18. Alan Taylor, "The Divided Ground: Upper Canada, New York, and the Iroquois Six Nations, 1783–1815," *Journal of the Early Republic* 22, no. 1 (2002): 55–75. These disputes continue even today at passport and security-checkpoint standoffs: see Audra Simpson, *Mohawk Interruptus: Political Life across the Borders of Settler States* (Durham, NC: Duke University Press, 2014).

19. Anderson argues that clan mothers appointed male clan leaders in *Chain Her By One Foot*, 107.

20. Lafitau, *Customs of the American Indians*, vol. 1, p. 69.

21. Spittal's volume is the best source for tracing this debate: W. G. Spittal, ed., *Iroquois Women: An Anthology* (Ohsweken, ON: Iroqrafts, 1990).

22. Elizabeth Tooker, "Women in Iroquois Society," in *Extending the Rafters: Interdisciplinary Approaches to Iroquoian Studies*, ed. Michael K. Foster, Jack Campisi, and Marianne Mithun (Albany: State University of New York Press, 1984), 113.

23. Nancy Shoemaker, "The Rise or Fall of Iroquois Women," *Journal of Women's History* 2, no. 3 (1991): 40.

24. Jan V. Noel, "Revisiting Gender in Iroquoia," in *Gender and Sexuality in Indigenous North America*, ed. Sandra Slater and Fay A. Yarbrough (Columbia: University of South Carolina Press, 2011), 59.

25. Roland Viau, *Femmes de personne: Sexes, genres, et pouvoirs en Iroquoisie ancienne* (Montreal: Boreal, 2000). Translated by and quoted in Noel, "Revisiting Gender in Iroquoia," 59.

26. Barbara Alice Mann, "'They Are the Soul of the Councils': The Iroquoian Model of Woman-Power," in *Societies of Peace: Matriarchies Past, Present, and Future*, ed. Heide Goettner-Abendroth (Toronto: Inanna Publications and Education, 2003), 60. The standard history of the Iroquois League is William Fenton, *The Great*

Law and the Longhouse: A Political History of the Iroquois Confederacy (Norman: University of Oklahoma Press, 1998).

27. Heide Goettner-Abendroth, ed., "Introduction," in *Societies of Peace: Matriarchies Past, Present, and Future* (Toronto: Inanna Publications and Education, 2003), 1.

28. Mann, "They Are the Soul," 61.

29. Tooker, "Women in Iroquois Society," 119.

30. On the eighteenth-century development of a recognizable separate-spheres doctrine, see Moran, "Commerce of the Sexes"; Rendall, "Clio, Mars, and Minerva"; Tomaselli, "Civilization, Patriotism, and Enlightened Histories"; Sylvana Tomaselli, "The Enlightenment Debate on Women," *History Workshop* 20 (1985): 101–24.

31. John Mohawk, "The Power of Seneca Women and the Legacy of Handsome Lake," in *Native Voices: American Indian Identity and Resistance*, ed. Richard A. Grounds, George E. Tinker, and David E. Wilkins (Lawrence: University of Kansas Press, 2003), 26.

32. Ibid., 28.

33. Judith K. Brown, "Economic Organization and the Position of Women among the Iroquois," *Ethnohistory* 17, no. 3–4 (1970): 151–67.

34. Tom Porter, *And Grandma Said . . . Iroquois Teachings as Passed Down through the Oral Tradition* (Bloomington, IN: Xlibris, 2008).

35. Thomas Proctor, "Narrative of the Journey of Col. Thomas Proctor to the Indians of the North-West," *Pennsylvania Archives* 4 (1876 [1791]), 551–622.

36. Richter, *Ordeal of the Longhouse;* Gordon M. Sayre, *Les Sauvages Americains: Representations of Native Americans in French and English Colonial Literature* (Chapel Hill: University of North Carolina Press, 1997).

37. For a persuasive account of the freedoms Haudenosaunee life offered Eunice Williams, see John Demos, *The Unredeemed Captive: A Family Story from Early America* (New York: Vintage Books, 1995). Mary Jemison's story is reprinted in James Seaver, "A Narrative of the Life of Mrs. Mary Jemison," in *Women's Indian Captivity Narratives*, ed. Kathryn Zabelle Derounian-Stodola (New York: Penguin, 1998), 117–210.

38. Brooke, *Emily Montague*, 40.

39. William Robertson, *The History of America* (Dublin: Messrs. Price Whitestone W. Watson R. Cross Corcoran, 1777), 108. Accessed June 12, 2007, on *Eighteenth-Century Collections Online*, ECCO.

40. Mark Duckworth, "An Eighteenth-Century Questionnaire: William Robertson on the Indians," *Eighteenth-Century Life* 11, no. 1 (1987): 36–49.

41. Ibid., 42.

42. H. P. Biggar, ed., *The Works of Samuel Champlain* (Toronto: Champlain Society, 1922–36), vol. 3, p. 136.

43. Brooke, *Emily Montague*, 15.

44. Ibid., 16.

45. Ibid., 52. In this scene, Arabella asks in French if the women are from Lorette: "They shook their heads: I repeated the question in English, when the oldest of the women told me, they were not; that their country was on the borders of New England; that, their husbands being on a hunting party in the woods, curiosity, and the desire of seeing their brethren the English who had conquered Quebec, had brought them

up the great river, down which they should return as soon as they had seen Montreal" (52–53). Because they are explicitly not Wendat and because Arabella describes the women's "privilege of chusing a chief" (59) and their customs of arranged marriage, I hypothesize that these women are Haudenosaunee—most likely Mohawk, traditionally known as "Keepers of the Eastern Door" of their homelands. While there is room for doubt, this attribution seems likely as most Algonquin groups further east were generally not as strongly matrilineal.

46. Ibid., 52, 58–59.

47. Henry Home Kames, *Sketches of the History of Man* (Dublin: James Williams, 1774). From sketch 6, "Progress of the Female Sex," p. 3. Accessed June 11, 2007, on *Eighteenth-Century Collections Online, ECCO.*

48. Ingrid H. Tague, "Love, Honor, and Obedience: Fashionable Women and the Discourse of Marriage in the Early Eighteenth Century," *Journal of British Studies* 40, no. 1 (2001), 76–106.

49. Jodi L. Wyett, "'No Place Where Women Are of Such Importance': Female Friendship, Empire, and Utopia in *The History of Emily Montague*," *Eighteenth-Century Fiction* 16, no. 1 (2003): 42.

50. Mohawk, "Power of Seneca Women," 28.

51. Lewis Henry Morgan, *League of the Iroquois* (Secaucus, NJ: Citadel Press, 1962), 320–22.

52. Judith Brown elaborates on Morgan's conflicting opinions of women's status in "Economic Organization," 152–55.

53. Henry Dearborn, "Henry A. S. Dearborn Journals (1838–1839)," *Publications of the Buffalo Historical Society* 7 (1904): 111–14. Quoted in Noel, "Revisiting Gender in Iroquoia," 67 (emphasis mine).

54. Johannes Fabian, *Time and the Other: How Anthropology Makes Its Object* (New York: Columbia University Press, 2002).

55. Elizabeth Povinelli, *The Empire of Love: Toward a Theory of Intimacy, Genealogy, and Carnality* (Durham, NC: Duke University Press, 2006), 183.

56. Plane offers fascinating readings of fragments of colonial record keeping to recover Native marriage practices in early New England: see Plane, *Colonial Intimacies.*

57. Devon A. Mihesuah, ed., "Commonality of Difference: American Indian Women and History," in *Natives and Academics: Researching and Writing about American Indians* (Lincoln: University of Nebraska Press, 1998), 47.

58. With the assistance of Herne and local officials, I was directed to Mitchell and McDonald, current office holders of traditional spiritual and community organization in their clans. For more on Mohawk border politics, see Simpson, *Mohawk Interruptus.*

59. Norman K. Denzin and Yvonna S. Lincoln, "Preface," in *Handbook of Critical and Indigenous Methodologies,* ed. Norman K. Denzin, Yvonna S. Lincoln, and Linda Tuhiwai Smith (Los Angeles: Sage, 2008), xi.

60. Radhakrishnan, "Why Compare?," 454.

61. I hope more scholars will begin the work of treating Native oral history as serious historical evidence. See Melissa Adams-Campbell, "*Life of Black Hawk*: A Sauk and Mesquakie Archive," *Settler Colonial Studies* (2014), doi:10.1080/22014

73X.2014.957259; Andrew Newman, *On Records: Delaware Indians, Colonists, and the Media of History and Memory* (Lincoln: University of Nebraska Press, 2012).

62. On the Longhouse faith, see Chief Jake Thomas and Terry Boyle, *Teachings from the Longhouse* (Toronto: Stoddard, 1994); Anthony F. Wallace, *The Death and Rebirth of the Seneca* (repr., New York: Vintage Books, 1972). Not all Haudenosaunee people adopted Handsome Lake's Code; there is considerable disagreement over it to this day.

63. Mohawk, "Power of Seneca Women," 28. On this point, John Mohawk cites William Fenton, ed., *Parker on the Iroquois: Iroquois Uses of Maize and Other Food Plants, the Code of Handsome Lake, the Seneca Prophet, the Constitution of the Five Nations* (Syracuse, NY: Syracuse University Press, 1968), 72.

64. Personal interview, July 25, 2012.

65. Gerald Vizenor and others elaborate on the significance of this concept in *Survivance: Narratives of Native Presence* (Lincoln: University of Nebraska Press, 2008).

66. Personal interview, July 25, 2012.

67. Brown, "Economic Organization," 155.

68. Personal interview, July 26, 2012.

69. Mohawk notes that "The rights of individual young men and women were clearly subordinated to the perceived needs of the group by custom, and in this case, the defined group was the extended female family occupying the longhouse of the wife." "Power of Seneca Women," 26; see also n. 35, p. 34.

70. Personal interview, July 26, 2012.

71. Personal interview, July 26, 2012.

72. McDonald draws on historical records and scholarship in these statements about eighteenth-century women's choices; however, W. G. Spittal notes that Jesuit accounts of women's premarital sex are imprecise about whether these practices were witnessed among the Wendat or the Haudenosaunee or both (*Iroquois Women*, 8). It is useful to keep in mind that sexual customs in the eighteenth century were significantly altered after the adoption of Handsome Lake's Code in the nineteenth century. John Mohawk discusses changes to women's roles in the wake of Handsome Lake's Code in "Power of Seneca Women."

73. Personal interview, July 25, 2012.

74. Morgan claims, "In ancient times, the young warrior was always united to a woman several years his senior, on the supposition that he needed a companion experienced in the affairs of life. . . . Thus, it often happened that the young warrior at twenty-five was married to a woman of forty, and often times a widow; while the widower at sixty was joined to the maiden at twenty." Morgan, *League of the Iroquois*, 322.

75. Personal interview, July 26, 2012.

76. Robert Merrett, "The Politics of Romance in *The History of Emily Montague*," *Canadian Literature* 133 (Summer 1992): 106.

77. Julie K. Ellison, "There and Back: Transatlantic Novels and Anglo-American Careers," in *The Past as Prologue: Essays to Commemorate the 25th Anniversary of ASECS*, ed. Carla H. Hay and Sydney M. Conger (New York: AMS Press, 1995), 303.

78. Tague, "Love, Honor, and Obedience," 76–106.

79. Povinelli, *Empire of Love*, 4.

80. Ibid., 183.

81. Ibid., 201.

3. Making Room for Coquettes and Fallen Women

1. See Joan Dayan, *Haiti, History, and the Gods* (Berkeley: University of California Press, 1995), 165–82; Michael Drexler, "Brigands and Nuns: The Vernacular Sociology of Collectivity after the Haitian Revolution," in *Messy Beginnings: Postcoloniality and Early American Studies,* ed. Malini Johar Schueller and Edward Watts (New Brunswick, NJ: Rutgers University Press, 2003), 175–99; Elizabeth Dillon, "The Secret History of the Early American Novel: Leonora Sansay and Revolution in Saint Domingue," *Novel* 40, no. 1–2 (2006): 77–103; Gretchen Woertendyke, "Romance to Novel: A Secret History," *Narrative* 17, no. 3 (2009): 255–73; Tessie P. Liu. "The Secret beyond White Patriarchal Power: Race, Gender, and Freedom in the Last Days of Colonial Saint-Domingue," *French Historical Studies* 33, no. 3 (2010): 387–416; Michael Drexler, "Leonora Sansay's Anatopic Imagination," in *Urban Identity and the Atlantic World,* ed. Elizabeth Faye and Leonard Morze (New York: Palgrave Macmillan, 2013), 143–57.

2. Saint-Domingue, now Haiti, was the most profitable colony of the late eighteenth century. After Columbus claimed the island for Spain, naming it Hispaniola, it was later divided between Spain and France in the 1697 Treaty of Ryswick. The French-occupied portion was called Saint-Domingue. Sansay, like many US citizens, referred to the territory as St. Domingo (also San Domingo). During the French Revolution, when the colony's enslaved population rebelled and declared themselves free citizens, Britain and Spain made their own unsuccessful attempts to acquire the colony. Eventually, the insurgent former slaves and the free black population, led by Dessalines, claimed independence from France and from slavery, largely expunging the white population and renaming the country Haiti. According to *Secret History,* the Sansays arrived in Saint-Domingue on the eve of Toussaint-Louverture's arrest. There are many important studies of the Haitian Revolution and the French Caribbean; I have found the following especially useful: C. L. R. James, *The Black Jacobins: Toussaint L'Ouverture and the San Domingo Revolution* (New York: Vintage Books, 1989); Carolyn Fick, *The Making of Haiti: The Saint-Domingue Revolution from Below* (Knoxville: University of Tennessee Press, 1990); Dayan, *Haiti, History, and the Gods*; David Barry Gaspar and David Patrick Geggus, eds., *A Turbulent Time: The French Revolution and the Greater Caribbean* (Bloomington: Indiana University Press, 1997); David P. Geggus, ed., *The Impact of the Haitian Revolution in the Atlantic World* (Columbia: University of South Carolina Press, 2001); Laurent Dubois, *Avengers of the New World: The Story of the Haitian Revolution* (Cambridge, MA: Belknap Press of Harvard University, 2004); Dorris Garraway, *The Libertine Colony: Creolization in the Early French Caribbean* (Durham, NC: Duke University Press, 2005).

3. For a timeline of Sansay's life, see Michael Drexler, ed., "Introduction" and "Chronology," in *Secret History; or, The Horrors of St. Domingo and Laura,* 10–37, 38–54 (Peterborough, ON: Broadview Editions, 2007).

4. Sansay, *Secret History,* 61, 63–64.

5. John Adams, "June 2, 1778," in *Diary and Autobiography of John Adams*, ed. Lyman H. Butterfield (Cambridge, MA: Belknap Press of Harvard University Press, 1962), 4:123. The widespread connection between individual companionate marriages and the nation's good can be traced to Scottish Enlightenment philosophy and further still to Montesquieu's *Spirit of the Law*. See chapter 1 of this book and Moran, "Commerce of the Sexes."

6. See A Friend to the Fair Sex, "To the Editor of the Columbian Magazine," *Columbian Magazine* 1, no. 10 (1787): 491–97.

7. Sansay, *Secret History*, 77, 79, 80.

8. Ibid., 96.

9. See Hannah Foster, *The Coquette* (New York: Oxford University Press, 1986); Dillon, *Gender of Freedom*, 184–96. Dillon's work on both *The Coquette* and *Secret History* have been formative to my reading of Sansay.

10. These descriptions and quotes are all from Sansay, *Secret History*, 95.

11. Ibid., 87.

12. Ibid., 91–92.

13. A sergeant in Toussaint-Louverture's army, Sanite Belair's bravery in death is also discussed in works by C. L. R. James and Joan Dayan, among others. Her picture appears on the Haitian ten gourdes note. See James, *Black Jacobins*, 352; Dayan, *Haiti, History, and the Gods*, 158–59.

14. Zuline is the likely model for another fictional mulatto heroine of the Haitian Revolution, Zelica. Based on the characters in *Secret History*, *Zelica, the Creole* (1820) may have been authored by Sansay. For an argument on Sansay's authorship, see Phillip Lapsansky, "Afro-Americana: Rediscovering Leonora Sansay," in *The Annual Report of the Library Company of Philadelphia for the Year 1992* (Philadelphia: Library Company, 1993). For a reading of *Zelica*, see Carol Smith-Rosenberg, "Black Gothic: The Shadowy Origins of the American Bourgeoisie," in *Possible Pasts: Becoming Colonial in Early America*, ed. Robert Blair St. George (Ithaca, NY: Cornell University Press, 2000), 243–69.

15. Sansay, *Secret History*, 131.

16. Ibid., 92.

17. Winthrop D. Jordan, *White Over Black: American Attitudes toward the Negro, 1550–1812* (Chapel Hill: University of North Carolina Press, 1968), 167–78.

18. Sansay, *Secret History*, 119.

19. Ibid., 120.

20. Ibid., 138–39.

21. Maria Elena Diaz, *The Virgin, the King, and the Royal Slaves of El Cobre: Negotiating Freedom in Colonial Cuba, 1670–1780* (Stanford, CA: Stanford University Press, 2002).

22. Sansay, *Secret History*, 140.

23. Ibid., 140.

24. Ibid., 149.

25. In modern usage the term *Creole* marks a hybrid cultural identity and *creolization* is the process of syncretism or fusion between different cultures and ethnicities. Following Doris Garraway and Sean Goudie, I use the late eighteenth-century colonial

meaning of *Creole*, which referred to locally born white "Americans" (North, South, and Caribbean). Garraway cites the *Dictionnaire Littré*, where *créole* is defined as "'homme blanc, femme blanche, originaire des colonies' and the *Petit Robert*, where even today the word's primary meaning is a 'person of the white race, born in the tropical colonies, notably the Antilles.'" See Garraway, *Libertine Colony*, 20; Sean X. Goudie, *Creole America: The West Indies and the Formation of Literature and Culture in the New Republic* (Philadelphia: University of Pennsylvania Press, 2006), 8–9.

26. Felicity Nussbaum demonstrates how colonial economic practices displace sexuality on exotic women; Sharon Harrow tracks concerns about the spread of Caribbean moral vices "back home"; and Sean Goudie observes how the Caribbean becomes a foil for US claims of moral and political superiority in the Early Republic: see Nussbaum, *Torrid Zones: Maternity, Sexuality, and Empire in Eighteenth-Century English Narratives* (Baltimore: Johns Hopkins University Press, 1995); Harrow, *Adventures in Domesticity*; Goudie, *Creole America*.

27. For one of many such reports, see Baron de Wimpffen, *A Voyage to Saint Domingo in the Years 1788, 1789, and 1790* (London: T. Caldwell, 1797), 112–13.

28. Sansay, *Secret History*, 95.

29. As a "feme covert," married women were legally "covered" or subsumed under a husband's legal identity; see Cott, "Marriage and Women's Citizenship in the United States."

30. Sansay, *Secret History*, 70–71.

31. Ibid., 73.

32. Pennsylvania passed the Gradual Abolition Bill in 1780. Any children born of slave mothers after that date had to serve a lengthy "indenture," but were freed after the age of twenty-eight. The state's census records for 1810 record 795 enslaved persons living in Pennsylvania. See Joe W. Trotter and Eric L. Smith, eds. *African Americans in Pennsylvania: Shifting Historical Perspectives* (University Park: Pennsylvania State University Press, 1997), 44.

33. Sansay, *Secret History*, 95.

34. James, *Black Jacobins*, 32.

35. John Stedman's description of his relationship with his "Surinam wife" Joanna, in *Narrative of a Five Years Expedition in Surinam* (1791), is one of the most extensive accounts of this type of arrangement; see: John Gabriel Stedman, *Narrative of a Five Years Expedition against the Revolted Negroes of Surinam* (repr., Baltimore: Johns Hopkins University Press, 1988).

36. See Garraway, *Libertine Colony*, 235; Susan M. Socolow, "Economic Roles of the Free Women of Color of Cap Français," in *More Than Chattel: Black Women and Slavery in the Americas*, ed. David Barry Gaspar and Darlene Clark Hine (Bloomington: Indiana University Press, 1996), 279–97; David P. Geggus, "Slave and Free Colored Women in Saint Domingue," in *More Than Chattel: Black Women and Slavery in the Americas*, ed. David Barry Gaspar and Darlene Clark Hine (Bloomington: Indiana University Press, 1996), 259–78.

37. Justin Girod de Chantrans, *Voyage d'un Suisse dans les colonies d'Amérique* (1785; repr., Paris: Librairie Jules Tallendier, 1980), 153, quoted in Garraway, *Libertine Colony*, 235.

38. Garraway, *Libertine Colony*, 229–30.

39. Gyssels observes that French Creole women in Saint-Domingue have received the least amount of historical scrutiny, in part because records from the period have so little to say about them. She turns to more recent "historical metafiction" to consider the complex psychological interiorities of French Creole planters' wives in slave-holding Saint-Domingue. See Kathleen Gyssels, "'Les Créoles Galantes?' White Women and the Haitian Revolution," *Echoes of the Haitian Revolution, 1804–2004* (Kingston, Jamaica: University of the West Indies Press, 2008), 95–110.

40. Caribbean mulatto woman's sexuality should not be equated with US black women's sexuality. Caribbean women of color, as a class, were generally free (though mulattos could be enslaved). They functioned as an intermediary class, maintaining the distance between racial slavery and white hegemony. Although women of color experienced real inequalities of power in their relations with white men, they were generally not violently coerced into such relations in the way that enslaved black women working on plantations frequently were. My concern here is to maintain the important distinctions between "black" US women (of all racial mixtures) and Caribbean women of color (generally a specific class of free women).

41. The quotes and descriptions appear in Sansay, *Secret History*, 95.

42. For more on Caribbean women's economic position, see Socolow, "Economic Roles," 279–97; Sidney Mintz, "Economic Role and Cultural Tradition," in *The Black Woman Cross-Culturally*, ed. Filomina Chioma Steady (Cambridge, MA: Schenkman, 1981), 523; Dominique Rogers and Stewart King, "Housekeepers, Merchants, Rentières: Free Women of Color in the Port Cities of Colonial Saint-Domingue, 1750–1790," in *Women in Port: Gendering Communities, Economies, and Social Networks in Atlantic Port Cities, 1500–1800*, ed. Douglas Catterall and Jodi Campbell (Leiden, Netherlands: Brill, 2012), 357–97.

43. Garraway, *Libertine Colony*, 236.

44. Garraway, *Libertine Colony*, 194–239. Similarly, Dayan observes that mulatto mistresses "became the concrete signifier for lust that could be portrayed as 'love'"; Dayan, *Haiti, History, and the Gods*, 56.

45. Michel-René Hilliard d'Auberteuil, *Considérations sur l'état présent de la colonie françoise de Saint-Domingue* (Paris: Chez Grangé, 1776), quoted in Garraway, *Libertine*, 230.

46. Both Hilliard d'Auberteuil and Moreau de Saint-Méry place the problem of interracial desire on mixed-race women who dominate white men. See Moreau de Saint-Méry, *Description topographique, physique, civile, politique, et historique de la partie française de l'isle Saint-Domingue* (1797; repr., Paris: Société de l'histoire des Colonies Françaises et Librairie Larose, 1958), 1:77, quoted in Garraway, *Libertine Colony*, 230.

47. Julien Raimond, "Observations on the Origin and Progression of the White Colonists' Prejudice against Men of Color," in *Slave Revolution in the Caribbean, 1789–1804: A Brief History with Documents*, ed. Laurent Dubois and John Garrigus (Boston: Bedford/St. Martin's, 2006), 80.

48. Sansay, *Secret History*, 95–96.

49. Sandra Lee Evenson, "Indian Madras Plaids as Real India," in *Dress Sense: Emotional and Sensory Experiences of the Body and Clothes*, ed. Donald Clay Johnson and Helen Bradley Foster (London: Berg, 2008), 96–108.

50. Dillon, "Secret History," 13.

51. Wimpffen, *Voyage to Saint Domingo,* 113–14, quoted in Dayan, *Haiti, History, and the Gods,* 175.

52. Sansay, *Secret History,* 96.

53. Ibid., 153.

54. Chakkalakal, *Novel Bondage,* 6.

55. Serge-Henri Vieux, *Le Plaçage: Droit coutumier et famille en Haïti* (Paris: Agence de Coopération Culturelle et Technique, 1989).

56. George Simpson estimates that in the early twentieth century, the percentage of couples living in *plaçage* versus marriage is 80/20; see "Sexual and Familial Institutions in Northern Haiti," *American Anthropologist* 44, no. 4 (1942): 655–74. Haiti's class divisions are also racial divisions created precisely through this historic division between wealthy free people of color (who often acquired their wealth through inheritances from white planter relations) and poor black peasants (primarily the descendants of former enslaved peoples). Haiti's wealthy mulatto population was (and is) more likely to participate in civil and religiously recognized marriage. Even Toussaint-Louverture's 1801 *Constitution* sanctions this division of official "institutional" marriage as it "encourages the purity of morals, and therefore those spouses who practice the virtues their status demands of them will always be distinguished and specially protected by the government." See Toussaint-Louverture, "From *Constitution of the French Colony of Saint-Domingue,* 1801," in *Slave Revolution in the Caribbean, 1789–1804: A Brief History with Documents,* ed. Laurent Dubois and John Garrigus (Boston: Bedford/St. Martin's, 2006), 167–70.

57. Dayan, *Haiti, History, and the Gods,* 130–39.

58. Mintz, "Economic Role," 523.

59. Ibid., 520.

60. Drexler, "Introduction," 27–29.

61. Aaron Burr, *Memoirs of Aaron Burr with Miscellaneous Selections of His Correspondence* (New York: Harper and Brothers, 1836), 2:326, quoted in Drexler, "Introduction," 27.

62. Drexler, "Introduction," 27.

63. Sansay, *Secret History,* 95.

64. See, for instance, Dror Wahrman, *The Making of the Modern Self: Identity and Culture in Eighteenth-Century England* (New Haven, CT: Yale University Press, 2004); Roxann Wheeler, *The Complexion of Race: Categories of Difference in Eighteenth-Century British Culture* (Philadelphia: University of Pennsylvania Press, 2000).

65. Sansay, *Laura,* 193, 194.

66. Drexler, "Introduction," 35. Sansay describes the factory in a letter to Burr included in appendix A of the Broadview Editions publication.

67. Sansay, *Laura,* 222.

68. Ibid.

4. A Postcolonial Heroine "Writes Back"

1. Three extant reviews, all published in 1810, are collected in appendix F of *The Woman of Colour: A Tale,* ed. Lyndon J. Dominique (Petersborough, ON: Broadview

Editions, 2008). They include a March review in the *British Critic*, a May review in the *Critical Review*, and a June review in the *Monthly Review*. As Dominique observes, this is a remarkable amount of reviews in a year (1808) when more than one hundred novels were published, an unusually high number. In a flood of contemporary novels, then, *The Woman of Colour* stood out as review-worthy; Lyndon J. Dominique, "Introduction," in *Woman of Colour*, 20.

2. For more examples of Romantic-period representations of women in the West Indies, see Harrow, *Adventures in Domesticity*.

3. Armstrong, *Desire and Domestic Fiction*, 79.

4. See, for instance, Armstrong, *Desire and Domestic Fiction*; Boone, *Tradition Counter Tradition*; Flint, *Family Fictions*.

5. Bannet, *Domestic Revolution*.

6. Thompson, *Ingenuous Subjection*, 12–13.

7. Armstrong, *Desire and Domestic Fiction*, 79.

8. *Woman of Colour*, 91, 92–93.

9. Ibid., 93.

10. Ibid., 92.

11. See appendix F in *Woman of Colour*, 257.

12. This and the preceding quote are taken from DuPlessis, *Writing beyond the Ending*, 5.

13. See Dominique, "Introduction," in *Woman of Colour*, 21. See also Goudie, *Creole America*; Garraway, *Libertine Colony*.

14. *Woman of Colour*, 77.

15. Ibid., 79.

16. Ibid., 85, 72–73.

17. One such example of the way that white creole women imitated mulatto women can be found in Baron de Wimpffen. He claims that mulatto women "are the envy and despair of the white ladies, who aspire to imitate them, and who do not see that it is impossible for the strong and glaring colours [of their clothes], calculated to animate the monotonous and livid hue of the mulatto, to harmonize with the alabaster and the rose of Europe!" Wimpffen, *Voyage to Saint Domingo*, 113–14, quoted in Dayan, *Haiti, History, and the Gods*, 175.

18. Harrow, *Adventures in Domesticity*, 2.

19. See Homi K. Bhabha, *The Location of Culture* (New York: Routledge, 1994), 145–74.

20. *Woman of Colour*, 82.

21. Ibid., 73, 88.

22. See Oliver Goldsmith, *The Citizen of the World; or, Letters from a Chinese Philosopher, Residing in London, to His Friends in the East* (Dublin: G. and A. Ewing, 1762).

23. *Woman of Colour*, 110.

24. Ibid., 110–11.

25. Ibid., 111.

26. bell hooks, *Black Looks: Race and Representation* (Cambridge, MA: South End Press, 1999), 23.

27. Ibid., 31.

28. In the introduction to *The Woman of Colour,* Dominique cites the work of Garside, Raven, and Schowerling to debunk the attribution of *The Woman of Colour* to E. M. Foster, the author of the novels listed on *The Woman of Colour*'s title page, an attribution most likely placed there as a common publishing strategy for boosting sales. Such a move would give the impression that a new author was actually an established one. Dominique speculates that because the "editor" of the novel is specifically acknowledged to be a woman, the author is likely female; moreover, there were certainly a number of highly educated and relatively wealthy people of color living in London at the end of the eighteenth century, any one of whom *could* have written this novel. Although we may never know who wrote the novel, Dominique offers a tantalizing lead for the story's origin: the real case of Andrew Wright, a white English planter from Jamaica, who died in 1806 leaving a strange clause in his will relative to his two illegitimate daughters of color. Wright insisted that both Ann and Rebecca Wright marry "in England" (presumably guaranteeing that they would marry white men in England). See Dominique, "Introduction," in *Woman of Colour*, 11–42; Peter Garside, James Raven, and Rainer Schowerling, eds., *The English Novel, 1770–1829: A Bibliographic Survey of Prose Fiction Published in the British Isles*, vol. 2, *1800–1829* (New York: Oxford University Press, 2000), 69–70.

29. Bill Ashcroft, Gareth Griffiths, and Helen Tiffen, eds., *The Empire Writes Back: Theory and Practice in Post-Colonial Literatures*, 2nd ed. (New York: Routledge, 2002).

30. *Woman of Colour,* 154. Olivia is quoting from the Bible, Mark 12:25 and Rev. 21:4.

31. Ibid., 165.

32. Child, *Hobomok,* 141.

33. I thank Nicole Clifton for pointing out this effect of Olivia's "widowing."

34. *Woman of Colour,* 182, emphasis mine.

35. See Stone, *Family, Sex and Marriage,* 329–30.

36. *Woman of Colour,* 72.

37. This and the preceding quote are from ibid., 106, 107.

38. Ibid., 148.

39. Quoted in Bannet, *Domestic Revolution,* 36.

40. Socolow, "Economic Roles."

41. Socolow, "Economic Roles," 292–93.

5. Bungling Bundling

1. "Lexington March" at the Henry E. Huntington Library under the heading and title, "Collection, Songs, English Songs" (n.p., c. 1720–80). Quoted in J. A. Leo Lemay, "The American Origins of 'Yankee Doodle,' *William and Mary Quarterly* 33, no. 3 (1976): 435–65. Both Richard Godbeer and Dana Doten note a tradition of antibundling songs that attempted to shame bundlers: Godbeer, *Sexual Revolution in Early America* (Baltimore: Johns Hopkins University Press, 2002); Doten, *The Art of Bundling: Being an Inquiry into the Nature & Origins of That Curious but Universal Folk-Custom, with an Exposition of the Rise & Fall of Bundling in the Eastern Part of*

No. America (New York: Countryman Press/Farrar and Rinehart, 1938). The American Antiquarian Society digitized two different broadsides of an antibundling ballad: "A New bundling song," *Isaiah Thomas Broadside Ballads Project*, accessed January 30, 2015, http://www.thomasballads.org/items/show/169; "A New bundling song: or A reproof to those young country women, who follow that reproachful practice, and to their mothers for upholding them therein," *Isaiah Thomas Broadside Ballads Project*, accessed January 30, 2015, http://www.thomasballads.org/items/show/170.

2. For demographics on premarital pregnancy, see Daniel Scott Smith and Michal S. Hindus, "Premarital Pregnancy in America 1640–1971: An Overview and Interpretation," *Journal of Interdisciplinary History* 5 (1975): 537–70. One study of the church records in Groton, Massachusetts, between 1761 and 1775 indicates that of two hundred persons owning the baptismal covenant, no less than sixty-six confessed to fornication before marriage. Quoted in Doten, *Art of Bundling,* 110–12. On early American sex, see Godbeer, *Sexual Revolution in Early America*; Clare Lyons, *Sex among the Rabble: An Intimate History of Gender and Power in the Age of Revolution, Philadelphia, 1730–1830* (Chapel Hill: University of North Carolina Press, 2006); Susan E. Klepp, *Revolutionary Conceptions: Women, Fertility, and Family Limitation in America, 1760–1820* (Chapel Hill: University of North Carolina Press, 2009); John D'Emilio and Estelle B. Freedman, eds. *Intimate Matters: A History of Sexuality in America,* 3rd ed. (Chicago: University of Chicago Press, 2012). On the history of bundling, see Richard Godbeer, *Sexual Revolution in Early America*; Doten, *Art of Bundling*; Henry Reed Stiles, *Bundling: Its Origin, Progress, and Decline in America* (Albany, NY: Knickerbocker, 1871).

3. Lemay, "American Origins," 444–45.

4. Early Americanists are some of the nicest academics; thanks to Ed White, who generously recommended the bundling episode in *The Life and Adventures of Obadiah Benjamin Franklin Bloomfield, M.D.* and to the other members of the Society of Early Americanists (SEA) listserv who suggested additional instances of bundling while I was researching chapter 5.

5. See, for example, my discussion of *Hymen: An Accurate Description of the Ceremonies Used in Marriage, by Every Nation in the Known World* (1760) by "Uxorious" in chapter 1. The quotation is taken from Hymen's subtitle.

6. O'Connell, "'Matrimonial Ceremonies Displayed.'" There is a growing body of literature considering the postrevolutionary era as a postcolonial transition era. For instance, Kariann Akemi Yokota describes a political change that had outpaced cultural separation from Britain in *Unbecoming British: How Revolutionary America Became a Postcolonial Nation* (New York: Oxford University Press, 2011), 12. See also Goudie, *Creole America*; David Kazanjian, *The Colonizing Trick: National Culture and Imperial Citizenship in Early America* (Baltimore: Johns Hopkins University Press, 2004); Malini Johar Schueller and Edward Watts, eds., *Messy Beginnings: Postcoloniality and Early American Studies* (New Brunswick, NJ: Rutgers University Press, 2003); Robert Blair St. George, ed., *Possible Pasts: Becoming Colonial in Early America* (Ithaca, NY: Cornell University Press, 2000); Edward S. Watts, *Writing and Postcolonialism in Early America* (Charlottesville: University of Virginia Press, 1998). Not a traditionally recognized postcolonial society, the United States has more recently

been theorized as a settler state, both formerly colonized and colonizer to internally colonized Native and African diasporic peoples. For an overview of setter colonialism, see Lorenzo Veracini, *Settler Colonialism: A Theoretical Overview* (New York: Palgrave Macmillan, 2010). See also Ashcroft, Griffiths, and Tiffin, *Empire Writes Back*; Bill Ashcroft, Gareth Griffiths, and Helen Tiffin, eds., *The Postcolonial Studies Reader* (London: Routledge, 1994); Lawrence Buell, "American Literary Emergence as a Postcolonial Phenomenon," *American Literary History* 4 (1992): 411–42; Stuart Hall, "When Was 'The Post-Colonial'? Thinking at the Limits," in *The Post-Colonial Question: Common Skies, Divided Horizons*, ed. Iain Chambers and Lidia Curti (New York: Routledge, 1996), 242–60; Alan Lawson, "A Cultural Paradigm for the Second World," *Australian and Canadian Studies* 9, no. 1 (1991): 67–78; Alan Lawson, "Comparative Studies and Post-Colonial 'Settler' Cultures," *Australian and Canadian Studies* 10, no. 2 (1992): 153–58; Jenny Sharpe, "Is the United States Postcolonial? Transnationalism, Immigration, and Race," *Diaspora* 4, no. 2 (1995): 181–99.

7. A Friend to the Fair Sex, "To the Editor," 491, 496, 497.

8. William Ellery Channing offers two reasons for "the barrenness of American Literature": its continued use of the English language (the United States had no "native" language of its own) and its support of "foreign literature" over local productions. See "Essay on American Language and Literature," *North American Review* 1, no. 3 (1815): 307–14.

9. On Walter Scott's nationalism, see Katie Trumpner, *Bardic Nationalism: The Romantic Novel and the British Empire* (Princeton, NJ: Princeton University Press, 1997), esp. chap. 3; Ian Duncan, *Scott's Shadow: The Novel in Romantic Edinburgh* (Princeton, NJ: Princeton University Press, 2007).

10. Edward Said, *Culture and Imperialism* (London: Vintage, 1993), 66.

11. Thomas Anburey, *Travels through the Interior Parts of America* (London: William Lane, 1789), 2:41–43.

12. Laurel Thatcher Ulrich and Lois K. Stabler, "'Girling of it' in Eighteenth-Century New Hampshire," in *Families and Children*, ed. Peter Benes (Boston: Boston University Press, 1987), 24–36.

13. Andrew Burnaby, *Burnaby's Travels through North America*, ed. Rufus Rockwell Wilson (repr., New York: A. Wessels, 1904), 141–43, quoted in Godbeer, *Sexual Revolution*, 247.

14. Johann David Schoepf, *Travels in the Confederation, 1783–1784*, trans. and ed. Alfred J. Morrison (Philadelphia: William Campbell, 1911), 101, quoted in Godbeer, *Sexual Revolution*, 247.

15. Rev. Samuel Peters, LL.D., *General History of Connecticut: From Its First Settlement [. . .]*, ed. Samuel Jarvis McCormick (New York: D. Appleton, 1877), 228, 226–27.

16. On the trend toward companionate marriage in New England, see Anya Jabour, *Marriage in the Early Republic: Elizabeth and William Wirt and the Companionate Ideal* (Baltimore: Johns Hopkins University Press, 1998); Mary Beth Norton, *Liberty's Daughters: The Revolutionary Experience of American Women, 1750–1800* (Ithaca, NY: Cornell University Press, 1996); Coontz, *Marriage, a History*; Carl Deglar, *At Odds: Women and the Family in America from the Revolution to the Present* (New York: Oxford University Press, 1980).

17. Smith and Hindus, "Premarital Pregnancy in America."

18. R.W.G. Vail, "*Adventures of Jonathan Corncob, Loyal American Refugee:* A Commentary," *Papers of the American Bibliographical Society* 50 (2nd Quarter 1956), 106.

19. Henri Petter, *The Early American Novel* (Columbus: Ohio State University Press, 1971), 29.

20. Davidson, *Revolution and the Word,* 169; *Adventures of Jonathan Corncob, Loyal American Refugee, Written by Himself* (London: Printed for the Author, 1787), 164. One modern edition of *Corncob* exists: Noel Perrin, ed., *The Adventures of Jonathan Corncob, Loyal American Refugee, Written by Himself,* illust. Mark Livingston (Boston: David Godine, 1976). Perrin notes the following reviews of the novel: "Harkee!," *Critical Review* (February 1788): 150; *General Magazine* (January 1788): 35; *Gentleman's Magazine* (December 1787): 1095; *European Magazine* (December 1787): 466; *Monthly Review* (December 1787): 495. The book was not reviewed in the United States.

21. *Jonathan Corncob,* 19–20. Noel Perrin notes that "slawbunk" is a corrupt pronunciation of the Dutch phrase *slaap bancke,* or sleeping bench, an interesting and apt surname; Perrin, "Preface," in *Jonathan Corncob,* xi.

22. *Jonathan Corncob,* 21, 22.

23. Ibid., 101–2.

24. Cameron C. Nickels, *New England Humor: From the Revolutionary War to the Civil War* (Nashville: University of Tennessee Press, 1993), 8. See also Winifred Morgan, *An American Icon: Brother Jonathan and American Identity* (Cranbury, NJ: Associated University Presses, 1988).

25. Thomas Green Fessenden, "Jonathan's Courting, or, The Country Lovers," in *Cyclopedia of American Literature,* ed. Evert A. Duyckinck and George L. Duyckinck (Philadelphia: William Rutter, 1880), 1:597–99.

26. On the relationships between the urban and rural in early America, see Ed White, *The Backcountry and the City: Colonization and Conflict in Early America* (Minneapolis: University of Minnesota Press, 2005).

27. Royall Tyler, *The Contrast,* in *Early American Drama,* ed. Jeffrey Richards (New York: Penguin, 1997), 38. Ten years later, Tyler returned to the literary market with his novel, *The Algerine Captive,* and another reference to bundling: "An Algerine courtship would be as disagreeable to the hale youth of New England, as a common bundling would be disgusting to the Mussulman"; see Royall Tyler, *The Algerine Captive* (New York: Modern Library, 2002), 174.

28. Nickels, *New England Humor,* 9.

29. For John Adams's remarks on bundling, see Adams, *Diary and Autobiography of John Adams,* 1:195–96 and 1:221. We cannot be sure that Abigail and John bundled, but we do know that they took a trip together before marriage, seemingly unchaperoned, and shortly after they were making plans for marriage. See Alaric Miller, "Serious Jesting: A Close Inspection of the Smith-Adams Epistolary Courtship Based on Their Early Love-Letters, 1762–1764," *Theses, Dissertations, Professional Papers,* paper 3531 (University of Montana, 1997).

30. Washington Irving, *A History of New York,* ed. Michael Black and Nancy Black (Boston: Twayne Publishers, 1983), 119–20.

31. Ibid.

32. Georges-Louis Leclerc, Comte de Buffon, *Histoire naturelle, générale, et particulière* (Paris: de l'Imprimerie Royale, 1749–1809). Thomas Jefferson repudiated Buffon's theories in his *Notes on the State of Virginia*.

33. Irving, *History of New York*, 123.

34. Ibid. Dana Doten argues that Yankee bundling was adapted from the Dutch practice of *questing* in *Art of Bundling*, 33–52.

35. I am drawing on the work of Homi Bhabha, *Location of Culture*. For a more historical account of collective consumer politics during the revolution, see T. H. Breen, *The Marketplace of Revolution: How Consumer Politics Shaped American Independence* (New York: Oxford University Press, 2005).

36. Alan Taylor, "Martyr's to Venus," *New Republic* 227, no. 18 (October 28, 2002): 36.

37. Davidson, *Revolution and the Word*, 111.

38. John Adams to William Cunningham, March 15, 1804, quoted in Jay Fliegelman, *Prodigals and Pilgrims: The American Revolution against Patriarchal Authority, 1750–1800* (Cambridge: Cambridge University Press, 1982), 237. On seduction in early America, see Rodney Hessinger, *Seduced, Abandoned, and Reborn: Visions of Youth in Middle-Class America, 1780–1850* (Philadelphia: University Press of Pennsylvania, 2005); Jennifer Baker, *Securing the Commonwealth: Debt, Speculation, and Writing in the Making of Early America* (Baltimore: Johns Hopkins University Press, 2005); Karen Weyler, *Intricate Relations: Sexual and Economic Desire in American Fiction, 1789–1814* (Iowa City: University of Iowa Press, 2005); Davidson, *Revolution and the Word*; Ruth H. Bloch, "Religion, Literary Sentimentalism, and Popular Revolutionary Ideology," in *Gender and Morality in Anglo-American Culture, 1650–1800* (Berkeley: University of California Press, 2003); Godbeer, *Sexual Revolution*; Julia Stern, *The Plight of Feeling: Sympathy and Dissent in the Early American Novel* (Chicago: University of Chicago Press, 1997); Elizabeth Barnes, *States of Sympathy: Seduction and Democracy in the Early American Novel* (New York: Columbia University Press, 1997); Carroll Smith-Rosenberg, "Domesticating 'Virtue': Coquettes and Revolutionaries in Young America," in *Literature and the Body: Essays on Populations and Persons* ed. Elaine Scarry (Baltimore: Johns Hopkins University Press, 1988), 243–69; Ruth H. Bloch, "The Gendered Meanings of Virtue in Revolutionary America," *Signs* 13, no. 1 (Autumn 1987): 37–58; Jan Lewis, "The Republican Wife: Virtue and Seduction in the Early Republic," *William and Mary Quarterly* 44, no. 4 (1987): 689–721.

39. Toni Bowers, *Force or Fraud: British Seduction Stories and the Problem of Resistance, 1660–1760* (New York: Oxford University Press, 2011).

40. Leonard Tennenhouse, *The Importance of Feeling English: American Literature and the British Diaspora: 1750–1850* (Princeton, NJ: Princeton University Press, 2007).

41. Bowers and Chico, *Atlantic Worlds*, 2.

42. Steven Shapiro, *The Culture and Commerce of the Early American Novel: Reading the Atlantic World-System* (University Park: Pennsylvania State University Press, 2008), 6.

43. Cathy N. Davidson, "Introduction," in *Charlotte Temple* (New York: Oxford University Press, 1986).

44. On *Charlotte Temple* and Rowson, see Marion Rust, *Prodigal Daughters: Susanna Rowson's Early American Women* (Chapel Hill: University of North Carolina Press, 2008); Melissa Homestead and Camryn Hansen, "Susanna Rowson's Transatlantic Career," *Early American Literature* 45, no. 3 (November 2010): 619–54; Michael Zuckerman, "*Charlotte*: A Tale of Truth, A Premonition of American Revolutions," in *Atlantic Worlds in the Long Eighteenth Century: Seduction and Sentiment,* ed. Toni Bowers and Tita Chico (New York: Palgrave Macmillan, 2012); Jill Anderson, "Tomes of Travel and Travesty: The Didactic of Captivity in Susanna Rowson's *Charlotte Temple* and Mary Rowlandson's *The Sovereignty and Goodness of God*," *Women's Studies: An Interdisciplinary Journal* 38, no. 4 (2009): 429–48; Giddeon Maillor, "The History of *Charlotte Temple* as an American Bestseller," in *Must Read: Rediscovering American Bestsellers from* Charlotte Temple *to* The DaVinci Code, ed. Sarah Churchwell and Thomas Ruys Smith (London: Continuum, 2013), 59–77; Angela Monsam, "Charlotte Temple, an Autopsy: The Physiology of Seduction," in *Death Becomes Her: Cultural Narratives of Femininity and Death in Nineteenth-Century America,* ed. Elizabeth Dill and Sheri Weinstein (Newcastle Upon Tyne: Cambridge Scholars, 2008), 73–88; Shelly Jarenski, "The Voice of the Preceptress: Female Education in and as Seduction Novel," *Journal of the Midwest Modern Language Association* 37, no. 1 (2004): 59–68; Gareth Evans, "Rakes, Coquettes, and Republican Patriarchs: Class, Gender, and Nation in Early American Sentimental Fiction," *Canadian Review of American Studies* 25, no. 3 (1995): 41–62; Nancy Armstrong, "Why Daughters Die: The Racial Logic of American Sentimentalism," *Yale Journal of Criticism: Interpretation in the Humanities* 7, no. 2 (1994): 1–24; Stern, *Plight of Feeling;* Eva Cherniavsky, "Charlotte Temple's Remains," in *Discovering Difference: Contemporary Essays in American Culture,* ed. Christopher K. Lohmann (Bloomington: Indiana University Press, 1993), 35–47; Davidson, *Revolution and the Word;* Davidson, "Introduction," in *Charlotte Temple*. For a roundup of recent scholarship on Rowson's other works, see Jennifer Desiderio, ed., "Special Issue: Beyond *Charlotte Temple*," *Studies in American Fiction* 38, no. 1–2 (2011): 1–287.

45. On sensibility, see Sarah Knott, *Sensibility and the American Revolution* (Chapel Hill:University of North Carolina Press, 2009); Anne Jessie Van Sant, *Eighteenth-Century Sensibility and the Novel: The Senses in Social Context* (Cambridge: Cambridge University Press, 2004); Mark Salber Phillips, *Society and Sentiment: Genres of Historical Writing in Britain, 1740–1820* (Princeton, NJ: Princeton University Press, 2000); G. J. Barker-Benfield, *The Culture of Sensibility: Sex and Society in Eighteenth-Century Britain* (Chicago: University of Chicago Press, 1992); Janet Todd, *Sensibility: An Introduction* (New York: Routledge, 1986). On racialized forms of sensibility, see Lynn Festa, *Sentimental Figures of Empire in Britain and France* (Baltimore: Johns Hopkins University Press, 2006); Glenn Hendler, *Public Sentiments: Structures of Feeling in Nineteenth-Century American Literature* (Chapel Hill: University of North Carolina Press, 2001); Julie K. Ellison, *Cato's Tears and the Making of Anglo-American Emotion* (Chicago: University of Chicago Press, 1999).

46. Martha Meredith Read, *Margaretta; or, The Intricacies of the Heart,* ed. Rich-

ard Pressman (San Antonio, TX: Early American Reprints, 2012); Richard Pressman, "Introduction: *Margaretta* as Federalist Fantasy," in *Margaretta* (San Antonio, TX: Early American Reprints, 2012), 31. Pressman draws on the work of Shirley Samuels to describe the conflation of national and bodily symbolics: Samuels, *Romances of the Republic: Women, the Family, and Violence in the Literature of the Early American Nation* (New York: Oxford University Press, 1996). Other studies of the novel include Joseph Fichtelberg, "Heart-Felt Verities: The Feminism of Martha Meredith Read," *Legacy* 15, no. 2 (1998): 125–38; Joseph Fichtelberg, *Critical Fictions: Sentiment and the American Market, 1780–1870* (Athens: University of Georgia Press, 2003); Matthew Pethers, "Poverty, Providence, and the State of Welfare," *Early American Literature* 49, no. 3 (2014): 707–40; Duncan Faherty, "'Murder, robbery, rape, adultery, and incest': Martha Meredith Read's *Margaretta* (1807) and the Function of Federalist Fiction," in *Warring for America* (forthcoming 2015).

47. Edward Franklin, *The Life and Adventures of Obadiah Benjamin Franklin Bloomfield, M.D.: A Native of the United States of America, Now on the Tour of Europe. Interspersed with Episodes, and Remarks, Religious, Moral, Public Spirited, and Humorous* (Philadelphia: Published for the Proprietor, 1818). In his 1969 bibliography, Lyle Wright tentatively attributes the novel to its copyright holder, Edward Franklin; however, because I have been unable to locate any evidence of an Edward Franklin living in Philadelphia in 1818, I assume this name is a pseudonym. See Lyle H. Wright, *American Fiction, 1774–1850* (San Marino, CA: Huntington Library, 1969), 47. I have found no reviews of the novel, and only one advertisement for the book by bookseller E. Goodale in the February 2, 1820, *Hallowell Gazette* (7, no. 5: 3), Hallowell, Maine. Accessed on March 21, 2013, through *America's Historical Newspapers*.

48. In a separate essay in progress, I address Franklin and Sterne as Atlantic world models of self-fashioning in *Obadiah*. Notably, *Jonathan Corncob* also draws on Sterne's suggestive breaks and pauses in the narrative to indicate sexual activity.

49. On the picaresque in early American fiction, see Davidson, *Revolution and the Word*. On the British picaresque, see Watt, *Rise of the Novel*.

50. Baartman's death in 1815, just three years before the publication of *Obadiah*, could be an impetus for this scene. For more on Baartman, see Elizabeth Alexander, *The Venus Hottentot* (Charlottesville: University of Virginia Press, 1990); Clifton Crais and Pamela Scully, *Sarah Baartman and the Hottentot Venus: A Ghost Story and a Biography* (Princeton, NJ: Princeton University Press, 2009); Janell Hobson, *Venus in the Dark: Blackness and Beauty in Popular Culture* (New York: Routledge, 2005); Deborah Willis, ed., *The Black Venus 2010: They Called Her "Hottentot"* (Philadelphia: Temple University Press, 2010).

51. *Hymen* includes an account of a "Hottentot" wedding replete with a priest who repeatedly "pisses" on the bride and groom; see "Uxorious," *Hymen*, 197–98.

52. Italics in original. Franklin, *Obadiah*, 3–4.

53. Ibid.

54. Ibid., 93–94.

55. Ibid., 93–94, 95.

56. I have italicized the Yankee's dialogue for clarity; ibid., 97.

57. Joseph Roach, *Cities of the Dead: Circum-Atlantic Performance* (New York: Columbia University Press, 1996), 3.

58. Mikhail Bakhtin, *The Dialogic Imagination: Four Essays,* trans. Vadin Liapunov and Kenneth Bromstrom (Austin: University of Texas Press, 1982).

59. Cott summarizes how the rhetoric of mutual conjugal affection became a central metaphor for describing the system of governance imagined by the new nation's founders in the late eighteenth century; both marriage and government were conceived as "voluntary union[s] based on consent." See Cott, *Public Vows,* 10; Fliegelman, *Prodigals and Pilgrims,* esp. chap. 4; Lewis, "Republican Wife."

60. Cott, *Public Vows,* 18.

61. Dillon, *Gender of Freedom,* 124, 125.

62. On gender performance, see Judith Butler, *Gender Trouble: Feminism and the Subversion of Identity* (New York: Routledge, 1990).

63. As such, the meanings of courtship are figured differently for white male and white female subjects in early national literature. Whereas Benjamin Franklin famously characterizes his premarital sexual activity as "errata," the narrative trajectory of popular early American seduction novels makes the same premarital sexuality fatal for women. Dillon, *Gender of Freedom,* 130.

64. Obadiah's father's initial intention of setting him out for a religious career echoes Benjamin Franklin's account of his father's desire to "tithe" him to the church.

65. All of the preceding quotes come from Franklin, *Obadiah,* 25. The text leaves blank what Yorick catches hold of.

66. On the grand tour, see Jeremy Black, *France and the Grand Tour* (New York: Palgrave Macmillan, 2003); Jeremy Black, *Italy and the Grand Tour* (New Haven, CT: Yale University Press, 2003); Clare Hornsby, *The Impact of Italy: The Grand Tour and Beyond* (London: British School of Rome, 2000); Annette Woolard, "Nineteenth-Century Delawareans and the Grand Tour," *Delaware History* 22, no. 3 (1987): 125–57; Christopher Herbert, *The Grand Tour* (New York: Putnam, 1969). Obadiah doesn't mention where he will go on his grand tour, but he may have in mind a bit of literary tourism, especially given his love of Sterne. On literary tourism in the Romantic period, see Paul Westover, *Necromanticism: Traveling to Meet the Dead, 1750–1860* (New York: Palgrave Macmillan, 2012).

Epilogue

1. Laurie Essig, "Same Love, Mass Weddings, and the Culture of Romance," *Love, Inc.* (blog), accessed January 21, 2014, http://www.psychologytoday.com/blog/love-inc/201401/same-love-mass-weddings-and-the-cult-romance.

2. On self-marriage or informal marriage, see Cott, *Public Vows,* esp. chap. 2; Otto E. Koegel, *Common Law Marriage and Its Development in the United States* (Washington, DC: John Byrne, 1922); John E. Semonche, "Common-Law Marriage in North Carolina: A Study in Legal History," *American Journal of Legal History* 9 (1965): 324–41; Hendrik Hartog, "Marital Exits and Marital Expectations in Nineteenth-Century America," *Georgetown Law Journal* 80, no. 1 (October 1991): 95–129.

3. Strong quoted in Norma Basch, "From the Bonds of Empire to the Bonds of Matrimony," in *Devising Liberty: Preserving and Creating Freedom in the New Amer-*

ican Republic, ed. David Thomas Konig (Stanford, CA: Stanford University Press, 1995), 228–29.

4. On married women's property law, see Richard H. Chused, "Married Women's Property Law, 1800–1850," *Georgetown Law Journal* 71, no. 5 (1983): 1359–1425; Norma Basch, *In the Eyes of the Law: Women, Marriage, and Property in Nineteenth-Century New York* (Ithaca, NY: Cornell University Press, 1982).

5. Rifkin, *When Did Indians Become Straight?*

6. Gregory Evans Dowd, "Spinning Wheel Revolution," in *The Revolution of 1800: Democracy, Race, and the New Republic,* ed. Jan Ellen Lewis, James Horn, and Peter S. Onuf (Charlottesville: University of Virginia Press, 2002), 265–86. See also Theda Perdue, *Cherokee Women: Gender and Culture Change, 1700–1835* (Lincoln: University of Nebraska Press, 1998); Carol Mason, "Eighteenth-Century Culture Change among the Lower Creeks," *Florida Anthropologist* 16, no. 3 (1963): 65–80; Kathryn E. Holland Braund, "Guardians of Tradition and Handmaidens to Change: Women's Roles in Creek Economic and Social Life during the Eighteenth Century," *American Indian Quarterly* 14, no. 3 (1990): 239–58. For similar policy changes in the Southwest, see Ramón A. Gutiérrez, *When Jesus Came, the Corn Mothers Went Away: Marriage, Sexuality, and Power in New Mexico, 1500–1846* (Stanford, CA: Stanford University Press, 1991); Mary E. Young, "Women, Civilization, and the Indian Question," in *Clio Was a Woman: Studies in the History of American Women,* ed. Mabel E. Deutrich and Virginia Purdy (Washington, DC: Howard University Press, 1980), 98–110.

7. Rose Stremlau, "'To Domesticate and Civilize Wild Indians': Allotment and the Campaign to Reform Indian Families, 1875–1887," *Journal of Family History* 30 (2005): 265–86.

8. Brenda E. Stevenson, *Life in Black and White: Family and Community in the Slave South* (New York: Oxford University Press, 1997).

9. Foster, '*Til Death or Distance Do Us Part.* On slave marriage in literature, see Chakkalakal, *Novel Bondage.*

10. Cott, *Public Vows,* 90. On the passing of the Thirteenth Amendment, see Amy Dru Stanley, *From Bondage to Contract: Wage Labor, Marriage, and the Market in the Age of Slave Emancipation* (Cambridge: Cambridge University Press, 1998).

11. Cott, *Public Vows,* 113.

12. On the development of the idea of race in an Anglophone context, see Wheeler, *Complexion of Race*; in the United States, see Theodore Allen, *The Invention of the White Race,* vols. 1–2, 2nd ed. (London: Verso, 2012).

13. John L. Brooke, *Refiner's Fire: The Making of Mormon Cosmology, 1644–1844* (Cambridge: Cambridge University Press, 1994), 290–91. On the Reynolds decision, see Carol Weisbrod and Pamela Sheingorn, "Reynolds v. United States: Nineteenth-Century Forms of Marriage and the Status of Women," *Connecticut Law Review* 10, no. 4 (Summer 1978): 828–58; Sarah Barringer Gordon, *The Mormon Question: Polygamy and Constitutional Conflict in Nineteenth-Century America* (Chapel Hill: University of North Carolina Press, 2002).

14. Cott, *Public Vows,* 54.

15. Brownstein, *Becoming a Heroine,* xxi; Boone, *Tradition Counter Tradition,* 6.

16. Freedom to Marry, Inc., "Why Marriage Matters," accessed January 21, 2014, http://www.whymarriagematters.org/.

17. "Poll: Support Grows for Gay Marriage in Illinois," accessed January 7, 2014, http://news.siu.edu/2013/02/021513par13026.html. For a comprehensive analysis of how same-sex marriage activists turned the tide of public opinion, see Marc Solomon, *Winning Marriage: The Inside Story of How Same-Sex Couples Took on the Politicians and Pundits—and Won* (Lebanon, NH: ForeEdge, 2014).

18. I have found the following particularly helpful: Michael Warner, *The Trouble with Normal: Sex, Politics, and the Ethics of Queer Life* (Cambridge, MA: Harvard University Press, 1999); Beyond Marriage, *Beyond Same-Sex Marriage: A New Strategic Vision for All Our Families and Relationships* (2006), accessed January 21, 2014, www.beyondmarriage.org/full-Statement.html; Nancy D. Polikoff, *Beyond (Straight and Gay) Marriage: Valuing All Families under the Law* (Boston: Beacon Press, 2009); Nicola Barker, *Not the Marrying Kind: A Feminist Critique of Same-Sex Marriage* (New York: Palgrave Macmillan, 2012); Mary Bernstein and Verta Taylor, eds., *The Marrying Kind? Debating Same-Sex Marriage within the Lesbian and Gay Movement* (Minneapolis: University of Minnesota Press, 2013).

19. Law Commission of Canada, *Beyond Conjugality: Recognizing and Supporting Close Personal Adult Relationships* (2001), accessed January 17, 2014, http://tabletology.com/docs/beyond_conjugality.pdf.

20. Ibid., xi.

21. Suzanna Danutta Walters, "Alter-ed Expectations," accessed January 21, 2014, http://www.fromthesquare.org/?p=5096.

22. For a strident critique of Macklemore's hit song, see Karen Tongsen, "Same Love? Same Old Shit," accessed January 21, 2014, http://www.fromthesquare.org/?p=5005.

BIBLIOGRAPHY

"A New bundling song." Isaiah Thomas Broadside Ballads Project. Accessed January 30, 2015. http://www.thomasballads.org/items/show/169.

"A New bundling song: or, A reproof to those young country women, who follow that reproachful practice, and to their mothers for upholding them therein." Isaiah Thomas Broadside Ballads Project. Accessed January 30, 2015. http://www.thomasballads.org/items/show/170.

Abbott, Elizabeth. *A History of Marriage: From Same Sex Unions to Private Vows and Common Law, the Surprising Diversity of a Tradition.* New York: Penguin, 2010.

Adams, Abigail. "Letter from Abigail Adams to John Adams, March 31, 1776." In *The Letters of John and Abigail Adams.* Edited by Frank Shuffleton, 147–49. New York: Penguin Classics, 2004.

Adams, John. *Diary and Autobiography of John Adams.* Edited by Lyman H. Butterfield. 4 vols. Cambridge, MA: Belknap Press of Harvard University Press, 1961.

Adams-Campbell, Melissa. "*Life of Black Hawk:* A Sauk and Mesquakie Archive." *Settler Colonial Studies* (2014). doi:10.1080/2201473X.2014.957259.

Adventures of Jonathan Corncob, Loyal American Refugee, Written by Himself. London: Printed for the Author, 1787.

Alexander, Elizabeth. *The Venus Hottentot.* Charlottesville: University of Virginia Press, 1990.

Alexander, William. *The History of Women.* London: W. Strahan and T. Cadell, 1779. Reprint, New York: AMS Press, 1976.

Allen, Theodore. *The Invention of the White Race.* 2 vols. 2nd ed. London: Verso, 2012.

Anburey, Thomas. *Travels through the Interior Parts of America.* 2 vols. London: William Lane, 1789.

Anderson, Benedict. *Imagined Communities: Reflections on the Origin and Spread of Nationalism.* New York: Verso, 1991.

Anderson, Jill. "Tomes of Travel and Travesty: The Didactic of Captivity in Susanna Rowson's *Charlotte Temple* and Mary Rowlandson's *The Sovereignty and Goodness of God.*" *Women's Studies: An Interdisciplinary Journal* 38, no. 4 (2009): 429–48.

Anderson, Karen. *Chain Her By One Foot: The Subjugation of Native Women in Seventeenth-Century New France.* New York: Routledge, 1991.

Arch, Stephen Carl. "The Female American; The Interesting Narrative of the Life of Olaudah Equiano." *Eighteenth-Century Fiction* 14, no. 2 (2002): 240–43.

Armstrong, Nancy. *Desire and Domestic Fiction: A Political History of the Novel.* New York: Oxford University Press, 1987.

———. "Why Daughters Die: The Racial Logic of American Sentimentalism." *Yale Journal of Criticism: Interpretation in the Humanities* 7, no. 2 (1994): 1–24.

Ashcroft, Bill, Gareth Griffiths, and Helen Tiffen, eds. *The Empire Writes Back: Theory and Practice in Post-Colonial Literatures.* 2nd ed. New York: Routledge, 2002.

———, *The Postcolonial Studies Reader.* London: Routledge, 1994.

Baker, Jennifer. *Securing the Commonwealth: Debt, Speculation, and Writing in the Making of Early America.* Baltimore: Johns Hopkins University Press, 2005.

Bakhtin, Mikhail. *The Dialogic Imagination: Four Essays.* Translated by Vadin Liapunov and Kenneth Bromstrom. Austin: University of Texas Press, 1982.

Bannet, Eve Tavor. *The Domestic Revolution: Enlightenment Feminisms and the Novel.* Baltimore: Johns Hopkins University Press, 2000.

Barker, Nicola. *Not the Marrying Kind: A Feminist Critique of Same-Sex Marriage.* New York: Palgrave Macmillan, 2012.

Barker-Benfield, G. J. *The Culture of Sensibility: Sex and Society in Eighteenth-Century Britain.* Chicago: University of Chicago Press, 1992.

Barnes, Elizabeth. *States of Sympathy: Seduction and Democracy in the Early American Novel.* New York: Columbia University Press, 1997.

Basch, Norma. "From the Bonds of Empire to the Bonds of Matrimony." In *Devising Liberty: Preserving and Creating Freedom in the New American Republic.* Edited by David Thomas Konig, 217–42. Stanford, CA: Stanford University Press, 1995.

———. *In the Eyes of the Law: Women, Marriage, and Property in Nineteenth-Century New York.* Ithaca, NY: Cornell University Press, 1982.

Baym, Nina. *Woman's Fiction: A Guide to Novels by and about Women in America, 1820–1870.* Ithaca, NY: Cornell University Press, 1978.

Bernstein, Mary, and Verta Taylor, eds. *The Marrying Kind? Debating Same-Sex Marriage within the Lesbian and Gay Movement.* Minneapolis: University of Minnesota Press, 2013.

Beyond Marriage. *Beyond Same-Sex Marriage: A New Strategic Vision for All Our Families and Relationships.* 2006. Accessed January 21, 2014. www.beyondmarriage.org/full-Statement.html.

Bhabha, Homi K. *The Location of Culture.* New York: Routledge, 1994.

Biggar, H. P., ed. *The Works of Samuel Champlain.* Vol. 3. Toronto: Champlain Society, 1922–36.

Black, Jeremy. *France and the Grand Tour.* New York: Palgrave Macmillan, 2003.

———. *Italy and the Grand Tour.* New Haven, CT: Yale University Press, 2003.

Bloch, Ruth H. "Religion, Literary Sentimentalism, and Popular Revolutionary Ideology." In *Gender and Morality in Anglo-American Culture, 1650–1800.* Berkeley: University of California Press, 2003.

———. "The Gendered Meanings of Virtue in Revolutionary America." *Signs* 13, no. 1 (Autumn 1987): 37–58.

Boone, Joseph Allen. *Tradition Counter Tradition: Love and the Form of Fiction.* Chicago: University of Chicago Press, 1987.

Bowen, Scarlet. "Via Media: Transatlantic Anglicanism in *The Female American*." *Eighteenth-Century: Theory and Interpretation* 53, no. 2 (2012): 189–207.

Bowers, Toni. *Force or Fraud: British Seduction Stories and the Problem of Resistance, 1660–1760*. New York: Oxford University Press, 2011.

Bowers, Toni, and Tita Chico, eds. *Atlantic Worlds in the Long Eighteenth Century: Seduction and Sentiment*. New York: Palgrave Macmillan, 2012.

Bowles, Paul. "John Millar, the Four-Stages Theory, and Women's Position in Society." *History of Political Economy* 16, no. 4 (1984): 619–38.

Braund, Kathryn E. Holland. "Guardians of Tradition and Handmaidens to Change: Women's Roles in Creek Economic and Social Life during the Eighteenth Century." *American Indian Quarterly* 14, no. 3 (1990): 239–58.

Brickhouse, Anna. *The Unsettlement of America: Translation, Interpretation, and the Story of Don Luis de Velasco, 1560–1945*. New York: Oxford University Press, 2014.

Breen, T. H. *The Marketplace of Revolution: How Consumer Politics Shaped American Independence*. New York: Oxford University Press, 2005.

Brooke, Frances. *The History of Emily Montague*. Toronto: McClelland and Stewart, 1995.

Brooke, John L. *Refiner's Fire: The Making of Mormon Cosmology, 1644–1844*. Cambridge: Cambridge University Press, 1994.

Brown, Harry. "'The Horrid Alternative': Miscegenation and Madness in the Frontier Romance." *Journal of American and Comparative Cultures* 24, no. 3–4 (2001): 137–51.

Brown, Judith K. "Economic Organization and the Position of Women among the Iroquois." *Ethnohistory* 17, no. 3–4 (1970): 151–67.

Brown, Stuart. *British Philosophy and the Age of Enlightenment*. Vol. 5 of *Routledge History of Philosophy*. Edited by G. H. R. Parkinson and S. G. Shanker. London: Routledge, 2003.

Brownstein, Rachel. *Becoming a Heroine: Reading about Women in Novels*. New York: Columbia University Press, 1994.

Bryson, Gladys. *Man and Society: The Scottish Inquiry of the Eighteenth Century*. Princeton, NJ: Princeton University Press, 1945.

Buckley, Jerome. *Season of Youth: The Bildungsroman from Dickens to Golding*. Cambridge, MA: Harvard University Press, 1974.

Buell, Lawrence. "American Literary Emergence as a Postcolonial Phenomenon." *American Literary History* 4 (1992): 411–42.

Buffon, Georges-Louis Leclerc, Comte de. *Histoire naturelle, générale, et particulière*. Paris: de L'Imprimerie Royale, 1749–1809.

Burnaby, Andrew. *Burnaby's Travels through North America*. Edited by Rufus Rockwell Wilson. New York: A. Wessels, 1904.

Burnham, Michelle, ed. *The Female American; or, The Adventures of Unca Eliza Winkfield*. Petersborough, ON: Broadview Editions, 2001.

Burr, Aaron. *Memoirs of Aaron Burr with Miscellaneous Selections of His Correspondence*. 2 vols. New York: Harper and Brothers, 1836.

Butler, Judith. *Gender Trouble: Feminism and the Subversion of Identity*. New York: Routledge, 1990.

Campbell, R. H., and Andrew S. Skinner, eds. *The Origins and Nature of the Scottish Enlightenment*. Edinburgh: John Donald Publishers, 1982.

Chakkalakal, Tess. *Novel Bondage: Slavery, Marriage, and Freedom in Nineteenth-Century America*. Urbana: University of Illinois Press, 2011.

Chantrans, Justin Girod de. *Voyage d'un Suisse dans les colonies d'Amérique*. Paris: Librairie Jules Tallendier, 1980.

Channing, William Ellery. "Essay on American Language and Literature." *North American Review* 1, no. 3 (1815): 307–14.

Cherniavsky, Eva. "Charlotte Temple's Remains." In *Discovering Difference: Contemporary Essays in American Culture*. Edited by Christopher K. Lohmann, 35–47. Bloomington: Indiana University Press, 1993.

Child, Lydia Maria. *Hobomok and Other Writings on Indians*. Edited by Carolyn L. Karcher. New Brunswick, NJ: Rutgers University Press, 1986.

Chused, Richard H. "Married Women's Property Law, 1800–1850." *Georgetown Law Journal* 71, no. 5 (1983): 1359–1425.

Coontz, Stephanie. *Marriage, a History: How Love Conquered Marriage*. New York: Penguin, 2005.

Cott, Nancy. *The Bonds of Womanhood: "Woman's Sphere" in New England, 1780–1835*. New Haven, CT: Yale University Press, 1977.

———. "Marriage and Women's Citizenship in the United States, 1830–1934." *American Historical Review* 103, no. 5 (1998): 1440–74.

———. *Public Vows: A History of Marriage and the Nation*. Cambridge, MA: Harvard University Press, 2000.

Crais, Clifton, and Pamela Scully. *Sarah Baartman and the Hottentot Venus: A Ghost Story and a Biography*. Princeton, NJ: Princeton University Press, 2009.

Davidson, Cathy N. "Introduction." In *Charlotte Temple*. New York: Oxford University Press, 1986.

———. *Revolution and the Word: The Rise of the Novel in America*. New York: Oxford University Press, 1986.

Davidson, Cathy N., and Jessamyn Hatcher, eds. *No More Separate Spheres! A Next Wave American Studies Reader*. Durham, NC: Duke University Press, 2002.

Dayan, Joan. *Haiti, History, and the Gods*. Berkeley: University of California Press, 1995.

Dearborn, Henry. "Henry A. S. Dearborn Journals (1838–1839)." *Publications of the Buffalo Historical Society* 7 (1904): 111–14.

D'Emilio, John, and Estelle B. Freedman, eds. *Intimate Matters: A History of Sexuality in America*. 3rd ed. Chicago: University of Chicago Press, 2012.

Deglar, Carl. *At Odds: Women and the Family in America from the Revolution to the Present*. New York: Oxford University Press, 1980.

Demos, John. *The Unredeemed Captive: A Family Story from Early America*. New York: Vintage Books, 1995.

Denzin, Norman K., and Yvonna S. Lincoln. "Preface." In *Handbook of Critical and Indigenous Methodologies*. Edited by Yvonna Lincoln, Norman Denzin, and Linda Tuhiwai Smith, ix–xv. Los Angeles: Sage, 2008.

Desiderio, Jennifer, ed. "Special Issue: Beyond *Charlotte Temple*." *Studies in American Fiction* 38, no. 1–2 (2011): 1–287.

Diaz, Maria Elena. *The Virgin, the King, and the Royal Slaves of El Cobre: Negotiating Freedom in Colonial Cuba, 1670–1780.* Stanford, CA: Stanford University Press, 2002.

Dillon, Elizabeth Maddock. *The Gender of Freedom: Fictions of Liberalism and the Literary Public Sphere.* Stanford, CA: Stanford University Press, 2004.

———. "The Secret History of the Early American Novel: Leonora Sansay and Revolution in Saint Domingue." *Novel* 40, no. 1–2 (2006): 77–103.

Dippie, Brian W. *The Vanishing American: White Attitudes and US Indian Policy.* Middletown, CT: Wesleyan University Press, 1982.

Dominique, Lyndon J., ed. *The Woman of Colour: A Tale.* Peterborough, ON: Broadview Editions, 2008.

Doten, Dana. *The Art of Bundling: Being an Inquiry into the Nature & Origins of That Curious but Universal Folk-Custom, with an Exposition of the Rise & Fall of Bundling in the Eastern Part of No. America.* New York: Countryman Press/ Farrar and Rinehart, 1938.

Dowd, Gregory Evans. "Spinning Wheel Revolution." In *The Revolution of 1800: Democracy, Race, and the New Republic.* Edited by Jan Ellen Lewis, James Horn, and Peter S. Onuf, 265–86. Charlottesville: University of Virginia Press, 2002.

Drexler, Michael. "Brigands and Nuns: The Vernacular Sociology of Collectivity after the Haitian Revolution." In *Messy Beginnings: Postcoloniality and Early American Studies.* Edited by Malini Johar Schueller and Edward Watts, 175–99. New Brunswick, NJ: Rutgers University Press, 2003.

———, ed. "Introduction" and "Chronology." In *Secret History; or, The Horrors of St. Domingo and Laura.* 10–37, 38–54. Peterborough, ON: Broadview Editions, 2007.

———. "Leonora Sansay's Anatopic Imagination." In *Urban Identity and the Atlantic World.* Edited by Elizabeth Faye and Leonard Morze, 143–57. New York: Palgrave Macmillan, 2013.

Dubois, Laurent. *Avengers of the New World: The Story of the Haitian Revolution.* Cambridge, MA: Belknap Press of Harvard University, 2004.

DuCille, Anne. *The Coupling Convention: Sex, Text, and Tradition in Black Women's Fiction.* New York: Oxford University Press, 1993.

Duckworth, Mark. "An Eighteenth-Century Questionnaire: William Robertson on the Indians." *Eighteenth-Century Life* 11, no. 1 (1987): 36–49.

Duncan, Ian. *Scott's Shadow: The Novel in Romantic Edinburgh.* Princeton, NJ: Princeton University Press, 2007.

DuPlessis, Rachel Blau. *Writing beyond the Ending: Narrative Strategies of Twentieth-Century Women Writers.* Bloomington: Indiana University Press, 1985.

Duvall, Adrienne. "The Ethics of Enterprise: Imagining Colonization in Eighteenth-Century Novels of Colonial Encounter." PhD diss., University of Oregon, 2008.

Dwyer, John. *The Age of Passions: An Interpretation of Adam Smith and Scottish Enlightenment Culture.* East Lothian, Scotland: Tuckwell Press, 1998.

Edmondson, Belinda. "The Black Romance." *Women's Studies Quarterly* 35, no. 1–2 (2007): 191–211.

Ellison, Julie K. *Cato's Tears and the Making of Anglo-American Emotion.* Chicago: University of Chicago Press, 1999.

————. "There and Back: Transatlantic Novels and Anglo-American Careers." In *The Past as Prologue: Essays to Commemorate the 25th Anniversary of ASECS*. Edited by Carla H. Hay and Sydney M. Conger, 303–23. New York: AMS Press, 1995.

Elmer, Jonathan. *On Lingering and Being Last: Race and Sovereignty in the New World*. New York: Fordham University Press, 2008.

Essig, Laurie. "Same Love, Mass Weddings, and the Culture of Romance." *Love, Inc.* (blog). http://www.psychologytoday.com/blog/love-inc/201401/same-love-mass-wed dings-and-the-cult-romance. Accessed January 21, 2014.

Eugenides, Jeffrey. Interview for audiobook. In *The Marriage Plot*. New York: Macmillan Audio, 2011.

Evans, Gareth. "Rakes, Coquettes, and Republican Patriarchs: Class, Gender, and Nation in Early American Sentimental Fiction." *Canadian Review of American Studies* 25, no. 3 (1995): 41–62.

Evenson, Sandra Lee. "Indian Madras Plaids as Real India." In *Dress Sense: Emotional and Sensory Experiences of the Body and Clothes*. Edited by Donald Clay Johnson and Helen Bradley Foster, 96–108. London: Berg, 2008.

Everhart, Darlene. "Accounting and Authorship in Eighteenth-Century Island Narratives." PhD diss., Carnegie Mellon University, 2009.

Fabian, Johannes. *Time and the Other: How Anthropology Makes Its Object*. New York: Columbia University Press, 2002.

Faherty, Duncan. *Remodeling the Nation: The Architecture of American Identity, 1776–1858*. Durham: University of New Hampshire Press, 2009.

————. "'Murder, robbery, rape, adultery, and incest': Martha Meredith Read's *Margaretta* (1807) and the Function of Federalist Fiction." In *Warring for America*. (Forthcoming 2015)

Fenton, William. *The Great Law and the Longhouse: A Political History of the Iroquois Confederacy*. Norman: University of Oklahoma Press, 1998.

————, ed. *Parker on the Iroquois: Iroquois Uses of Maize and Other Food Plants, the Code of Handsome Lake, the Seneca Prophet, the Constitution of the Five Nations*. Syracuse, NY: Syracuse University Press, 1968.

Fessenden, Thomas Green. "Jonathan's Courting, or, The Country Lovers." In *Cyclopedia of American Literature*. Vol. 1. Edited by Evert A. Duyckinck and George L. Duyckinck, 597–99. Philadelphia: William Rutter, 1880.

Festa, Lynn. *Sentimental Figures of Empire in Britain and France*. Baltimore: Johns Hopkins University Press, 2006.

Fichtelberg, Joseph. *Critical Fictions: Sentiment and the American Market, 1780–1870*. Athens: University of Georgia Press, 2003.

————. "Heart-Felt Verities: The Feminism of Martha Meredith Read." *Legacy* 15, no. 2 (1998): 125–38.

Fick, Carolyn. *The Making of Haiti: The Saint-Domingue Revolution from Below*. Knoxville: University of Tennessee Press, 1990.

Fiedler, Leslie. *Love and Death in the American Novel*. Champaign, IL: Dalkey Archive Press, 2003.

Firestone, Shulamith. *The Dialectic of Sex: The Case for Feminist Revolution*. New York: Farrar, Straus and Giroux, 2003.

Fliegelman, Jay. *Prodigals and Pilgrims: The American Revolution against Patriarchal Authority 1750–1800*. Cambridge: Cambridge University Press, 1982.

Flint, Christopher. *Family Fictions: Narrative and Domestic Relations in Britain, 1688–1798*. Stanford, CA: Stanford University Press, 2000.

Fluck, Winfried, Donald E. Pease, and John Carlos Rowe, eds. *Re-Framing the Transnational Turn in American Studies*. Lebanon, NH: Dartmouth College Press, 2011.

Foster, Frances Smith. *'Til Death or Distance Do Us Part: Love and Marriage in African America*. New York: Oxford University Press, 2010.

Foster, Hannah. *The Coquette*. New York: Oxford University Press, 1986.

Fraiman, Susan. *Unbecoming Women: British Women Writers and the Novel of Development*. New York: Columbia University Press, 1993.

Franklin, Edward. *The Life and Adventures of Obadiah Benjamin Franklin Bloomfield, M.D.: A Native of the United States of America, Now on the Tour of Europe. Interspersed with Episodes, and Remarks, Religious, Moral, Public Spirited, and Humorous*. Philadelphia: Published for the Proprietor, 1818.

Freedom to Marry, Inc. "Freedom to Marry." Accessed January 21, 2014. http://www.freedomtomarry.org/.

———. "Why Marriage Matters." Accessed January 21, 2014. http://www.whymarriagematters.org/.

Friedman, Susan Stanford. *Mappings: Feminism and the Cultural Geographies of Encounter*. Princeton, NJ: Princeton University Press, 1998.

A Friend to the Fair Sex. "To the Editor of the Columbian Magazine." *Columbian Magazine* 1, no. 10 (June 1787): 491–97.

Gage, Matilda Joslyn. *Women, Church, and State*. Watertown, MA: Persephone Press, 1980.

Garraway, Doris. *The Libertine Colony: Creolization in the Early French Caribbean*. Durham, NC: Duke University Press, 2005.

Garside, Peter, James Raven, and Rainer Schowerling, eds. *The English Novel, 1770–1829: A Bibliographic Survey of Prose Fiction Published in the British Isles*. Vol. 2, *1800–1829*. New York: Oxford University Press, 2000.

Gaspar, David Barry, and David Patrick Geggus, eds., *A Turbulent Time: The French Revolution and the Greater Caribbean*. Bloomington: Indiana University Press, 1997.

Geggus, David P. "Slave and Free Colored Women in Saint Domingue." In *More Than Chattel: Black Women and Slavery in the Americas*. Edited by David Barry Gaspar and Darlene Clark Hine, 259–78. Bloomington: Indiana University Press, 1996.

———, ed. *The Impact of the Haitian Revolution in the Atlantic World*. Columbia: University of South Carolina Press, 2001.

Giles, Paul. *The Global Remapping of American Literature*. Princeton, NJ: Princeton University Press, 2011.

———. *Virtual Americas: Transnational Fictions and the Transatlantic Literary Imagination*. Durham, NC: Duke University Press, 2002.

———. *Transatlantic Insurrections: British Culture and the Formation of American Literature, 1730–1860*. Philadelphia: University of Pennsylvania Press, 2001.

Gillis, John R. *For Better or Worse: British Marriages, 1600 to the Present*. New York: Oxford University Press, 1985.

Godbeer, Richard. *Sexual Revolution in Early America*. Baltimore: Johns Hopkins University Press, 2002.

Goettner-Abendroth, Heide, ed. "Introduction." In *Societies of Peace: Matriarchies Past, Present, and Future*. 1–14. Toronto: Inanna Publications and Education, 2003.

Goldsmith, Oliver. *The Citizen of the World; or, Letters from a Chinese Philosopher, Residing in London, to His Friends in the East*. Dublin: G. and A. Ewing, 1762.

Golightly, Jennifer. *The Family, Marriage, and Radicalism in British Women's Novels of the 1790s*. Lewisburg, PA: Bucknell University Press, 2012.

Gordon, Sarah Barringer. *The Mormon Question: Polygamy and Constitutional Conflict in Nineteenth-Century America*. Chapel Hill: University of North Carolina Press, 2002.

Goudie, Sean X. *Creole America: The West Indies and the Formation of Literature and Culture in the New Republic*. Philadelphia: University of Pennsylvania Press, 2006.

Green, Katherine Sobba. *The Courtship Novel, 1740–1820*. Lexington: University Press of Kentucky, 1991.

Gustafson, Sandra M. *Eloquence Is Power: Oratory and Performance in Early America*. Chapel Hill: University of North Carolina Press, 2000.

Gutiérrez, Ramón A. *When Jesus Came, the Corn Mothers Went Away: Marriage, Sexuality, and Power in New Mexico, 1500–1846*. Stanford, CA: Stanford University Press, 1991.

Gyssels, Kathleen. "'Les Créoles Galantes?' White Women and the Haitian Revolution." In *Echoes of the Haitian Revolution, 1804–2004*. Edited by Martin Munro and Elizabeth Walcott-Hackshaw, 95–110. Kingston, Jamaica: University of the West Indies Press, 2008.

Habermas, Jürgen. *Structural Transformation of the Public Sphere*. Cambridge, MA: MIT Press, 1989.

Hall, Stuart. "When Was 'The Post-Colonial'? Thinking at the Limits." In *The Post-Colonial Question: Common Skies, Divided Horizons*. Edited by Iain Chambers and Lidia Curti, 242–60. New York: Routledge, 1996.

Harrow, Sharon. *Adventures in Domesticity: Gender and Colonial Adulteration in Eighteenth-Century British Literature*. New York: AMS Press, 2004.

Hartog, Hendrik. "Marital Exits and Marital Expectations in Nineteenth-Century America." *Georgetown Law Journal* 80, no. 1 (October 1991): 95–129.

Hendler, Glenn. *Public Sentiments: Structures of Feeling in Nineteenth-Century American Literature*. Chapel Hill: University of North Carolina Press, 2001.

Herbert, Christopher. *The Grand Tour*. New York: Putnam, 1969.

Hessinger, Rodney. *Seduced, Abandoned, and Reborn: Visions of Youth in Middle-Class America, 1780–1850*. Philadelphia: University Press of Pennsylvania, 2005.

Hilliard d'Auberteuil, Michel-René. *Considérations sur l'état présent de la colonie françoise de Saint-Domingue*. Paris: Chez Grangé, 1776.

Hinz, Evelyn J. "Hierogamy versus Wedlock: Types of Marriage Plots and Their Relationships to Genres of Prose Fiction." *PMLA* 91 (1976): 900–913.

Hobson, Janell. *Venus in the Dark: Blackness and Beauty in Popular Culture*. New York: Routledge, 2005.

Homestead, Melissa, and Camryn Hansen. "Susanna Rowson's Transatlantic Career." *Early American Literature* 45, no. 3 (November 2010): 619–54.

hooks, bell. *Black Looks: Race and Representation.* Cambridge, MA: South End Press, 1999.

Hornsby, Clare. *The Impact of Italy: The Grand Tour and Beyond.* London: British School of Rome, 2000.

Irving, Washington. *A History of New York.* Edited by Michael Black and Nancy Black. Boston: Twayne Publishers, 1983.

Jabour, Anya. *Marriage in the Early Republic: Elizabeth and William Wirt and the Companionate Ideal.* Baltimore: Johns Hopkins University Press, 1998.

James, C. L. R. *The Black Jacobins: Toussaint L'Ouverture and the San Domingo Revolution.* New York: Vintage Books, 1989.

Jarenski, Shelly. "The Voice of the Preceptress: Female Education in and as Seduction Novel." *Journal of the Midwest Modern Language Association* 37, no. 1 (2004): 59–68.

Jefferson, Thomas. *Notes on the State of Virginia.* Chapel Hill: University of North Carolina Press, 1982.

Jónasdóttir, Anna G. "Feminist Questions, Marx's Method and the Theorisation of 'Love Power.'" In *The Political Interests of Gender Revisited: Redoing Theory and Research with a Feminist Face,* edited by Anna G. Jónasdóttir and Kathleen B. Jones, 58–83. Tokyo: United Nations University Press, 2009.

Jordon, Winthrop D. *White Over Black: American Attitudes toward the Negro, 1550–1812.* Chapel Hill: University of North Carolina Press, 1968.

Joseph, Betty. "Re(Playing) Crusoe/Pocahontas: Circum-Atlantic Stagings in *The Female American.*" *Criticism* 42, no. 3 (2000): 317–35.

Kames, Henry Home. *Sketches of the History of Man.* Dublin: James Williams, 1774.

Karcher, Carolyn L. *The First Woman in the Republic: A Cultural Biography of Lydia Maria Child.* Durham, NC: Duke University Press, 1994.

———, ed. "Introduction." In *Hobomok and Other Writings on Indians.* New Brunswick, NJ: Rutgers University Press, 1986.

Kazanjian, David. *The Colonizing Trick: National Culture and Imperial Citizenship in Early America.* Baltimore: Johns Hopkins University Press, 2004.

Klepp, Susan E. *Revolutionary Conceptions: Women, Fertility, and Family Limitation in America, 1760–1820.* Chapel Hill: University of North Carolina Press, 2009.

Knott, Sarah. *Sensibility and the American Revolution.* Chapel Hill: University of North Carolina Press, 2009.

Koegel, Otto E. *Common Law Marriage and Its Development in the United States.* Washington, DC: John Byrne, 1922.

Kulman, Keely Susan. "Transatlantic Travel and Cultural Exchange in the Early Colonial Era: The Hybrid *American Female* and Her New World Colony." PhD diss., Washington State University, 2006.

Lafitau, Father Joseph-François. *Customs of the American Indians Compared with Customs of Primitive Times.* Edited by William Fenton and Elizabeth Moore. Toronto: Champlain Society, 1977.

Lahontan, Louis Armand de Lom d'Arce, Baron de. *Mémoires de l'Amérique Septentrionale ou la Suite des Voyages de Mr. Le Baron de Lahontan,* vol 2., tome second. The Hague: Chez les Frères l'Honoré Marchands Libraries, 1703.

———. *New Voyages to North America*. Edited by Reuben Gold Thwaites. 2 vols. Chicago: A. C. McClurg, 1905.

———. "A Conference or Dialogue between the Author and Adario, a Noted Man among the Savages, Containing a Circumstantial View of the Customs and Humors of That People." In *New Voyages to North America*. Edited by Reuben Gold Thwaites. Vol. 2. Chicago: A. C. McClurg, 1905.

Langford, Paul. *Public Life and the Propertied Englishman, 1689–1798*. New York: Oxford University Press, 1991.

———. *A Polite and Commercial People: England, 1727–1783*. New York: Oxford University Press, 1983.

Lapsansky, Phillip. "Afro-Americana: Rediscovering Leonora Sansay." In *The Annual Report of the Library Company of Philadelphia for the Year 1992*. Philadelphia: Library Company, 1993.

Law Commission of Canada. *Beyond Conjugality: Recognizing and Supporting Close Personal Adult Relationships*. 2001. Accessed January 17, 2014. http:// tabletology.com/docs/beyond_conjugality.pdf.

Lawson, Alan. "A Cultural Paradigm for the Second World." *Australian and Canadian Studies* 9, no. 1 (1991): 67–78.

———. "Comparative Studies and Post-Colonial 'Settler' Cultures." *Australian and Canadian Studies* 10, no. 2 (1992): 153–58.

Leites, Edmund. *The Puritan Conscience and Modern Sexuality*. New Haven, CT: Yale University Press, 1986.

Lemay, J. A. Leo. "The American Origins of 'Yankee Doodle.'" *William and Mary Quarterly* 33, no. 3 (1976): 435–65.

Lemmings, David. "Marriage and the Law in the Eighteenth Century: Hardwicke's Marriage Act of 1753." *Historical Journal* 39 (1996): 339–60.

Lewis, Jan. "The Republican Wife: Virtue and Seduction in the Early Republic." *William and Mary Quarterly* 44, no. 4 (1987): 689–721.

Liu, Tessie P. "The Secret beyond White Patriarchal Power: Race, Gender, and Freedom in the Last Days of Colonial Saint-Domingue." *French Historical Studies* 33, no. 3 (2010): 387–416.

Luhmann, Niklas. *Love as Passion: The Codification of Intimacy*. Translated by Jeremy Gaines and Doris L. Jones. Stanford, CA: Stanford University Press, 1998.

———. *Love: A Sketch*. Edited by Andre Kieserling and translated by Kathleen Cross. Malden, MA: Polity Press, 2010.

Lyons, Clare. *Sex among the Rabble: An Intimate History of Gender and Power in the Age of Revolution, Philadelphia, 1730–1830*. Chapel Hill: University of North Carolina Press, 2006.

Lystra, Karen. *Searching the Heart: Women, Men, and Romantic Love in Nineteenth-Century America*. New York: Oxford University Press, 1992.

Macfarlane, Alan. *The Origins of English Individualism: The Family, Property, and Social Transition*. London: Blackwell, 1978.

———. *Marriage and Love in England: Modes of Reproduction, 1300–1840*. New York: Blackwell Publishers, 1986.

Maddox, Lucy. "American Indians, Civilized Performance, and Civil Rights." *European Contributions to American Studies* 57 (2004): 53–59.

Maillor, Giddeon. "The History of *Charlotte Temple* as an American Bestseller." In *Must Read: Rediscovering American Bestsellers from* Charlotte Temple *to* The DaVinci Code. Edited by Sarah Churchwell and Thomas Ruys Smith, 59–77. London: Continuum, 2013.

Mann, Barbara Alice. *Iroquoian Women: The Gantowisas*. New York: Peter Lang, 2006.

———. "'They Are the Soul of the Councils': The Iroquoian Model of Woman-Power." In *Societies of Peace: Matriarchies Past, Present, and Future*. Edited by Heide Goettner-Abendroth, 57–79. Toronto: Inanna Publications and Education, 2003.

Mason, Carol. "Eighteenth-Century Culture Change among the Lower Creeks." *Florida Anthropologist* 16, no. 3 (1963): 65–80.

McDowell, Tremaine. "An American Robinson Crusoe." *American Literature* 3 (1929): 307–9.

McMullen, Lorraine. *An Odd Attempt in a Woman: The Literary Life of Frances Brooke*. Vancouver: University of British Columbia Press, 1983.

McMurran, Mary Helen. "Realism and the Unreal in *The Female American*." *Eighteenth-Century: Theory and Interpretation* 52, no. 3–4 (2011): 323–42.

Meek, Ronald. *Social Science and the Ignoble Savage*. Cambridge: Cambridge University Press, 1976.

Merrett, Robert. "The Politics of Romance in *The History of Emily Montague*." *Canadian Literature* 133 (Summer 1992): 92–108.

Mihesuah, Devon A., ed. "Commonality of Difference: American Indian Women and History." In *Natives and Academics: Researching and Writing about American Indians*. 37–54. Lincoln: University of Nebraska Press, 1998.

Millar, John. *The Origin of the Distinction of Ranks; or, An Inquiry into the Circumstances Which Give Rise to Influence and Authority, in the Different Members of Society*. Indianapolis: Liberty Fund, 2006.

Miller, Alaric. "Serious Jesting: A Close Inspection of the Smith-Adams Epistolary Courtship Based on Their Early Love-Letters, 1762–1764." *Theses, Dissertations, Professional Papers*. Paper 3531. University of Montana, 1997.

Miller, Nancy K. *The Heroine's Text: Readings in the French and English Novel, 1722–1782*. New York: Columbia University Press, 1980.

Mintz, Sidney. "Economic Role and Cultural Tradition." In *The Black Woman Cross-Culturally*. Edited by Filomina Chioma Steady, 515–34. Cambridge, MA: Schenkman, 1981.

Modleski, Tania. *Loving with a Vengeance: Mass-Produced Fantasies for Women*. New York: Routledge, 1990.

Mohawk, John. "The Power of Seneca Women and the Legacy of Handsome Lake." In *Native Voices: American Indian Identity and Resistance*. Edited by Richard A. Grounds, George E. Tinker, and David E. Wilkins, 20–34. Lawrence: University of Kansas Press, 2003.

Monsam, Angela. "*Charlotte Temple,* an Autopsy: The Physiology of Seduction." In
    *Death Becomes Her: Cultural Narratives of Femininity and Death in Nineteenth-
    Century America.* Edited by Elizabeth Dill and Sheri Weinstein, 73–88. Newcastle
    Upon Tyne: Cambridge Scholars, 2008.
Moran, Mary Catherine. "The Commerce of the Sexes: Gender and the Social Sphere
    in Scottish Enlightenment Accounts of Civil Society." In *Paradoxes of Civil Soci-
    ety: New Perspectives on Modern German and British History.* Edited by Frank
    Trentmann, 61–85. New York: Berghahn Books, 2000.
Moreau de Saint-Méry, M. L. E. *Description topographique, physique, civile, poli-
    tique et historique de la partie française de l'isle Saint-Domingue.* 2 vols. Paris:
    Société de l'histoire des Colonies Françaises et Librairie Larose, 1958.
Morgan, Edmund Sears. "The Puritan's Marriage with God." *South Atlantic Quar-
    terly* 49 (1949): 107–12.
Morgan, Lewis Henry. *League of the Iroquois.* Secaucus, NJ: Citadel Press, 1962.
Morgan, Jennifer L. *Laboring Women: Reproduction and Gender in New World
    Slavery.* Philadelphia: University of Pennsylvania Press, 2004.
Morgan, Winifred. *An American Icon: Brother Jonathan and American Identity.*
    Cranbury, NJ: Associated University Presses, 1988.
Newman, Andrew. *On Records: Delaware Indians, Colonists, and the Media of
    History and Memory.* Lincoln: University of Nebraska Press, 2012.
Nickels, Cameron C. *New England Humor: From the Revolutionary War to the
    Civil War.* Nashville: University of Tennessee Press, 1993.
Noel, Jan V. "Revisiting Gender in Iroquoia." In *Gender and Sexuality in Indigenous
    North America.* Edited by Sandra Slater and Fay A. Yarbrough, 54–73. Columbia:
    University of South Carolina Press, 2011.
Nordius, Janina. "'Thus Might I Reason with a Heathen . . . ': The Gothic Moment in
    The Female American." *Nordic Journal of English Studies* 7, no. 2 (2008): 1–18.
Norton, Mary Beth. *Liberty's Daughters: The Revolutionary Experience of American
    Women, 1750–1800.* Ithaca, NY: Cornell University Press, 1996.
Nussbaum, Felicity. *Torrid Zones: Maternity, Sexuality, and Empire in Eighteenth-
    Century English Narratives.* Baltimore: Johns Hopkins University Press, 1995.
O'Connell, Lisa. "'Matrimonial Ceremonies Displayed': Popular Ethnography and
    Enlightened Imperialism." *Eighteenth-Century Life* 26, no. 3 (Fall 2002): 98–116.
Okin, Susan Moller. "Women and the Making of the Sentimental Family." *Philoso-
    phy and Public Affairs* 11, no. 1 (1982): 65–88.
Parmentar, Jon. *The Edge of the Woods: Iroquoia, 1534–1701.* East Lansing: Michi-
    gan State University Press, 2010.
Parrish, Susan Scott. *American Curiosity: Cultures of Natural History in the Colonial
    British Atlantic World.* Chapel Hill: University of North Carolina Press, 2006.
Pateman, Carol. *The Sexual Contract.* Stanford, CA: Stanford University Press, 1988.
Pease, Donald E., and Robyn Wiegman, eds. *The Futures of American Studies.* Dur-
    ham, NC: Duke University Press, 2002.
Perdue, Theda. *Cherokee Women: Gender and Culture Change, 1700–1835.* Lincoln:
    University of Nebraska Press, 1998.
Perrin, Noel, ed. "Preface." In *The Adventures of Jonathan Corncob, Loyal Ameri-

can Refugee, Written by Himself. Illustrated by Mark Livingston. Boston: David Godine, 1976.

Perry, Ruth. *Novel Relations: The Transformation of Kinship in English Literature and Culture, 1748–1818.* Cambridge: Cambridge University Press, 2004.

Peters, Rev. Samuel, LL.D. *General History of Connecticut: From Its First Settlement [. . .].* Edited by Samuel Jarvis McCormick. New York: D. Appleton, 1877.

Pethers, Matthew. "Poverty, Providence, and the State of Welfare." *Early American Literature* 49, no. 3 (2014): 707–40.

Petter, Henri. *The Early American Novel.* Columbus: Ohio State University Press, 1971.

Phillips, Mark Salber. *Society and Sentiment: Genres of Historical Writing in Britain, 1740–1820.* Princeton, NJ: Princeton University Press, 2000.

Phillipson, N. T., and Rosalind Mitchison, eds. *Scotland in the Age of Improvement; Essays in Scottish History in the Eighteenth Century.* Edinburgh: Edinburgh University Press, 1970.

Plane, Ann Marie. *Colonial Intimacies: Indian Marriage in Early New England.* Ithaca, NY: Cornell University Press, 2002.

Pocock, J. G. A. *Virtue, Commerce, and History: Essays on Political Thought and History, Chiefly in the Eighteenth Century.* Cambridge: Cambridge University Press, 1985.

Polikoff, Nancy D. *Beyond (Straight and Gay) Marriage: Valuing All Families under the Law.* Boston: Beacon Press, 2009.

"Poll: Support Grows for Gay Marriage in Illinois." Accessed January 7, 2014. http://news.siu.edu/2013/02/021513par13026.html.

Porter, Tom. *And Grandma Said . . . Iroquois Teachings as Passed Down through the Oral Tradition.* Bloomington, IN: Xlibris, 2008.

Porterfield, Amanda. *Female Piety in Puritan New England: The Emergence of Religious Humanism.* New York: Oxford University Press, 1992.

Povinelli, Elizabeth. *The Empire of Love: Toward a Theory of Intimacy, Genealogy, and Carnality.* Durham, NC: Duke University Press, 2006.

Pressman, Richard, ed. "Introduction: *Margaretta* as Federalist Fantasy." In *Margaretta; or, The Intricacies of the Heart.* 13–41. San Antonio, TX: Early American Reprints, 2012.

Proctor, Thomas. "Narrative of the Journey of Col. Thomas Proctor to the Indians of the North-West." *Pennsylvania Archives* 4 (1876 [1791]), 551–622.

Radhakrishnan, R. "Why Compare?" *New Literary History* 40, no. 3 (Summer 2009): 453–71.

Radway, Janice. *Reading the Romance: Women, Patriarchy, and Popular Literature.* Chapel Hill: University of North Carolina Press, 1984.

Raimond, Julien. "Observations on the Origin and Progression of the White Colonists' Prejudice against Men of Color." In *Slave Revolution in the Caribbean, 1789–1804: A Brief History with Documents.* Edited by Laurent Dubois and John Garrigus, 78–81. Boston: Bedford/St. Martin's, 2006.

Read, Martha Meredith. *Margaretta; or, The Intricacies of the Heart.* Edited by Richard Pressman. San Antonio, TX: Early American Reprints, 2012.

Reilly, Matthew. "'No Eye Has Seen, or Ear Heard': Arabic Sources for Quaker Subjectivity in Unca Eliza Winkfield's *The Female American.*" *Eighteenth-Century Studies* 44, no. 2 (2011): 261–83.

Rendall, Jane. "Clio, Mars, and Minerva: The Scottish Enlightenment and the Writing of Women's History." In *Eighteenth-Century Scotland: New Perspectives.* Edited by Thomas M. Devine and John R. Young, 134–51. East Lothian, Scotland: Tuckwell Press, 1999.

———, ed. *The Origins of the Scottish Enlightenment, 1707–1776.* Basingstoke: Macmillan, 1978.

Richter, Daniel K. *The Ordeal of the Longhouse: The People of the Iroquois League in the Era of European Colonization.* Chapel Hill: University of North Carolina Press, 1991.

Rifkin, Mark. *When Did Indians Become Straight? Kinship, the History of Sexuality, and Native Sovereignty.* New York: Oxford University Press, 2011.

Roach, Joseph. *Cities of the Dead: Circum-Atlantic Performance.* New York: Columbia University Press, 1996.

Robertson, William. *The History of America.* Dublin: Messrs. Price Whitestone W. Watson R. Cross Corcoran, 1777. Accessed on *Eighteenth-Century Collections Online, ECCO,* June 12, 2007.

Rogers, Dominique, and Stewart King. "Housekeepers, Merchants, Rentières: Free Women of Color in the Port Cities of Colonial Saint-Domingue, 1750–1790." In *Women in Port: Gendering Communities, Economies, and Social Networks in Atlantic Port Cities, 1500–1800.* Edited by Douglas Catterall and Jodi Campbell, 357–97. Leiden, Netherlands: Brill, 2012.

Roof, Judith. *Come as You Are: Sexuality and Narrative.* New York: Columbia University Press, 1996.

Rothman, Ellen K. *Hands and Hearts: A History of Courtship in America.* New York: Basic Books, 1984.

Rust, Marion. *Prodigal Daughters: Susanna Rowson's Early American Women.* Chapel Hill: University of North Carolina Press, 2008.

Said, Edward. *Culture and Imperialism.* London: Vintage, 1993.

Samuels, Shirley. *Romances of the Republic: Women, the Family, and Violence in the Literature of the Early American Nation.* New York: Oxford University Press, 1996.

Sansay, Leonora. *Secret History; or, The Horrors of St. Domingo* and *Laura.* Edited by Michael Drexler. Peterborough, ON: Broadview Editions, 2007.

Sayre, Gordon M. *Les Sauvages Americains: Representations of Native Americans in French and English Colonial Literature.* Chapel Hill: University of North Carolina Press, 1997.

Schoepf, Johann David. *Travels in the Confederation, 1783–1784.* Translated and edited by Alfred J. Morrison. Philadelphia: William Campbell, 1911.

Schueller, Malini Johar, and Edward Watts, eds. *Messy Beginnings: Postcoloniality and Early American Studies.* New Brunswick, NJ: Rutgers University Press, 2003.

Schweitzer, Ivy. *Perfecting Friendship: Politics and Affiliation in Early American Literature.* Chapel Hill: University of North Carolina Press, 2006.

Seaver, James. "A Narrative of the Life of Mrs. Mary Jemison." In *Women's Indian Captivity Narratives*. Edited by Kathryn Zabelle Derounian-Stodola, 117–210. New York: Penguin, 1998.

Semonche, John E. "Common-Law Marriage in North Carolina: A Study in Legal History." *American Journal of Legal History* 9 (1965): 324–41.

Shapiro, Stephen. *The Culture and Commerce of the Early American Novel: Reading the Atlantic World-System*. University Park: Pennsylvania State University Press, 2008.

Sharpe, Jenny. "Is the United States Postcolonial? Transnationalism, Immigration, and Race." *Diaspora* 4, no. 2 (1995): 181–99.

Shoemaker, Nancy. "The Rise or Fall of Iroquois Women." *Journal of Women's History* 2, no. 3 (1991): 40.

Simpson, Audra. *Mohawk Interruptus: Political Life across the Borders of Settler States*. Durham, NC: Duke University Press, 2014.

Simpson, George. "Sexual and Familial Institutions in Northern Haiti." *American Anthropologist* 44, no. 4 (1942): 655–74.

Smith, Adam. *Lectures on Jurisprudence*. In *The Glasgow Edition of the Works and Correspondence of Adam Smith*. Edited by Ronald L. Meek, D. D. Raphael, and Peter Stein. Vol. 5. Oxford: Clarendon Press, 1978.

Smith, Daniel Scott, and Michael S. Hindus, "Premarital Pregnancy in America 1640–1971: An Overview and Interpretation." *Journal of Interdisciplinary History* 5 (1975): 537–70.

Smith-Rosenberg, Caroll. "Black Gothic: The Shadowy Origins of the American Bourgeoisie." In *Possible Pasts: Becoming Colonial in Early America*. Edited by Robert Blair St. George, 243–69. Ithaca, NY: Cornell University Press, 2000.

———. "Domesticating 'Virtue': Coquettes and Revolutionaries in Young America." In *Literature and the Body: Essays on Populations and Persons*. Edited by Elaine Scarry, 160–84. Baltimore: Johns Hopkins University Press, 1988.

Smits, David D. "The 'Squaw Drudge': A Prime Index of Savagism." *Ethnohistory* 29, no. 4 (1982): 281–306.

Socolow, Susan M. "Economic Roles of the Free Women of Color of Cap Français." In *More Than Chattel: Black Women and Slavery in the Americas*. Edited by David Barry Gaspar and Darlene Clark Hine, 279–97. Bloomington: Indiana University Press, 1996.

Solomon, Marc. *Winning Marriage: The Inside Story of How Same-Sex Couples Took on the Politicians and Pundits—and Won*. Lebanon, NH: ForeEdge, 2014.

Spadafora, David. *The Idea of Progress in Eighteenth-Century Britain*. New Haven, CT: Yale University Press, 1990.

Spittal, W. G., ed. *Iroquois Women: An Anthology*. Ohsweken, ON: Iroqrafts, 1990.

Spivack, Gayatri. "Can the Subaltern Speak?" In *Marxism and the Interpretation of Culture*. Edited by Cary Nelson and Lawrence Grossberg, 271–313. Urbana: University of Illinois Press, 1988.

Stanley, Amy Dru. *From Bondage to Contract: Wage Labor, Marriage, and the Market in the Age of Slave Emancipation*. Cambridge: Cambridge University Press, 1998.

Staves, Susan. *Players' Scepters: Fictions of Authority in the Restoration*. Lincoln: University of Nebraska Press, 1970.

Stedman, John Gabriel. *Narrative of a Five Years Expedition against the Revolted Negroes of Surinam.* Baltimore: Johns Hopkins University Press, 1988.

Stern, Julia. *The Plight of Feeling: Sympathy and Dissent in the Early American Novel.* Chicago: University of Chicago Press, 1997.

Stevens, Laura M. *The Poor Indians: British Missionaries, Native Americans, and Colonial Sensibility.* Philadelphia: University of Pennsylvania Press, 2004.

———. "Reading the Hermit's Manuscript: The Female American and Female Robinsonades." In *Approaches to Teaching Defoe's Robinson Crusoe.* Edited by Maximillian Novak and Carl Fisher, 140–51. New York: MLA, 2005.

Stevenson, Brenda E. *Life in Black and White: Family and Community in the Slave South.* New York: Oxford University Press, 1997.

St. George, Robert Blair, ed. *Possible Pasts: Becoming Colonial in Early America.* Ithaca, NY: Cornell University Press, 2000.

Stiles, Henry Reed. *Bundling: Its Origin, Progress, and Decline in America.* Albany, NY: Knickerbocker, 1871.

Stremlau, Rose. "'To Domesticate and Civilize Wild Indians': Allotment and the Campaign to Reform Indian Families, 1875–1887." *Journal of Family History* 30 (2005): 265–86.

Stone, Lawrence. *The Family, Sex and Marriage in England, 1500–1800.* New York: Harper and Row, 1977.

Stuart, Gilbert. *A View of Society in Europe, in Its Progress from Rudeness to Refinement.* Edinburgh: Bell, 1778.

Swanson, Diana. "Subverting Closure: Compulsory Heterosexuality and Compulsory Endings in Middle-Class British Women's Novels." In *Sexual Practice, Textual Theory: Lesbian Cultural Criticism.* Edited by Susan J. Wolfe and Julia Penelope, 150–63. Cambridge, MA: Blackwell Publishers, 1993.

Tague, Ingrid H. "Love, Honor, and Obedience: Fashionable Women and the Discourse of Marriage in the Early Eighteenth Century." *Journal of British Studies* 40, no. 1 (2001): 76–106.

Tanner, Tony. *Adultery in the Novel: Contract and Transgression.* Baltimore: Johns Hopkins University Press, 1979.

Tawil, Ezra. "Domestic Frontier Romance, or, How the Sentimental Heroine Became White." *Novel: A Forum on Fiction* 32, no. 1 (1998): 99–124.

Taylor, Alan. "The Divided Ground: Upper Canada, New York, and the Iroquois Six Nations, 1783–1815." *Journal of the Early Republic* 22, no. 1 (2002): 55–75.

———. "Martyr's to Venus." *New Republic* 227, no. 18 (October 28, 2002): 33–37.

Taylor, Barbara. "Feminists Versus Gallants: Sexual Manners and Morals in Enlightenment Britain." In *Women, Gender, and Enlightenment.* Edited by Sarah Knott and Barbara Taylor, 30–52. Basingstoke: Palgrave Macmillan, 2005.

Tennenhouse, Leonard. *The Importance of Feeling English: American Literature and the British Diaspora: 1750–1850.* Princeton, NJ: Princeton University Press, 2007.

Tennyson, G. B. "The *Bildungsroman* in Nineteenth-Century English Literature." In *Medieval Epic to the "Epic Theater" of Brecht.* Edited by Rosario P. Armato and John M. Spalek, 135–46. Los Angeles: University of Southern California Press, 1968.

Thomas, Chief Jake, and Terry Boyle. *Teachings from the Longhouse.* Toronto: Stoddard, 1994.

Thompson, E. P. "Happy Families." *Radical History Review* 20 (1979): 42–50.

Thompson, Helen. *Ingenuous Subjection: Compliance and Power in the Eighteenth-Century Domestic Novel.* Philadelphia: University of Pennsylvania Press, 2005.

Thwaites, Reuben Gold, ed. *The Jesuit Relations and Allied Documents: Travels and Explorations of the Jesuit Missionaries in New France, 1610–1791.* 73 vols. Cleveland, OH: Burrows Brothers, 1898.

Todd, Janet. *Sensibility: An Introduction.* New York: Routledge, 1986.

Tomaselli, Sylvana. "Civilization, Patriotism, and Enlightened Histories of Woman." In *Women, Gender, and Enlightenment.* Edited by Sarah Knott and Barbara Taylor, 117–35. Basingstoke: Palgrave Macmillan, 2005.

———. "The Enlightenment Debate on Women." *History Workshop* 20 (1985): 101–24.

Tongsen, Karen. "Same Love? Same Old Shit." Accessed January 21, 2014. http://www.fromthesquare.org/?p=5005.

Tooker, Elizabeth. "Women in Iroquois Society." In *Extending the Rafters: Interdisciplinary Approaches to Iroquoian Studies.* Edited by Michael K. Foster, Jack Campisi, and Marianne Mithun, 109–23. Albany: State University of New York Press, 1984.

Toussaint-Louverture. "From *Constitution of the French Colony of Saint-Domingue, 1801.*" In *Slave Revolution in the Caribbean, 1789–1804: A Brief History with Documents.* Edited by Laurent Dubois and John Garrigus, 167–70. Boston: Bedford/St. Martin's, 2006.

Tracey, Karen. *Plots and Proposals: American Women's Fiction, 1850–90.* Urbana: University of Illinois Press, 2000.

Trotter, Joe W., and Eric L. Smith, eds. *African Americans in Pennsylvania: Shifting Historical Perspectives.* University Park: Pennsylvania State University Press, 1997.

Trumbach, Randolph. *The Rise of the Egalitarian Family: Aristocratic Kinship and Domestic Relations in Eighteenth-Century England.* New York: Academic Press, 1978.

Trumpner, Katie. *Bardic Nationalism: The Romantic Novel and the British Empire.* Princeton, NJ: Princeton University Press, 1997.

Tyler, Royall. *The Algerine Captive.* New York: Modern Library, 2002.

———. *The Contrast.* In *Early American Drama.* Edited by Jeffrey Richards, 1–57. New York: Penguin, 1997.

Ulrich, Laurel Thatcher, and Lois K. Stabler. "'Girling of it' in Eighteenth-Century New Hampshire." In *Families and Children.* Edited by Peter Benes, 24–36. Boston: Boston University Press, 1987.

"Uxorious." *Hymen: An Accurate Description of the Ceremonies Used in Marriage, by Every Nation in the Known World. Shewing, the Oddity of Some, the Absurdity of Others, the Drollery of Many, and the Real or Intended Piety of All.* London: I. Pottinger, 1760. Accessed July 1, 2014. http://books.google.com/books/reader?id=JIDAAAAQAAJ&printsec=frontcover&output=reader&pg=GBS.PR1.

Vaccaro, Kristianne Kalata. "'Recollection . . . sets my busy imagination to work': Transatlantic Self-Narration, Performance, and Reception in *The Female American.*" *Eighteenth-Century Fiction* 20, no. 2 (2008): 127–50.

Vail, R. W. G. "*Adventures of Jonathan Corncob, Loyal American Refugee*: A Commentary." *Papers of the American Bibliographical Society* 50 (2nd Quarter 1956): 101–14.

Van Sant, Anne Jessie. *Eighteenth-Century Sensibility and the Novel: The Senses in Social Context*. Cambridge: Cambridge University Press, 2004.

Veracini, Lorenzo. *Settler Colonialism: A Theoretical Overview*. New York: Palgrave Macmillan, 2010.

Viau, Roland. *Femmes de personne: Sexes, genres et pouvoirs en Iroquoisie ancienne*. Montreal: Boreal, 2000.

Vickery, Amanda. *The Gentleman's Daughter: Women's Lives in Georgian England*. New Haven, CT: Yale University Press, 1998.

Vieux, Serge-Henri. *Le Plaçage: Droit coutumier et famille en Haïti*. Paris: Agence de Cooperation Culturelle et Technique, 1989.

Vizenor, Gerald, ed. *Survivance: Narratives of Native Presence*. Lincoln: University of Nebraska Press, 2008.

Wagner, Sally Roesch. "The Root of Oppression Is the Loss of Memory: The Iroquois and the Early Feminist Vision." In *Iroquois Women: An Anthology*. Edited by W. G. Spittal, 224. Ohsweken, ON: Iroqrafts, 1990.

———. *Sisters in Spirit: The Haudenosaunee (Iroquois) Influence on Early American Feminists*. Summertown, TN: Book, 2001.

Wahrman, Dror. *The Making of the Modern Self: Identity and Culture in Eighteenth-Century England*. New Haven, CT: Yale University Press, 2004.

Wallace, Anthony F. *The Death and Rebirth of the Seneca*. New York: Vintage Books, 1972.

Walters, Suzanna Danutta. "Alter-ed Expectations." Accessed January 21, 2014. http://www.fromthesquare.org/?p=5096.

Warner, Michael. *The Trouble with Normal: Sex, Politics, and the Ethics of Queer Life*. Cambridge, MA: Harvard University Press, 1999.

Watt, Ian. *The Rise of the Novel: Studies in Defoe, Richardson, and Fielding*. Berkeley: University of California Press, 1964.

Watts, Edward S. *Writing and Postcolonialism in Early America*. Charlottesville: University of Virginia Press, 1998.

Weisbrod, Carol, and Pamela Sheingorn. "Reynolds v. United States: Nineteenth-Century Forms of Marriage and the Status of Women." *Connecticut Law Review* 10, no. 4 (Summer 1978): 828–58.

Weisser, Susan Ostrov. *The Glass Slipper: Women and Love Stories*. New Brunswick, NJ: Rutgers University Press, 2013.

Westover, Paul. *Necromanticism: Traveling to Meet the Dead, 1750–1860*. New York: Palgrave Macmillan, 2012.

Weyler, Karen. *Intricate Relations: Sexual and Economic Desire in American Fiction, 1789–1814*. Iowa City: University of Iowa Press, 2005.

Wheeler, Roxann. *The Complexion of Race: Categories of Difference in Eighteenth-Century British Culture*. Philadelphia: University of Pennsylvania Press, 2000.

White, Ed. *The Backcountry and the City: Colonization and Conflict in Early America*. Minneapolis: University of Minnesota Press, 2005.

Willis, Deborah, ed. *The Black Venus 2010: They Called Her "Hottentot."* Philadelphia: Temple University Press, 2010.

Wimpffen, Baron de. *A Voyage to Saint Domingo in the Years 1788, 1789, and 1790.* London: T. Caldwell, 1797.

Woertendyke, Gretchen. "Romance to Novel: A Secret History." *Narrative* 17, no. 3 (2009): 255–73.

Wolfe, Stephen. "Unifying Misnomers: Unca Eliza Winkfield's *The Female American.*" *American Studies in Scandinavia* 36, no. 2 (2004): 17–34.

Wood, William. *New England's Prospect.* London: Thomas Cotes for John Bellamie, 1634. Reprint, Boston: John Wilson and Son, 1865.

Woolard, Annette. "Nineteenth-Century Delawareans and the Grand Tour." *Delaware History* 22, no. 3 (1987): 125–57.

Wright, Lyle H. *American Fiction, 1774–1850.* San Marino, CA: Huntington Library, 1969.

Wyett, Jodi L. "'No Place Where Women Are of Such Importance': Female Friendship, Empire, and Utopia in *The History of Emily Montague.*" *Eighteenth-Century Fiction* 16, no. 1 (2003): 33–57.

Yeazell, Ruth Bernard. *Fictions of Modesty: Women and Courtship in the English Novel.* Chicago: University of Chicago Press, 1991.

Yokota, Kariann Akemi. *Unbecoming British: How Revolutionary America Became a Postcolonial Nation.* New York: Oxford University Press, 2011.

Young, Mary E. "Women, Civilization, and the Indian Question." In *Clio Was a Woman: Studies in the History of American Women.* Edited by Mabel E. Deutrich and Virginia Purdy, 98–110. Washington, DC: Howard University Press, 1980.

Zuckerman, Michael. "*Charlotte:* A Tale of Truth, a Premonition of American Revolutions." In *Atlantic Worlds in the Long Eighteenth Century: Seduction and Sentiment,* Edited by Toni Bowers and Tita Chico, 65–80. New York: Palgrave Macmillan, 2012.

INDEX

Adams, Abigail, 44, 45, 68, 69; and bundling, 123, 170n29; "Remember the Ladies," 42
Adams, John, 42, 73, 123, 127, 170n29
adultery, 75, 138
The Adventures of Jonathan Corncob, 114, 119–22, 132
agency, women's, 14, 26, 85; British, 47, 50; feminist theorization of, 9, 99; Native American, 46, 50, 51–52, 55, 68–69
Akwesasne Mohawk Reservation, 59–66
Alexander, William, 24, 25, 152n10
The Algerine Captive (Tyler), 170n27
"The American Origins of 'Yankee Doodle'" (Lemay), 113–14
Anburey, Thomas, 118, 125
Anderson, Karen, 156n8
Anthony, Susan B., 42
Apess, William, 151n37
Aravamudan, Srinivas, 98
Armstrong, Nancy, 7, 98–99, 154n30
arranged marriages: companionate marriages compared to, 3, 72, 73; among the Haudenosaunee, 46, 52, 55, 56, 60–61, 62, 64, 68, 159n45
Austen, Jane, 1, 56, 97, 126

Baartman, Saartjie "Sarah," 130, 173n50
Bakhtin, Mikhail, 135
Bannet, Eve Tavor, 99, 108
Barker, Nicola, 144
Beaver (Mourning) Wars, 47
Behn, Aphra, 10, 76

Belair, Sanite, 76, 162n13
Belinda (Edgeworth), 10
Beyond Conjugality (Law Commission of Canada), 144–45
Beyond Marriage movement, 144
Bhabha, Homi, 103–4
bigamy, 100, 108, 111, 138, 141, 143
Black Looks (hooks), 106–7
Boone, Joseph Allen, 7, 19, 98–99, 144
Bowers, Toni, 127
Bowles, Paul, 153n16
British Critic, 98, 101, 166n1
Brontë, Charlotte, 10
Brooke, Frances: Canadian stay of, 43, 44; *History of Emily Montague,* 2, 5–6, 18, 43–47, 54–56, 67, 69, 159n45
Brown, Judith, 51
Brown, Thomas, 22
Brownstein, Rachel, 8, 144
Buffon, Count (Georges-Louis Leclerc), 124
bundling, 118–25, 132; *Adventures of Jonathan Corncob* on, 114, 119–22; *The Contrast* on, 114, 122–23; disappearance of, 126; *A History of New York* on, 114, 123–25; *Obadiah* on, 133–35, 136; as practice and tradition, 14, 19, 113, 114, 117, 118–19; in "Yankee Doodle," 113–14
Burnaby, Andrew, 118
Burr, Aaron, 72, 92

capitalism, 28
Chakkalakal, Tess, 90–91

Channing, William Ellery, 117, 126,
    169n8
Charlevoix, Pierre François Xavier de,
    45
Charlotte Temple (Rowson), 126, 128
chastity, 27–28
Cherokee peoples, 141–42
Chico, Tita, 127
Child, Lydia Maria: biographical
    background, 150n29; ethnographic
    detail by, 12, 150n31; *The First
    Settlers of New England*, 151n37;
    *The History of the Condition
    of Women, in Various Ages and
    Nations*, 150n29; *Hobomok*, 11–12,
    14–18, 150–51n32; *The Progress of
    Religious Ideas through Successive
    Ages*, 150n29
chivalry and gallantry, 27, 28, 29,
    154n31
The Citizen of the World (Goldsmith),
    104
colonial alterity, 81, 103, 106, 118, 119
colonialism, justifications for, 25,
    152–53n11, 163n26
common-law marriage, 99, 141
*Considérations sur l'état présent de la
    colonie française de Saint-Domingue*
    (Hilliard d'Auberteuil), 86
The Contrast (Tyler), 114, 122–23
Coontz, Stephanie, 4
Cooper, James Fenimore, 11
The Coquette (Foster), 74
coquettes, 73–74, 75, 92
Cott, Nancy, 141, 143, 174n59
courtship, 3; bundling and, 113–14,
    118–25, 126, 133–35, 136;
    eighteenth-century novel and, 7,
    34, 40, 80, 97, 135–36, 174n63;
    leisure time for, 27–28; Native
    American, 14–18
Creole identity, 80, 102, 162–63n25
Creole women, 75, 77–78, 82, 164n39;
    and mulatto women, 81–83, 87–88,
    103, 166n17

Critical Essays Concerning Marriage
    (Salmon), 22
Critical Review, 98
cultural tourism, 107–8
*Customs of the American Indians as
    Compared with Customs of Primitive
    Times* (Lafitau), 45, 48

Davidson, Cathy, 46, 120, 126
Dawes Act of 1887 (Allotment Act), 142
Dayan, Joan, 91, 164n44
Dearborn, Henry, 57, 66
decolonization, 59, 65, 134
Defoe, Daniel, 10, 121
Denzin, Norman, 59
Dillon, Elizabeth Maddock, 9, 74, 80,
    89, 135–36
division of labor, 49, 51, 53–54, 62
divorce, 141; Native Americans and, 17,
    23, 50–51, 60, 64, 151–52n42
domesticity, 28, 99; *The Female Amer-
    ican* on, 34–35; *Secret History* on,
    79–80, 81–93; *Woman of Colour*
    on, 19, 98, 100, 103–6, 108, 111,
    112
Dominique, Lyndon J., 166n1, 167n28
Dowd, Gregory, 141
Drexler, Michael, 92, 95
DuCille, Anne, 7
DuPlessis, Rachel Blau, 8, 34, 101, 108

Edgeworth, Maria, 10
Edmunds-Tucker Act, 143
Ellison, Julie, 67
The Empire of Love (Povinelli), 57–58
Engels, Friedrich, 154n33
Enlightenment, 24, 67–68
"Essay on American Language and Lit-
    erature" (Channing), 117, 169n8
Essig, Laurie, 140
Eugenides, Jeffrey, 1–2, 19

Fabian, Johannes, 30–31, 57
"fallen women," 85, 90, 92–93, 94, 95,
    101, 109

family, 98–99; Native American, 50, 141; nuclear, 4, 5, 44, 141, 142

The Family, Sex and Marriage in England (Stone), 4, 5, 148n7

The Female American ("Unca Eliza Winkfield"): alternate vision of marriage in, 2, 18, 21, 33–41; hybrid identity in, 22, 34–36, 37; plot summary, 33

Femmes de personne (Viau), 48–49

Fessenden, Thomas, 122

Firestone, Shulamith, 6

The First Settlers of New England (Child), 151n37

Flaubert, Gustave, 1

Flint, Christopher, 98–99

Foster, E. M., 167n28

Foster, Frances Smith, 142

Foster, Hannah, 74

Foucault, Michel, 68

Fowler, Lorenzo Niles, 22

Franklin, Benjamin, 129, 174n63

Franklin, Edward, 129, 173n47

Friedman, Susan Stanford, 6

Gage, Matilda Joslyn, 42

Garraway, Doris, 84, 86–87, 162–63n25

Gaya, Louis de, 22

The Gender of Freedom (Dillon), 74, 135

gender roles and relations: division of labor in, 49, 51, 53–54, 62; *The Female American* on, 35–39, 40–41; and gender differences, 4–5, 25–26, 71, 135–36, 174n63; Millar on, 25–28, 29–30, 31, 32–33; among Native Americans, 14, 33, 42, 44–45, 47–52, 141–42; northern European, 154n22; novels' shaping of, 98–99, 135–36, 174n63; Thomas Jefferson on, 154–55n37

Girod de Chantrans, Justin, 84

Godbeer, Richard, 113, 119, 126

Goettner-Abendroth, Heide, 49

Goldsmith, Oliver, 104

Goudie, Sean, 162–63nn25–26

Gradual Abolition Bill (Pennsylvania), 163n32

Greek myth, 32

Gyssels, Kathleen, 164n39

Habermas, Jürgen, 5, 68

Haitian Revolution, 70, 72, 76, 161n2

Handsome Lake, 60, 61, 160n62, 160n72

Hardwicke's Marriage Act, 23, 61, 99, 115

Harrow, Sharon, 103, 163n26

Haudenosaunee (Iroquois): arranged marriages among, 46, 52, 55, 56, 60–61, 62, 64, 68, 159n45; gender balance among, 47–52; marriage customs of, 56–57, 58–67; matrilineal social structure of, 26, 31, 47–48, 156n8; Millar on, 26, 30–31, 33, 153n16; name of, 50; political participation of, 5, 42, 66–67

Hays, Mary, 99, 108

H. D. (Hilda Doolittle), 8

Herne, Sue Ellen, 59, 62–63, 64–65

Hilliard d'Auberteuil, Michel-René, 82, 84, 86, 87, 164n46

The History of America (Robertson), 52–53

History of Emily Montague (Brooke): colonialist invocations in, 68, 69; comparative marriage plot of, 2, 5, 18, 43–47, 55; depiction of marriage in, 55–56, 67, 159n45; as long ignored, 5–6; plot summary, 43–44; Wendat depiction in, 44–46, 54–55

History of New France (Charlevoix), 45

A History of New York (Irving), 114, 123–25

History of Woman Suffrage, 42

The History of Women (Alexander), 24, 25, 152n10

Hobbes, Thomas, 26

Hobomok (Child), 11–12, 14–18, 150–51n32

hooks, bell, 106–7

"Hottentots," 24, 130–32, 173n51
Hume, David, 24
Hymen: An Accurate Description of the Ceremonies Used in Marriage ("Uxorious"), 18, 21; as marriage-rite anthology, 23–25, 130

illegitimate children, 99, 120, 167n28
interracial marriage, 11, 12, 14
interracial sexual relations, 82, 86, 87
Irving, Washington, 114, 123–25, 151n37

James, C. L. R., 83
James, Henry, 1
Jane Eyre (Brontë), 10
Jefferson, Thomas, 141, 154–55n37
Jemison, Mary, 52
Jesuit Relations, 45, 151n42
Jónasdóttir, Anna, 6
"Jonathan's Courting, or, The Country Lovers" (Fessenden), 114, 122

Kames, Lord, 25, 56, 153n12
kinship structure, 26, 44, 50, 51, 154n17

Lafitau, Father Joseph-François, 45, 48
Lahontan, Baron, 14, 13, 15, 16, 63, 151n33
Langford, Paul, 47
Laura (Sansay), 70, 93–96
League of the Iroquois (Morgan), 56–57, 65, 160n74
Leatherstocking Tales (Cooper), 11
Leites, Edmund, 3–4
Le Jeune, Father, 151–52n42
Lemay, J. A. Leo, 113–14
Lemmings, David, 47
liberalism, 57–58
The Life and Adventures of Obadiah Benjamin Franklin Bloomfield, M.D., 2, 19, 114–15, 129–39; authorship attributions, 173n47; bundling episode in, 133–35, 136; cosmopolitan literary tourism in, 138, 174n66;

"The Enchanted Hat" chapter in, 136–37; as marriage-rites anthology, 130–33; plot summary, 129–30; and seduction fiction, 130, 136; and women's sexuality, 136–38
The Life and Opinions of Tristram Shandy (Sterne), 130, 137
Lincoln, Yvonna, 59
local color, 126, 134
"locational" feminism, 6
Locke, John, 26, 99
Love, Inc. (Essig), 140
Luhmann, Niklas, 3, 68, 154n20

Macfarlane, Alan, 148n6
Macklemore, 145
madras headscarf, 88–89
Mann, Barbara, 48, 49
Margaretta; or, The Intricacies of the Heart (Read), 128–29
marriage: arranged, 3, 46, 52, 55–56, 60–62, 64, 68, 72–73, 159n45; British women and, 7, 41, 46, 47, 115; common-law, 99, 141; eighteenth-century transformation of, 3, 4, 23; emotional companionship in, 3–4, 41, 46, 69; freedom and, 5, 8, 16, 19, 68, 148n6; ideological function of, 9, 162n5; interracial, 11, 12, 14; Millar on, 28–29; mulatto women and, 82, 84; parental influence and control in, 3, 21, 67; polygamous, 23–24, 53, 100, 108, 111, 138, 141, 143; as relationship goal, 19; same-sex, 19, 143–45; slavery and, 10, 90–91, 142–43; as social ideal, 3–4, 7, 99; as voluntary union, 4, 135, 174n59
Marriage Act of 1753, 23, 61, 99, 115
Marriage Ceremonies (Brown), 22
Marriage: Its History and Ceremonies (Fowler), 22
The Marriage Plot (Eugenides), 1–2
marriage plots: diversity representation in, 2–3, 10–18, 24; in *The Female*

American, 34, 40, 41; feminist debates about, 7–9, 12; in *History of Emily Montague*, 2, 5, 18, 43–47, 55–56, 68–69, 158–59n45; and novel form, 1–2, 5, 99, 140; in *Secret History*, 71, 72–73, 75–76, 77–78; in *Woman of Colour*, 2, 100–101, 108–9

marriage rites and customs, 21–22, 57; anthology genre of, 22–25, 41, 73, 115–18; English, 24, 46; of "Hottentots," 24, 130, 132; *Hymen* as anthology of, 23–25, 130; *Life and Adventures of Obadiah Benjamin Franklin Bloomfield* as anthology of, 130–33; Native American, 11–12, 14–18, 23–24, 54–55, 56–57, 58–67, 151n36; in postcolonial US, 116

matriarchy, 48–49

matrilineal structure, 26, 31, 47–48, 156n8

Matrimonial Ceremonies Displayed (Brown), 22

"'Matrimonial Ceremonies Displayed': Popular Ethnography and Enlightened Imperialism" (O'Connell), 22

Matrimonial Customs (Gaya), 22

McDonald, Louise, 59, 62, 63, 65–66, 160n72

McMullen, Lorraine, 44

Mémoires de l'Amérique Septentrionale (Lahontan), 13, 14, 15, 16, 63, 151n33

ménagères, 71, 83–86, 87, 91–92

Merrett, Robert, 67

Mihesuah, Devon, 58–59

Millar, John, 152n10, 153n16; on gender differences, 25–26; *The Origin of the Distinction of Ranks*, 18, 25–33, 41; on patriarchy, 30, 154n33

mimicry, colonial: Bhaba theory of, 103–4; *Woman of Colour* and, 106–7, 108, 112

Mintz, Sidney, 91

miscegenation, 11, 84

missionary work, 36–38, 155n46

Mitchell, Richard, 59–63

Mohawk, John, 49–50, 56, 60, 63, 160n69

Mohawk oral tradition, 59, 60, 62

Moll Flanders (Defoe), 10, 121

monogamy, 9, 73, 75, 141, 142–43

Montesquieu, 162n5

More, Hannah, 99

Moreau de Saint-Méry, M. L. E., 82, 86, 87, 164n46

Morgan, Edmund Sears, 148n5

Morgan, Lewis Henry, 56–57, 65, 160n74

Morrill Bill of 1862, 143

mulatto women: domestic partnership model of, 81, 89–90; madras headscarf for, 88–89; as *ménagères*, 83–84, 85; power and agency by, 85, 86–87; sexual relationships of, 82, 84, 85, 86–87, 92, 164n40; social and economic role of, 111; white Creole women and, 81–83, 87–88, 103, 166n17

Napoleon Bonaparte, 72

national culture, 117

New England's Prospects (Wood), 16

Nickels, Cameron, 122, 123

Noel, Jan, 48

novel form: and gender roles, 98–99, 135–36, 174n63; marriage plots and, 1–2, 5, 140

nuclear family, 4, 5, 44, 141, 142

Nussbaum, Felicity, 163n26

"Observations on the Origin and Progression of the White Colonists' Prejudice against Men of Color" (Raimond), 87

O'Connell, Lisa, 22, 115

The Origin of the Distinction of Ranks (Millar), 18, 41; as stadial history, 25–33

The Origin of the Family, Private Property, and the State (Engels), 154n33

Oroonoko (Behn), 10, 76
otherness, 103, 106–8, 118, 119

Pamela (Richardson), 128, 129
Parker, Ely, 56
Pateman, Carol, 26
patriarchy, 6, 9, 47; Millar on, 26, 30, 31–32, 154n33
Perrin, Noel, 170n21
Peters, Rev. Samuel, 119
plaçage, 82, 84, 91–92, 165n56
Plane, Ann Marie, 151n36
Polikoff, Nancy, 144
polygamy, 23–24, 53, 143
Porter, Tom, 51
Porterfield, Amanda, 148n5
postcolonial eras, 115, 123, 168–69n6
postcolonial strategies, 19, 107, 108, 112
Povinelli, Elizabeth, 57–58, 67
premarital sex, 130, 137, 141, 174n63; and bundling, 119; Native Americans and, 14, 17, 63, 160n72; in *Secret History*, 94, 96
Proctor, Thomas, 51–52
Puritans, 4, 12, 148n5, 150–51n32

Quaker Church, 116

racism, 44, 82, 130; Child's rhetoric and, 11–12, 17; *Woman of Colour* and, 97, 98, 100, 102–3
Radhakrishnan, R., 21, 59
Raimond, Julien, 87
Read, Martha Meredith, 128–29
"Remember the Ladies" (Adams), 42
Rendall, Jane, 152n10
Reynolds v. United States, 143
Richardson, Samuel, 126, 128, 129
Richter, Daniel, 52
Rifkin, Mark, 12, 44, 45, 141, 154n17
Roach, Joseph, 135
Robertson, William, 24, 52–53, 153n12
romantic love, 6, 67, 68, 154n31; Millar on, 29, 32; Native Americans and,

52–53, 54, 55, 57, 62; as social ideal, 3–4
Roof, Judith, 5

Said, Edward, 118
Saint-Dominigue, 71, 161n2; *plaçage* in, 91–92. *See also* Haitian Revolution
Salmon, Thomas, 22
same-sex marriage, 19, 143–45
Sansay, Leonora, 161n2; as Burr mistress, 74, 92; *Laura*, 70, 93–96; *Secret History; or, The Horrors of St. Domingo*, 2, 18–19, 79–80, 81–93
Sayre, Gordon, 52
Schoepf, Johann, 118–19
Scott, Sir Walter, 117
The Secret Garden (Burnett), 106
Secret History; or, The Horrors of St. Domingo (Sansay), 2, 5–6, 18–19, 70; Caribbean domesticity in, 81–93; Clara's identity in, 73–74, 80; companionate marriage rhetoric in, 72–73; French Creole and mulatto women depicted by, 75, 77–78, 81–83, 87–88; Haitian Revolution depicted in, 70, 72, 76; reworking of courtship and seduction plots by, 18, 70–80, 81, 86, 90
seduction fiction and plot, 96, 126–27; *Charlotte Temple* and, 126, 128; coquettes and, 74–75; *Margaretta* and, 128–29; *Life and Adventures of Obadiah Benjamin Franklin Bloomfield* and, 130, 136; Sansay novels and, 18–19, 81, 93–96
self-marriage, 140–41
Seneca Falls Convention (1848), 42
A Sentimental Journal through France and Italy (Sterne), 136
Seven Years' War, 47
sexual assault, 78, 128–29, 142
sexual relations, 74, 132, 136–38; interracial, 82, 86, 87; of mulatto women, 82, 84, 85, 86–87, 92, 164n40; of Native Americans, 14, 17, 26–28, 63,

141, 160n72; premarital, 14, 17, 63, 94, 96, 119, 130, 137, 141, 160n72, 174n63
Shapiro, Steven, 127
Shoemaker, Nancy, 48
Simpson, George, 165n56
Sisters in Spirit (Wagner), 42
Sketches of the History of Man (Kames), 25, 56
Sky Woman, 49, 63
slavery, 83, 163n32; and marriage, 10, 90–91, 142–43
Smith, Adam, 24, 25, 153n12
Smits, David, 16, 28
Socolow, Susan, 111–12
Spenser, Edmund, 27
Spittal, W. G., 160n72
Spivack, Gayatri, 152–53n11
"squaw drudge" stereotype, 16, 28, 31, 54, 57
stadial histories, 25–33, 41
Stanton, Elizabeth Cady, 42
Sterne, Laurence, 126, 129, 132, 173n48, 174n66; *The Life and Opinions of Tristram Shandy*, 130, 137; *A Sentimental Journal through France and Italy*, 136
Stevens, George Alexander, 133
Stone, Lawrence, 4, 5, 148n7, 157n15
Strong, Abigail, 141
Stuart, Gilbert, 154n22

Tague, Ingrid, 67
Taylor, Alan, 126
Taylor, Barbara, 154n31
Tennenhouse, Leonard, 127
"They Are the Soul of the Councils" (Mann), 49
Thompson, Helen, 9, 99
Tolstoy, Leo, 1
Tomaselli, Sylvana, 152n10
Tom Jones (Fielding), 130
Tooker, Elizabeth, 48
Toussaint-Louverture, François-Dominique, 72, 165n56

Travels through the Interior Parts of America (Anburey), 118
Tyler, Royall, 114, 122–23, 170n27

"Unca Eliza Winkfield." See *The Female American*
"Uxorious." See *Hymen: An Accurate Description of the Ceremonies Used in Marriage*

Vail, R. W. G., 120
Viau, Roland, 48–49
Vieux, Henri, 91
Vindications of the Rights of Woman (Wollstonecraft), 154n31
Vizenor, Gerald, 61
vulnerability, 93, 126–27

wage labor, 4
Wagner, Sally Roesch, 42
Walters, Suzanna Danutta, 145
Warner, Michael, 144
Watt, Ian, 5, 147n1
Waverly (Scott), 117
Wendat (Huron), 5, 156n8; confederacy of, 47, 157n17; courtship and wedding customs of, 14–18; and divorce, 17, 151–52n42; *History of Emily Montague* on, 44, 45–46, 54–55; and romantic love, 52, 54
West, Jane, 99, 110
When Did Indians Become Straight? (Rifkin), 44, 45, 141
Whitman, Elizabeth, 74
"Why Compare?" (Radhakrishnan), 21, 59
Williams, Eunice, 52
Wimpffen, Baron de, 89, 166n17
Wollstonecraft, Mary, 99, 108, 154n31
Woman, Church, and State (Gage), 42
The Woman of Colour: authorship attributions, 167n28; Caribbean domesticity in, 104–6, 112; and colonial mimicry, 106–7, 108, 112; comparative marriage plot in, 2, 100–101, 108–9; critique of

British in, 8, 19, 104–6; new domestic world depicted in, 101–6; Olivia as tropicopolitan heroine in, 98–101, 108; plot summary, 97–98; postcolonial "writing back" strategy of, 19, 106–12; reviews of, 98, 100–101, 165–66n1
women of color. *See* mulatto women
Wood, William, 16
Woolf, Virginia, 8

Wright, Andrew, 167n28
Wright, Lyle, 173n47
Writing beyond the Ending (DuPlessis), 8, 34, 101, 108
Wyett, Jodi, 56

"Yankee Doodle," 113–14
Yokota, Kariann Akemi, 168n6

Zuline, 76–77, 162n14